knitting plus

mastering fit
+ plus-size style
+ 15 projects

LISA SHROYER

INTERWEAVE.
interweave.com

Editor
Ann Budd

Technical Editor
Lori Gayle

Art Director
Liz Quan

Cover + Interior Design
Pamela Norman

Photography
Joe Hancock

Stylist
Carol Beaver

Hair + Makeup
Kathy MacKay

Production
Katherine Jackson

Interweave Press LLC
201 East Fourth Street
Loveland, CO 80537-5655 USA
Interweave.com

Printed in China by Asia Pacific Offset Ltd.

Library of Congress Cataloging-in-
Publication Data

Shroyer, Lisa. Knitting plus : mastering
fit + plus-size style + 15 projects /
Lisa Shroyer.
p. cm. Includes index.
ISBN 978-1-59668-237-5 (pbk.)
ISBN 978-1-59668-493-5 (eBook)
  1. Knitting--Patterns. 2. Plus-size
women's clothing. I. Title.
TT820.S523 2011
  746.43'2--dc22

                            2010031787

10 9 8 7 6 5 4 3 2 1

acknowledgments

As a long-time creative writer, I never thought my first book would be a knitting reference text. But I find meaning in that fact—I've always been interested in the hard knowledge behind the softness we see as beauty. The feet in an iambic line; the chemical makeup of early Renaissance paints; the engineering of suspension bridges; the structure of knitted fabric. . . . The secret to craftsmanship is expert knowledge of the craft, applied with precision and artfulness. I see this book as a tribute to the beautiful things technique can realize.

I have to thank my mom, Nancy, for instilling a love of technique in me and for teaching me to knit to begin with. I also thank my partner, Laurie, for her continued support of all my endeavors, even when it means days spent knitting in the same chair without looking up. Thanks, too, to my editor Ann Budd for all her work on this book and also for her mentorship when I first began my career in how-to publishing.

A very big thanks is owed to the designers who contributed their projects to the book. This is a group of knitwear designers who are interested in designing for all women and dedicated to designing with body diversity in mind. The truth is, a knitter falls in love with a design, not with the idea of how it will fit her own body. A good designer, however, does think of this.

The true gatekeeper to any pattern is the technical editor. Thanks to Lori Gayle for all of her applied expertise on this book, united with a real interest in providing good things to the knitter.

Lastly, I want to thank you, the reader. This book was written with no judgment toward the end user; you are who you are, and you should feel good about your craft—and all of your pursuits. I wish you good health and good knitting!

contents

introduction

I WROTE THIS book because I'm a plus-size knitter, and I know some things about sweater construction. In these pages, I intend to give you the tools and information you need to knit sweaters that fit you, that achieve your knitting objectives, and that are fun to make. This is a book about knitting—not about fashion, self-confidence, or "what not to wear." Whether you are new to making sweaters or just want to advance your understanding of the mechanics, *Knitting Plus* will give you the rules of sweater construction and insight into what those rules mean for the plus-size. And there are some lovely patterns, too.

Working on the editorial staff of *Interweave Knits* and *Knitscene* magazines, my primary job has been manager of knitting patterns. In this job, I have studied many sweaters and learned many ways to construct a garment. In the end, most sweaters fall into five basic styles:

+ **drop shoulder (including modified drop shoulder)**
+ **set-in sleeve**
+ **raglan yoke**
+ **seamless round yoke**
+ **dolman (which encompasses a lot of variations)**

These construction styles all pivot around armhole and sleeve cap design. The body of a sweater can be shaped a myriad of ways, but the treatment of the sleeve-to-body join makes all the difference in fit, style, and final product. Sweaters in these styles usually follow general rules—learning these rules can help you throughout your knitting endeavors. This book

will particularly focus on these five styles and what they can do for the plus-size wearer.

Knitting Plus is divided into seven chapters. Chapter 01 explains the basic measurable parts of any sweater, how these parts affect each other, and how these parts relate to plus-size needs. If you've never understood why armholes get deeper with bust size, or why plus-size people need wider neck openings, you'll find this chapter highly informative. Chapter 02 covers taking measurements, choosing a size to knit, and tips on customizing patterns to fit your particular shape. The basic sweater styles are presented in the remaining five chapters. Within each of these chapters, I provide a basic sweater pattern in the relevant construction style—a design worked in stockinette without much adornment to illustrate the basic look and elements of that style. These basic designs are easy to customize for individual shape and can be considered a kind of template for plus-size sweaters. The basic sweater is followed by more involved designs that showcase the possibilities of the constructions. Although this book offers very detailed information about adjusting patterns, you should not feel daunted; not every plus-size woman will require this level of modification. And even those who do can begin with some of the simpler adjustments.

The information in this book will advance your knitting knowledge and your understanding of sweater making. It will give you valuable insight to make better sweaters that fit your own personal shape. I hope the collection of patterns will inspire you to start knitting *now*.

common sweater elements
+ what they mean for you

THIS CHAPTER explains the standard elements of a sweater, how they interact with each other, and the implications thereof for plus-size women.

bust circumference

We measure the bust circumference of a sweater just below the underarm. The sweater circumference below the underarm must be wide enough to accommodate the fullest part of the bust. In a sweater with hourglass shaping, the bust shaping reaches its full width below the armholes. For designs with body shaping, plus-size and/or busty women should have the widest bust circumference extend to about 5" (12.5 cm) below the underarm.

Most women's knitting patterns are sized by the bust circumference. The other measurements, such as cross-back width, shoulder width, upper arm circumference, and so on, relate to the bust circumference and are based on standards such as those provided by the Craft Yarn Council of America (CYCA; see Chapter 02).

Standardized measurements generally assume that a woman's torso has an hourglass shape—the bust and hips are roughly equal in girth with a narrower waist between. While many plus-size women do fit this template (but at a larger scale than their size-6 counterparts), many do not. We'll talk about other shapes and how to address them when we come to body shaping.

Body Width at Underarm

If the front and back of a sweater are worked in two separate pieces, the body doesn't have a circumference until it is seamed. Instead, the front and back have a bust width just below the armhole. This width is generally half the total bust circumference. But be aware that once you seam the front and back together, some fabric is lost in the seams and the finished bust circumference will be slightly less than two times the body width.

For some designs, especially cardigans, the front has a different width than the back. Always check the back width at the underarm for such projects to make sure that it is sufficiently wide for your body. In garments with unusual design elements on the front or very deep front necklines, or cardigans with fronts that don't close—such as the Audubon Shrug (page 104)—the back width at the underarm is the only way to determine the size of the garment. In such cases, multiply the back width by two to determine the intended bust circumference.

body length

Body length is the measurement from hem to underarm. This element is not as isolated as it may seem. If you're tall, you need a long sweater. But you have to pay attention to armhole depth as well. If the body length doesn't change from one size to the next but the armhole depth increases with each larger size, then the overall length of the sweater will

In a garment with waist shaping, the full bust girth must be reached before the armholes—preferably with a few inches worked even before the first underarm bind-off.

If the front and back are worked separately, multiply the body width (excluding the seaming selvedge stitches) at the underarm by two to get the total bust circumference.

The depth of the armhole is affected by the projection of the bust—the farther outward the fabric has to travel before it reaches the underarm, the deeper the armhole will have to be.

The depth of any shoulder shaping is not included in the armhole depth.

increase as well. If a designer progressively sizes her pattern to have both deeper armholes and longer body length with each size, the largest sizes may become too long overall.

For most women, a body length of less than 13" (33 cm) makes for a cropped sweater. A length between 13" (33 cm) and 15" (38 cm) makes for a fairly average hemline, a length between 15" (38 cm) and 19" (48.5 cm) makes for a longer line, and a length longer than 19" (48.5 cm) enters tunic and dress territory.

For plus-size women, however, body length is affected by the terrain the fabric has to cover. If your sweater has enough positive ease (see box on page 12) to hang loosely over your abdomen, nothing will interrupt the downward flow of the fabric and the width will not affect the length. But, if you have a highly contoured abdomen, the fabric has to go out as well as down to get over your body. In this case, body width does affect sweater length. If a sweater is to be fitted with zero or negative ease, the fabric won't have much slack for passing over contours, and those contours will draw up the length of the garment and create an upward-arching hemline. (Short-row shaping—the insertion of wedges of extra length at the most contoured area—can do wonders to alleviate this problem; see page 24.) Therefore, when I design fitted sweaters, I work some extra length into the lower body. How much length depends on how much negative ease I want (based on the widest body part: bust, belly, or hip). When designing for myself, I add about ½" (1.3 cm) of length for every 1" (2.5 cm) of negative ease. You'll want to experiment to see what works best for your particular shape.

armhole (+ yoke) depth
Armhole depth is measured from the base of the armhole to the outer edge of the top of the shoulder. Generally, the armhole depth is half

the armhole circumference, which encompasses both the back armhole depth and the front armhole depth.

In sweaters without shoulder shaping, the armhole depth is equal to the total yoke depth. However, in a sweater that has shaped shoulders, the armhole depth is shorter than the total yoke depth. In a sweater with 1" (2.5 cm) of shoulder shaping, for example, that 1" (2.5 cm) occurs above the top of the armhole. In raglan and seamless yoke sweaters, the armhole depth is roughly the same as the yoke depth because the sleeve extends all the way to the neck opening. Technically, at some unwritten point in

common elements

This schematic displays the most basic sweater elements, some or all of which can be identified in any knitted garment.

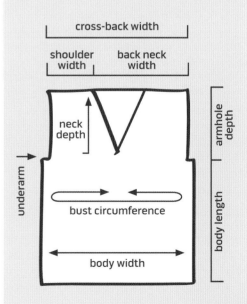

the yoke shaping, the sleeve fabric ceases to be sleeve fabric and becomes body fabric, thereby creating an undefined shoulder line, but not in such a way that the shoulder can be measured or drawn in a concrete way—we'll address the nebulous nature of yokes in later chapters.

Armhole depth is strictly a sweater element, not a body element. There is no way to measure an armhole on a bare body; we only know how deep armholes should be in relation to body measurements based on a set of accepted standards. In general, women with larger busts require deeper armholes, as the body fabric has to cover more contours between the underarm to shoulder line.

But, if the fullest part of the bust is covered by the fabric below the underarm, why does the fabric parallel to the armhole have to cover bust fullness? For this, you need to think in three dimensions. As the yoke fabric passes from the shoulder seam down the chest, it has to pass to the outside of the breast and under the arm

to reach the side seam below the underarm. The farther your breast extends out from your chest, the farther the yoke fabric has to travel to reach the side seam of the lower body and, therefore, the deeper the armhole must be. It can be assumed that a particular bust measurement is proportionate to other characteristics—the shoulder's fleshiness (a roundness that eats up length), the upper back fleshiness (a roundness that eats up length), and the upper arm circumference (a roundness that drives sleeve circumference, which is strongly tied to armhole depth).

In the simplest sweater construction—the drop shoulder—the total armhole circumference (measured in rows) is the same as the total sleeve circumference (measured in stitches). Because these two circles are seamed together, the armhole depth must measure half the total sleeve circumference. In a set-in sweater, the relationship between the sleeve cap and armhole is more complicated, but the total cap perimeter

yoke

The yoke refers to the depth of fabric between the base of the underarm and the neck or shoulder line, whichever is longer. All of the shaping from the underarm to the neck is worked during this distance.

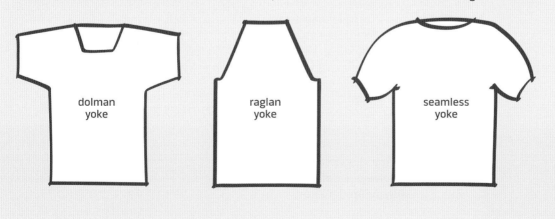

dolman yoke

raglan yoke

seamless yoke

(calculated through a series of formulas) must match the armhole perimeter. Consequently, the armhole depth must measure half of the calculated armhole perimeter. In raglan and seamless yoke designs, the armhole depth reflects the vertical distance in which the sleeve fabric (and the body fabric, for that matter) is decreased away. The wider the sleeve, the more yoke depth is required to accommodate all the decreases necessary to reach a reasonable neck circumference. Because the sleeve joins the body seamlessly in a dolman, the sleeve opening and the armhole opening are one and the same. Again, it follows that the armhole depth is half the sleeve circumference.

neck circumference

Neck circumference, as an isolated element, is mostly applicable to sweaters with raglan or seamless yoke shaping. For sweaters worked in pieces in which the front (or front and back) neck is shaped, the width across the back neck opening is more important. Neck circumference can vary widely based on design and styling—a boatneck has a wider neck opening than a crewneck, but both work as structural elements. Women's necks can vary in size, but not by a whole lot. The neck opening of a pullover should be large enough (or at least elastic enough) to fit over the head.

For boatneck pullovers, there is a simple way to determine your ideal neck circumference. Take a flexible tape measure and pinch the end back onto the tape to make a large loop. Put this loop over your head and stand in front of a mirror. Playing with the circumference of the loop, lay the loop on your shoulders to see how different sizes of openings will look. If your bra straps show or if the loop hangs to the outer part of your shoulder, the opening may be too wide for your liking. You can test the neck circumference for your chosen size from any pattern in this way ahead of time to determine if you want to customize the fit.

back neck width

The back neck edge typically forms a straight (or close to straight) line between the shoulders and is used as the standard for the neck width. In most cases, the front neck width is the same, but can vary in shape and depth, which makes the less-variable back a better guide for this measurement. If the back neck is narrow, the sides (shoulder edges) of the sweater will ride up on the neck. If it is too narrow, the fabric has to travel outward to get around the neck before traveling down to cover the body, causing puckers and fit problems.

ease

Ease describes the difference between your physical body measurement and the sweater measurement. If your bust measures 46" (117 cm), and your sweater measures 50" (127 cm), then the sweater has 4" (10 cm) positive ease, which provides a fairly roomy fit. If your sweater measures 46" (117 cm), there is zero ease, and the sweater will look fitted but not overly tight. If your sweater measures 42" (106.5 cm), it has 4" (10 cm) negative ease and will stretch over your body (but may still be quite comfortable to wear). If you have a lot of fleshy contours, a standard pattern might result in a garment with significantly different amounts of ease in different areas— from hip to belly to bust. For example, there may be 2" (5 cm) negative ease at the full part of your belly, 3" (7.5 cm) positive ease at the narrow point just under your bust, and 4" (10 cm) negative ease across your bust. If the inconsistency becomes too drastic, you'll want to customize the fit as described in Chapter 02.

01

Plus-size women don't necessarily need progressively wider neck openings, but they do need wider cross-back widths (see below).

shoulder width

The fabric that remains at the top of the yoke between the neck and the armhole forms the shoulder. This width can vary a lot with construction style, as well as from size to size. The shoulder of a drop-shoulder sweater is relatively wide because no stitches are decreased along the outside edge of the body at the armhole. The shoulder of a set-in sweater is narrower because the armhole is shaped to end at the top of the shoulder bone. In this construction, the shoulder of the sweater matches the actual body distance from the inside of the shoulder joint to the side of the neck. Plus-size women can have very different needs when it comes to shoulder width. In general, we do need a wider shoulder than a thin woman, but as for back neck width, this is related to the need for a wider cross-back width overall.

cross-back width

The cross-back width consists of the two shoulder widths plus the back neck width—it is the width of the remaining yoke fabric after all armhole shaping has been completed. This fabric has to be wide enough to span comfortably from arm to arm across the upper back. For drop-shoulder sweaters, the cross-back width measures the same as or very close to the body width at the underarm. For set-in sweaters, the cross-back width can be much narrower than the body width. We don't really talk about cross-back width in raglan or seamless yoke sweaters because the yoke in these constructions forms a cone shape that decreases continuously to the neck. For dolman sweaters, the cross-back width is generally the same as the body width, but there are so many variations in the dolman category, it's hard to make generalizations.

Plus-size women generally need wider cross-back widths than thin women because their all-around fleshiness and farther-protruding busts take up width across the yoke (just as in armhole depth, the fabric has farther to travel outside the breast to the side seam). Broad-shouldered women in particular need wide cross-backs. How wide you want your cross-back is a matter of personal preference, but err on the side of generosity—you never want the cross-back to be too narrow.

getting the **right fit**

IF A SWEATER HEM falls at the same point as the waistband of your pants (below, left), the effect can be unattractive. This highlights a fleshy abdomen and makes the sweater look too small overall. A hem that falls a few inches below the waistband (below, right) has a more flattering and refined look.

A longer body length has a slimming effect on plus-size women and can cover awkward areas like a lower belly pooch. If a hemline falls at the midline of your abdomen, it can highlight this wideness instead of drawing the eye onto other areas. Avoid having your sweater hem fall at the same point as the waistband on your pants—this line usually falls between two rolls of flesh. Both your pants and sweater are sucked into the space, which highlights the contours above and below. If you raise your arms or move around much, your sweater will creep up and expose your belly. For plus-size women, I recommend sweater hems that fall at least a couple of inches below the waistband.

The size and shape of a neck opening is mostly a design element and not so much dictated by fit and body measurements.

Again, plus-size women don't necessarily need progressively wider back necks and shoulders—these are not body elements that change drastically with dress size. However, the increased cross-back width for each larger size in a pattern is divided among the back neck and shoulder widths, making those progressively wider for each larger size.

neck depth

In general, the front neck of a sweater is a bit lower than the shoulder line to account for the natural forward curve of the body—the back of the neck is actually higher than the front of the neck—and to give the throat breathing room. A dropped, or shaped, front neck can be quite flattering, especially for plus-size women. The back neck can also be dropped for a more tailored fit and to accommodate neckband treatments. The depth and shape of the neckline is dependent on design, but it's important to understand how depth and width are interrelated in neck shaping.

If you bind off the center 25 stitches for the first row of neck shaping, then on subsequent rows, decrease one stitch at each neck edge three times, the total neck width consists of 31 stitches: the initial 25 stitches plus 6 decreased stitches (3 decreases on each side). Any stitches decreased along neck edges are part of the neck width, and the front neck has to consume the same number of stitches as the back neck. In this way, planning neck shaping relies on a set neck width.

If you have a large bust, a high bust, or a shelf bust (a bust that stands out from your chest wall at a right angle, either because it's so large or because the belly below pushes it upward), you need to consider the foreshortening effect this will have on the neckline. A dropped neck may look deep when the garment is laid flat, but look shallow when worn because the fabric travels outward across the bust instead of down toward

the ground. If you're busty, consider working dropped front necks a couple inches deeper than the pattern calls for, especially for V-neck and scoop-neck designs. But always review a pattern first to see if the pattern-writer accounted for this effect when sizing the pattern. One good way to determine the neck depth for your size is to follow the draw-your-own schematic instructions on page 20 .

A deep V-neck is generally flattering on busty women because it keeps the eye moving and frames the breasts in an attractive way. For such designs, I split the front at the level of the first underarm bind-off so that the front neck depth matches the total yoke depth, as in the Lystra Pullover (at right). For a shallower V-neck, begin the front neck split between 2" and 5" (5 and 12.5 cm) above the initial underarm bind-off. If you make the split more than 5" (12.5 cm) above the underarm bind-off, the V may be unattractively short and wide.

shoulder depth or slope

The shoulder depth, or slope, is the vertical difference between the armhole edge and the neck edge of the shoulder. A sweater with shoulder shaping is higher at the neck edge than the armhole edge, allowing for a tailored fit on the naturally sloping shoulder of the wearer. As long as the total yoke depth, armhole depth, and cross-back width of the sweater are adequate, shoulder shaping can be attractive for a plus-size woman. But if you're broad-shouldered, you might want to avoid drastic shoulder shaping. If your shoulder does not slope, a shaped shoulder might cause the armhole edge to be too snug.

underarm span

One element common to most construction styles is the underarm span—the straight bind-off worked at the beginning of the armhole shaping or the total width of fabric at the base of the armhole that spans between front and back in a finished, seamed sweater. For garments worked flat in pieces, the underarm bind-off equals about half the total width after seaming (the sum of the armhole bind-off for the front and back minus the width of the selvedge stitches lost in the seam). For garments worked in the round, the front and back armhole bind-offs are worked in a continuous section (and are not seamed) so that the underarm bind-off equals the total underarm span.

It's worth mentioning that stitches are not always bound off at the base of the underarm; sometimes the span stitches are placed on holders and then grafted to the corresponding sleeve underarm stitches in finishing.

Why do you need to set aside stitches for the underarm span? This "cut-out" width creates a notch for your arm and armpit. The fabric below this notch covers the side of your body (including the side "seam"). This fabric isn't needed above the armhole—it is replaced with the sleeve. The underarm span also accelerates the armhole decreases by getting rid of a number of stitches in one row (an important secondary function utilized by modified drop-shoulder, set-in, and yoked constructions).

In general, for garments knitted in pieces and seamed, the initial underarm bind-off should equal about 1" (2.5 cm) in width, resulting in a finished total span of 1¾" to 2" (4.5 to 5 cm) in the seamed garment. For plus-size garments, this initial bind-off is typically a bit wider (up to 2½" [6.5 cm] with a finished total span of 5" [12.5 cm]) so that the body width can be decreased more quickly to the desired cross-back width. Spans that are too wide become visible on the upper garment body—you may be plus-size, but your armpit is only so wide from front to back. For garments worked in the round, the initial underarm bind-off should equal about 1¾" to 2" (4.5 to 5 cm) in width, and certainly not more than 5" (12.5 cm).

LYSTRA PULLOVER [page 60]

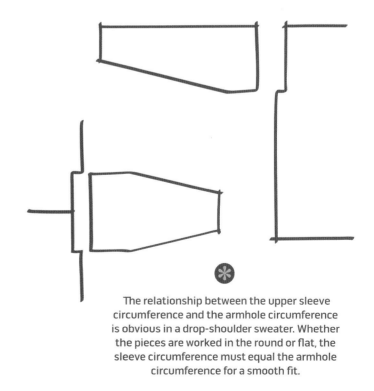

The relationship between the upper sleeve circumference and the armhole circumference is obvious in a drop-shoulder sweater. Whether the pieces are worked in the round or flat, the sleeve circumference must equal the armhole circumference for a smooth fit.

The underarm span is the sum of the distance bound off at the base of the armhole on the front and back.

sleeves

Sleeves vary widely from one construction style to the next—in length, ratio of sleeve circumference to armhole depth, and in cap width and length. The particular guidelines will be discussed in each garment-style chapter. For now, let's just cover the basics.

In general, plus-size women need shaped sleeves—sleeves that widen from cuff to upper arm. Otherwise, the cuff will be too voluminous at the wrist if the upper sleeve is wide enough to fit the fleshy arm. A straight sleeve that fits the wrist and forearm will probably have to stretch around the bicep. Plus-size women tend to carry weight in their upper arms, and for some women, this characteristic is quite pronounced. Measure your bicep and check the pattern schematics before knitting a sleeve. You may need to modify the upper sleeve width (or circumference) to fit your arm.

Use incremental increases to shape a sleeve from the cuff to the armhole. For the best results, work the increases evenly spaced over the length of the sleeve, ending 2" (5 cm) below the initial armhole bind-off. Although one increase row doesn't change the width much, the fabric will widen over many rows. Be sure to begin the increases in time for the increases to fit the shape of your arm. In general, increases should begin between 2" and 10" (5 and 25.5 cm) up from the cuff edge. The wider the sleeve needs to be, the sooner you'll start working increases, and at a faster pace.

Sleeves come in several length styles: extra-long (beyond the wrist), full-length (to the wrist), bracelet (to just above the wrist bone), three-quarter (halfway between wrist and elbow), elbow (what it sounds like), short (anywhere between elbow and shoulder), and cap (a sliver of fabric that cups the outer part of the shoulder). You'll see many styles used in this book, including sleeveless. What length looks good on you is a personal issue, as is what you like to wear. What are your preferences?

body shaping

Body shaping is the deliberate manipulation of stitch counts to affect fabric width. Changes in gauge are also manipulations of width, but, for our purposes, are not considered shaping. A sweater without body shaping but that does have a ribbed hem (which draws in) is still considered "unshaped."

An unshaped body silhouette forms a parallelogram. The body measures the same width from hem to waist to bust. An hourglass silhouette indents for the waist and expands outward for the bust. An A-line silhouette is wider at the hem, then tapers gradually to a narrower bust. A V-line silhouette is narrower at the hem and expands to a wider bust.

An unshaped body can range from a roomy fit to a slinky fit that creates its own curves via negative ease over the contours of the body. If you are square-bodied, an unshaped body gives a nice consistent fit.

An hourglass silhouette requires special attention to ensure the garment follows the body proportions exactly—narrowest where the

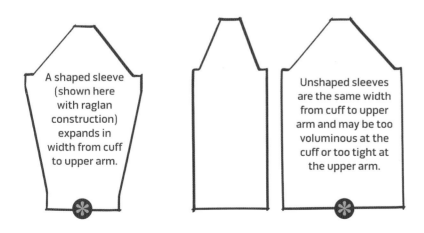

A shaped sleeve (shown here with raglan construction) expands in width from cuff to upper arm.

Unshaped sleeves are the same width from cuff to upper arm and may be too voluminous at the cuff or too tight at the upper arm.

body shapes

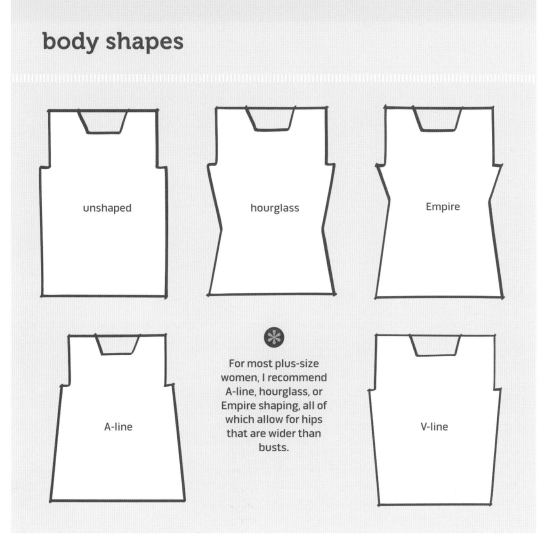

unshaped

hourglass

Empire

A-line

For most plus-size women, I recommend A-line, hourglass, or Empire shaping, all of which allow for hips that are wider than busts.

V-line

body is narrowest and widest where the body is widest. The hip and bust circumferences don't need to be equal.

An Empire waist is a modified hourglass, with the narrowest part raised closer to the bust, and the rate of shaping between the areas adjusted so that the body gradually decreases from the hem to the waist, then rapidly increases from the waist to the bust.

The A-line silhouette is a lovely choice for plus-size women. For a pear-shaped body, the sweater will have consistent ease along the body. If the line tapers to give little or negative ease at the bust, the garment will accentuate

the bust while still fitting around the hips comfortably. For a square-shaped body, the silhouette will create the illusion of the pear, which many consider a feminine shape (but be careful of too-roomy hemlines). For broad-shouldered women, the wider hem (especially when combined with a longer body length) will balance the upper body.

A V-line silhouette works best for large-busted but thin-hipped (apple shaped) women. Be aware that the V-line may accentuate the apple shape and that most plus-size women don't wear the V-line attractively (most thin women don't either!).

sweater + body measurements
standard + otherwise

Beyond bust circumference, there are many measurable expanses in a sweater, and there are accepted standards for most of them—for example, the length of a woman's set-in sleeve to the underarm is generally between 16" and 18" (40.5 and 45.5 cm). Having these standards at your fingertips can eliminate frustrating trial-and-error; why reinvent the wheel? While it is true that few women's bodies are "standard," these standards provide a starting point on which to base your own custom measurements. And we do have a standards list available in our sizes—the Craft Yarn Council of America (CYCA) has devised a table of standard measurements that range from a woman's 28" (71 cm) bust to a 62" (157.5 cm) bust.

The full chart is reproduced here, but you can always find it online at craftyarncouncil.com/womansize.html.

CYCA Chart of Standard Women's Measurements

Woman's size		X-Small	Small	Medium	Large	1X	2X	3X	4X	5X
BUST	inch	28–30	32–34	36–38	40–42	44–46	48–50	52–54	56–58	60–62
	cm	71–76	81.5–86.5	91.5–96.5	101.5–106.5	112–117	122–127	132–137	142–147.5	152.5–157.5
CENTER BACK NECK TO CUFF	inch	27–27½	28–28½	29–29½	30–30½	31–31½	31½–32	32½–33	32½–33	33–33½
	cm	68.5–70	71–72.5	73.5–75	76–77.5	78.5–80	80–81.5	82.5–84	82.5–84	84–85
BACK WAIST LENGTH	inch	16½	17	17¼	17½	17¾	18	18	18½	18½
	cm	42	43	44	44.5	45	45.5	45.5	47	47
CROSS BACK (shoulder to shoulder)	inch	14–14½	14½–15	16–16½	17–17½	17½	18	18	18½	18½
	cm	35.5–37	37–38	40.5–42	43–44.5	44.5	45.5	45.5	47	47
SLEEVE LENGTH TO UNDERARM	inch	16½	17	17	17½	17½	18	18	18½	18½
	cm	42	43	43	44.5	44.5	45.5	45.5	47	47
UPPER ARM	inch	9¾	10¼	11	12	13½	15½	17	18½	19½
	cm	25	26	28	30.5	34.5	39.5	43	47	49.5
ARMHOLE DEPTH	inch	6–6½	6½–7	7–7½	7½–8	8–8½	8½–9	9–9½	9½–10	10–10½
	cm	15–16.5	16.5–18	18–19	19–20.5	20.5–21.5	21.5–23	23–24	24–25.5	25.5–26.5
WAIST CIRCUMFERENCE	inch	23–24	25–26½	28–30	32–34	36–38	40–42	44–45	46–47	49–50
	cm	58.5–61	63.5–67.5	71–76	81.5–86.5	91.5–96.5	101.5–106.5	112–114.5	117–119.5	124.5–127
HIP CIRCUMFERENCE	inch	33–34	35–36	38–40	42–44	46–48	52–53	54–55	56–57	61–62
	cm	84–86.5	89–91.5	96.5–101.5	106.5–112	117–122	132–134.5	137–139.5	142–145	155–157.5

It's important to note that these measurements are for actual body parts, not finished sweater parts, except where specific sweaters elements are listed, such as sleeve length or armhole depth. These are listed because they don't necessarily correspond to a finite body measurement. It is also important to note that the sleeve lengths listed are based on set-in sleeve construction and don't always correspond to other styles. For example, a modified drop-shoulder sleeve should be worked a bit longer than a set-in (the CYCA standards would result in a sleeve that's too short for a modified drop-shoulder sweater). Finally, these measurements are for actual body measurements and do not include ease—it's up to you to add the desired amount of ease for the fit you want.

Standard measurement tools like the CYCA chart are great for designing your own sweaters and sizing the pattern. But I recommend you use it as a template to make your own personal

what is a schematic
+ how do I read it?

A schematic is a blueprint of a sweater design. The schematic reflects the garment as it would look if laid flat; either in one piece or in separate pieces, depending on the construction. It shows all the finite measurements based on the gauge(s), stitch counts, and the step-by-step instructions. Once you are familiar with the sweater elements discussed in Chapter 01, you'll understand the importance of each of the measurements marked on a schematic. Note that if the individual pieces (front or fronts, back, and sleeves) will be seamed during the finishing process, some fabric—and therefore width—will be lost in the seams. In these cases, the measurements in the schematic may differ slightly from the finished garment measurements. In general, pattern writers try to keep schematics as minimal as possible for space reasons, so a schematic will likely include only one sleeve and only one front of a cardigan.

A schematic will show measurements for all sizes in the pattern, but the drawing itself is usually rendered based on the proportions of the smallest size. If the larger sizes replicate the design identically, then the provided schematic should be sufficient for an understanding of the design and construction. It can be a useful practice (and a fun one) to draw your own schematic based on the proportions of your chosen size. You'll get a visual of the elements and how they interact, and you'll be best able to tweak the pattern for your particular body shape. Using graph paper and a scale of 1" (2.5 cm) of knitting, copy the provided schematic but draw the elements to the scale of the measurements for your size. Notice the silhouette differences between the smallest and the largest sizes of the Banstead Pullover, below.

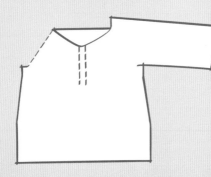

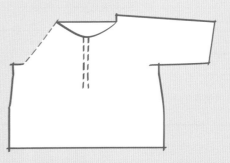

The body schematic for the Banstead Pullover (page 88) in size 42" (106.5 cm) bust (left) and size 66" (167.5 cm) bust (right).

measurements chart. Measure your body parts and record them in a copy of the chart so you can see, at a glance, how you compare to the "standard" woman who shares your bust circumference. This will help you see where to tweak sweater patterns to fit your particular shape—for example, if your upper arm is larger than that listed on the standards chart, you'll know that you'll need to adjust the upper sleeve width (or circumference) in the pattern.

A wonderful source for standard measurements, broken out by construction style, is Ann Budd's *The Knitter's Handy Guide to Sweater Patterns* (Interweave, 2004). Ann covers the general rules for drop shoulders, modified drop shoulders, set-ins, set-in saddle shoulders, raglans, and seamless yokes. She gives generic instructions for these styles (you pick your gauge) for adult sizes 36" to 54" (91.5 to 137 cm), as well as children's sizes. The schematics alone are valuable—at a glance, you can see the standard measurements for all the elements of sweaters in all the different construction styles. But because the larger sizes are geared for men, the sleeve lengths may be a little long for a plus-size woman.

In the following chapters, I have provided one basic design in each construction style. These may have unique design elements, such as the collar in the Farrington Pullover (page 30), but the body shapes are fairly generic in order to demonstrate the basic fit and construction elements. These patterns provide a set of standard measurements for plus sizes in each construction, and, at the same time, provide blank-slate projects into which you can incorporate your own design elements: body shaping, stitch patterns (which will require playing a bit with gauge and stitch counts), and any modifications needed to fit your shape.

what size do I knit?

Most knitting patterns list sizes by bust circumference. If you know your bust circumference and how much ease you want at the bust, choosing a size is fairly straightforward. But if your belly protrudes further than your bust, should you pick a size based on belly circumference? If you don't want the sweater to stretch over the bulge of your abdomen and emphasize its protrusion, then, yes, you should pick a size based on your belly. If you have one major problem area and don't want to customize your knitting, pick a size based on that particular part. Keep in mind that most patterns don't list sizes by elements other than bust circumference, so you'll need to review the schematics, gauge, and stitch counts in the pattern to figure out the size of the sweater at your problem area.

To determine your problem area(s), or if you have any, compare your measurements to the CYCA standards as directed on page 19. Are your other measurements in proportion to your bust? Or, do you have outliers that skew far from the CYCA standards for your bust size? If so, garments that follow your bust size won't fit these other areas because the pattern writer based the measurements on proportions that don't match yours. In general, not all pattern writers base sizing on CYCA standards, and some designs don't lend themselves to that type of exactitude in all areas. Always review all of the measurements on the schematic before choosing a size.

Some plus-size women address fit problems by making everything big. I have no argument with this. Sweaters are not shirts and don't need to be tailored to every body part. Positive ease is comfortable and hides lumps

If you like positive ease or choose to follow the big-sweater rule, I recommend drop-shoulder, seamless yoke, and dolman sweaters. If you want a tailored fit, I recommend set-in and, less emphatically, raglan sweaters. In any case, if you want custom fit, you will need to customize.

and bumps. A big sweater may make you look bigger, but in my opinion, a sweater that is too small will make you look even larger, while emphasizing every roll to boot. The big-sweater solution is fairly simple—if you have problem areas or want to distract from your shape, rather than show it off, an oversized sweater will do the trick. Choose a size with positive ease in relation to your problem areas and let everything else be hidden.

how to identify your non-standard measurements

To determine your problem areas in relation to a specific pattern, simply follow these four quick steps.

STEP 1 | Measure your bust and determine what size, based on wearing ease, you'd like to make for yourself.

STEP 2 | Find the measurements for the hip circumference, mid-abdomen circumference (waist, if there is waist shaping), and upper sleeve circumference of the finished garment. These are basic elements to any knitwear design and should be clearly labeled on a schematic that accompanies any pattern.

STEP 3 | Measure your own hip circumference, mid-abdomen circumference, and upper

sleeve circumference, and add the desired amount of ease to each.

STEP 4 | Align the numbers in columns to see the differences between the pattern measurements and your desired measurements.

According to the table below left, you've chosen to knit a sweater with zero ease at the bust. The problem is that your hips and arms are not in proportion to those used in the pattern. The finished garment will be 6" (15 cm) smaller than your hip circumference, 1" (2.5 cm) larger than your abdomen circumference, and 1½" (3.8 cm) smaller than your upper arm circumference. You now must choose whether to follow the instructions as written, knowing the sweater will end up too small in some areas, choose another size that accommodates your hip and arm circumferences, or customize the pattern to fit your exact shape.

Believe it or not, the biggest problem in this scenario is the too-small sleeve. Depending on the construction style, the sleeve width may greatly or minimally affect all the other sleeve and upper body elements. You can't just add stitches to the sleeve and then try to follow the pattern for the upper body and sleeve cap. Changing the sleeve stitch count means changing everything from the underarm up—tips for dealing with this problem are included in later chapters that focus on specific sweater constructions.

The name of the game is consistency. For a good-looking sweater, aim for consistent ease in all body parts. The exception to this rule can be the bust measurement. If you want to emphasize your feminine assets, you may prefer a closer fit around the bust than anywhere else. Regardless, you don't want to see the ease change drastically from part to part—6" (15 cm) of negative ease at the hips and 1" (2.5 cm) of positive ease at waist is going to ruin the graphic impact of your sweater.

Comparison of Pattern + Body Measurements

	PATTERN MEASUREMENTS	DESIRED MEASUREMENTS	DIFFERENCE
HIP	42" (106.5 cm)	46" (117 cm)	-6" (-15 cm)
ABDOMEN	42" (106.5 cm)	41" (104 cm)	1" (2.5 cm)
BUST	42" (106.5 cm)	42" (106.5 cm)	0
ARM	14" (35.5 cm)	15.5" (39.5 cm)	-1.5" (-3.8 cm)

02

What if the differences are more subtle? Let's say that instead of one major problem area, you have subtle disproportions. If your measurements will skew the overall fit toward negative ease—half an inch too small here, the exact size there, and so on—be realistic. Do you want a sweater that clings to your body and leaves little room for underlayers? Do not jump to the conclusion that this particular size will fit you. Beyond actually getting into the sweater, there are other aspects to fit. Drape, proportion, and ease of movement are altered when a sweater is tight. Go a size up or, you guessed it, customize.

basic steps for customizing + redesigning patterns

Many knitters are intimidated by the idea of altering patterns. If you know ahead of time what areas you'll need to rework and if you have an understanding of basic sweater construction, you do know enough to alter a pattern.

The best way to handle knitting challenges is to lay out all the information in an organized manner. Follow these steps to collect the necessary information to move forward with your sweater.

STEP 1 | Identify the construction style (see Chapters 03–07).

STEP 2 | Following the rules for that construction and your measurement needs, map out an idealized schematic.

STEP 3 | Compare your schematic to the original and identify which parts of the pattern can be worked as given and which need to be reworked (you may find that you can combine elements from different sizes in the pattern to make your custom size).

tweaking body shaping

If you want to simply tweak the body shaping (from hem to underarm), ask yourself the following two questions (before you buy the yarn!):

QUESTION 1. Is there a "blank space" at the side seams of the sweater into which the shaping can be worked? *Increases and decreases can be worked in "filler" stitches between the side seam and the stitch pattern without affecting the pattern repeats. These filler stitches are commonly worked in stockinette, reverse stockinette, ribbing, or another small-repeat pattern such as seed, moss, or basketweave stitch. Designers use these fillers to size the pattern, and they make it easy for you to modify the shape.*

QUESTION 2. If you adjust stitch counts, will you need to adjust pattern repeats? If so, can you do this within reason? *It will be more difficult to change numbers and maintain full pattern repeats for a pattern that repeats over 36 stitches than one that repeats over 8 stitches. If you can't adjust the pattern repeat within reason to accommodate your stitch count, you'll need to redesign the sweater, accept the provided shaping, make a different size, or move on to another project. Redesigning can be as simple as adding or subtracting filler stitches or as drastic as following the twelve customizing steps at left.*

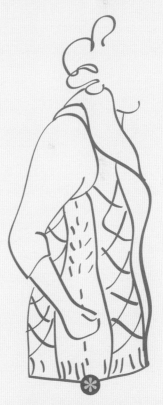

This cabled vest design uses stockinette "filler" stitches at the side seams. Side shaping can be worked within these filler stitches, leaving the patterned sections unaffected.

STEP 4 | Take the average stitch gauge of all patterns across a certain part—the sleeve cuff, lower body, cross-back, and so on—and determine roughly how many stitches you need to span the width of each part on your schematic. Write these numbers on your schematic.

STEP 5 | Take the average row/round gauge of all the stitch patterns up and down a certain part—body length to underarm, yoke depth from underarm to neck edge, and so on—and determine how many rows/rounds you need to fulfill your schematic lengths. Write these numbers on your schematic.

STEP 6 | Identify the limiting factors of the design: pattern repeats, design elements such as pockets and bands, internal devices such as short-rows or darts, and so on.

using short-rows for custom shaping

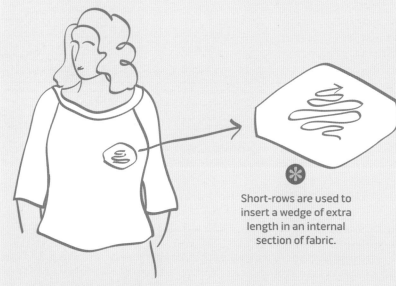

Short-rows are used to insert a wedge of extra length in an internal section of fabric.

A short-row is literally a short row, inserted between full-length rows to add height in an internal section. Check out *Big Girl Knits* (Potter Craft, 2006) for a great tutorial on short-rows geared to plus-size women.

You can use short-rows to add length at the bust, at the center of a sleeve cap, or anywhere you have isolated fullness. If the width of fabric in an area is not adequate for your fullness, you can address the problem by adding short-rows instead of following the instructions for a larger size. In this way, short-rows really work best in a garment with zero or negative ease, where the fabric is stretched over a full part, which would cause the length to draw up. Inserting a wedge of extra length at the fullest point alleviates the drawing up, while not actually adding to the width. The result is a more attractive fit.

Short-rows can also be used purely for their ability to fill vertical space—to raise the back neck of a seamless yoke, add inches to the back neck of a shawl collar, and so on.

However, short-rows don't come without complications. Used in baggy garments or used too liberally, short-rows can cause the fabric to pouch in strange ways—it's best to err on the side of too few short-rows than too many. Also be aware that short-rows, which interrupt a row of knitting, can be difficult to incorporate successfully into stitch patterns. Because so many popular sweater designs utilize stitch patterns, I find short-rows are not that practical as internal devices for custom shaping. In theory they're great, but in reality there are few times when they can be easily applied.

STEP 7 | Match these limiting factors to static points on the schematic such as hip width, upper sleeve width, shoulder depth, and so on. Tweak your stitch and row counts to work with the limiting factors. If you need to tweak a lot, consider using filler stitches and/or rows to reach your desired measurements. If you plan to keep static elements of the original pattern, start by placing these as the pattern states (for example, 20 repeats of the stitch pattern across the bust of a 76-round yoke).

STEP 8 | To transition from the isolated placement of limiting factors between each area of the schematic, configure what kind and how much shaping needs to be done—for example, gradual decreases, drastic increases the rate of 2 stitches every row for 10" (25.5 cm), raglan decreases every other round for the body but only every fourth round for the sleeves, and so on.

STEP 9 | Determine how many inches (centimeters) in length need to be worked even in each area.

STEP 10 | Determine how to work the shaping in pattern while maintaining the overall design.

STEP 11 | Record your stitch and row counts, the placement of design elements, and shaping instructions in an easy-to-follow pattern.

STEP 12 | Follow your own pattern to make the sweater.

adding sizes to a pattern

Mainstream knitting patterns often fall short for plus-size knitters. The same process described for customizing designs can be used for adding sizes to an inadequately sized pattern. Study the pattern, identify its key components, and generate a pattern that suits you while maintaining the design elements that attracted you to the original. In the end, you might become a designer yourself!

alternate modification: changing a sweater's construction

Sometimes, you can modify a sweater by changing the construction technique. For example, if you're broad-shouldered but have fallen in love with a set-in style, work it as a modified drop-shoulder silhouette instead. Similarly, work an oversized drop-shoulder sweater as a tailored set-in silhouette. Don't want to bother redesigning a set-in sleeve cap after modifying the sleeve circumference? Work the sweater with 1:1 raglan caps and armholes (i.e., the same number of rows in the sleeve cap and armhole depth), then seam the pieces together selvedge to selvedge. If you love the fit of a drop-shoulder sweater but don't like the obvious overhang of the cross-back width, work the sleeves with the body as for a dolman silhouette. If the diagonal tension along the armhole of a raglan is uncomfortable due to fleshy outer arms or broad shoulders, work the yoke with concentric shaping as for a seamless yoke (this is easy for simple stitch patterns but can cause problems with more complicated patterns). Once you identify the construction styles that work best for you, you can alter most patterns to fit those styles.

the drop-shoulder
sweater

The drop-shoulder is a classic style and one of the simplest constructions. A true drop-shoulder features no armhole shaping. A modified drop-shoulder has a single bound-off indentation at the underarm, then the armhole edges are worked even for the rest of the yoke.

Without the interference of shaping, the surfaces of drop-shoulder sweaters can be richly patterned without changes in pattern repeats—great for Aran and Fair Isle designs. The roomy fit is similar to that of a sweatshirt, making it ideal for women who like positive ease without customizing their knitting. The rectangular pieces make easy knitting for the beginner. The upper arm gets plenty of room, the fit is fairly universal, and, styled right, the look is fashionable.

who should wear the drop-shoulder style?

The pitfalls of drop-shoulder construction can ring especially true for women in the largest sizes—when bust circumferences approach the mid-50s (about 139 cm), the upper body becomes proportionately overwhelming. If the front bust width is 27½" (70 cm) wide and 1" (2.5 cm) of width is bound off at each underarm, the cross-back will measure a sizeable 25½" (65 cm). Whether or not this cross-back is too wide for a woman with a 55" (139.5 cm) bust circumference is hard to generalize. For some women, a wide cross-back is roomy but comfortable. But for others, it will lead to

drastic shoulder overhang. Before you decide to knit a drop-shoulder sweater, evaluate the proportionate difference between your bust and actual cross-back widths. If you're large-busted and narrow-framed, the drop shoulder may be particularly problematic for you.

In general, however, most women can wear a drop-shoulder sweater. The lack of tailoring makes it a one-size-fits-all construction. So it's roomy up top—that's the idea. You have to decide how roomy is too roomy. On the flip side, women with broad shoulders almost require drop-shoulder sweaters. The narrow shoulder of a set-in and the diagonal tension of a raglan can be unhappy constructions for the big-boned woman, whose thicker build puts stress on armhole seams, sleeve caps, and the fabric in the shoulder areas.

When I began exploring how different constructions fit plus-size women in real life, I had one preconceived assumption—plus-size women should avoid drop-shoulder sweaters. I assumed that because we need so much width at the bust, the resulting wide cross-back would be ridiculous and ill-fitting. To my astonishment, I found that drop-shoulder sweaters fit some women—those with broad, high shoulders—beautifully. The sweaters weren't oversized or disproportionate. In fact, they fit these women much better than the set-in sweaters (my assumed best-fit style for all plus-size women). Women, and especially tall women, with broad shoulders and a large frame benefit greatly from the wider shoulder and wider cross-back of the drop-shoulder construc-

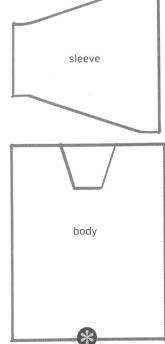

True drop-shoulder sweaters have no armhole shaping.

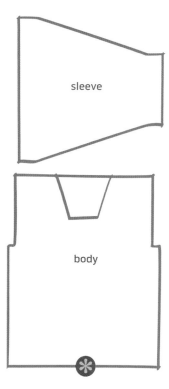

Modified drop-shoulder sweaters have short indentions at the underarms.

tion. They may require longer sleeves, but the body of the sweater fits quite nicely.

drop-shoulder construction

When knitting a drop-shoulder sweater, you can work the front and back in a single piece on a circular needle (as in the Vauxhall Tunic at right) or in separate pieces that are seamed together (as in the Farrington Pullover on page 30). The sleeves can be worked separately and sewn into the armholes (as for the Farrington Pullover), or stitches can be picked up around the armhole of the finished body and worked down to the cuff (as for the Vauxhall Tunic).

All three of the drop-shoulder sweaters in this chapter are worked as modified-drops with an underarm span. The Farrington Pullover, a basic prototype for the drop-shoulder, is worked flat in pieces, then seamed. The Waltham Cabled Cardigan (page 46) is also worked in pieces and seamed. The Vauxhall Pullover is worked in the round in stranded colorwork, with steeks for the neck and armhole openings. This design features top-down sleeves that are picked up around the armhole edges and worked to the cuffs—this sweater requires no seaming.

The Armhole

To partially alleviate the problem of the wide cross-back and to create a notch for the armhole, you can work an initial underarm bind-off to produce modified drop-shoulder shaping, as was done for all three of the drop-shoulder designs in this chapter. In general, the underarm span for a modified drop measures about 1" (2.5 cm) at each edge to give a final seamed span of 1¾" to 2" (4.5 to 5 cm). Cutting away a couple inches of the yoke in this way has one distinct benefit—the cross-back is not quite as wide as the bust. This makes the modified drop better for plus-size women, as the shoulders don't need to be as wide as the lower body of our sweaters.

For plus-size patterns, you might see underarm spans that measure over 5" (12.5 cm). This is usually done in an effort to create a narrower cross-back without formal set-in shaping, but

notable effects
of drop-shoulder construction

+ The cross-back width is the same as the bust width in true drop-shoulder construction; the back width is a bit narrower than the bust width in modified drop-shoulder construction.

+ The shoulder is wide and, on some women, overhangs the shoulder onto the upper arm.

+ The sleeve cap typically has no shaping.

+ The sleeve cap bind-off edge must fit around the armhole, stitches to rows, without the help of an extended cap; this means the upper sleeve has to be fairly wide.

+ The armhole depth measures half of the upper sleeve circumference.

+ A narrow fitted sleeve will only fit a shallow drop-shoulder armhole, which is not ideal for plus-size women.

+ The drop-shoulder sweater requires more yarn (and more knitting) than a set-in pullover.

+ The shapeless silhouette is not particularly flattering.

such drastic armholes can be problematic. Think of the indentation of the armhole—it is a right angle. The wider the bottom leg of the angle becomes, the more the point of that angle will creep onto your chest (see Underarm Span on page 14). Therefore, it's best to keep the underarm span under 5" (12.5 cm). In fact, the smaller your bust, the closer to 2" (5 cm) the span should be. If your goal is a sweater that doesn't swim in the shoulders and upper body, choose a set-in construction (see Chapter 04) instead.

The Sleeve

The sleeve on a drop-shoulder sweater, whether it's a true drop or modified, is longer than the actual arm length from wrist to underarm. In general, a drop-shoulder sleeve for a plus-size woman measures 20" to 21" (51 to 53.5 cm), while her arm typically measures about 18" (45.5 cm). To understand why the sleeve is longer than the arm measurement, it helps to compare the drop sleeve to a set-in sleeve.

For a size 44" (112 cm) pullover, a drop-shoulder sleeve is about 21" (53.5 cm) long, while its set-in counterpart is only about 17¾" (45 cm) long. The set-in closely matches the actual length of the arm (18" [45.5 cm]) because the part of the set-in sleeve worked to the sleeve cap clothes the arm just from the wrist to the underarm (the cap covers the distance from the underarm to the shoulder). A drop-shoulder sleeve, on the other hand, has to accommodate the length from wrist to underarm on the inside and, at the same time, the length from the wrist to the top of the shoulder on the outside. The extra length acts as a rudimentary cap, extending into the upper arm area. The specialized cap of a set-in sleeve covers that area and, combined together, a set-in sleeve can measure longer than a drop-shoulder sleeve. That is because the overhang of the drop-shoulder's wide cross-back accounts for some of the sleeve length—the body reaches down part way to meet the sleeve.

VAUXHALL TUNIC [page 36]

If you alter the upper sleeve width of a drop-shoulder sleeve, you will need to alter the armhole depth of the body as well. This is because the bind-off edge of the sleeve (the total width) has to match the selvedge edge of the armhole (the circumference). Do not attempt to match a true fitted sleeve with drop-shoulder construction—the shallow armhole, accompanied by a wide shoulder, will make for odd results in fit and appearance.

farrington pullover

DESIGNED BY **LISA SHROYER**

A dramatic slouch collar forms the focal point in this otherwise simple modified drop-shoulder sweater. The pieces are worked flat and then seamed; plain stockinette allows for custom body shaping. You'll find this seeded rib edging in a few of my designs—it makes a great non-curling edge that doesn't contract like traditional ribbing. In a chunky yarn and relaxed silhouette, this design is meant to be worn with positive ease for a comfortable outer layer. If you like the collar treatment but prefer a refined fit, try applying this collar to the Lystra Pullover on page 60. The V-neck shaping in both designs is similar and splits at about the same depth on the fronts.

FINISHED SIZE
About 47 (49, 52½, 54½, 58, 60, 63½)" (119.5 [124.5, 133.5, 138.5, 147.5, 152.5, 161.5] cm) bust circumference. Sweater shown measures 47" (119.5 cm).

YARN
Heavy worsted weight (#5 Bulky).

Shown here: Brown Sheep Lanaloft Worsted (100% wool; 160 yd [146 m]/100 g): #LL45 Manhattan mist (light blue), 8 (8, 9, 9, 10, 10, 11) balls.

NEEDLES
Body and sleeves: size U.S. 9 (5.5 mm): straight or 24" (60 cm) circular (cir).

Ribbing: size U.S. 8 (5 mm): straight.

Collar: size U.S. 9 (5.5 mm): 24" (60 cm) cir.

Adjust needle size if necessary to obtain the correct gauge.

NOTIONS
Stitch holders; markers (m); removable marker; tapestry needle.

GAUGE
14½ stitches and 20 rows = 4" (10 cm) in stockinette stitch.

notes

+ A 24" (60 cm) or shorter size U.S. 9 (5.5 mm) circular needle is recommended for working the collar, but if you use a circular needle for the body, the same needle can also be used for the collar.

+ The body length to the armhole gets progressively shorter with each size because the armhole depth gets progressively deeper with each size; the total length from cast-on edge to shoulder line for this project has been capped at 28" (71 cm), and the lengths for the individual sizes are 26¾ (27½, 28, 28, 28, 28, 28)" (68 [70, 71, 71, 71, 71, 71] cm).

+ Because the cross-back width gets progressively wider for the larger sizes, the sleeves get progressively shorter to prevent the cuff-to-cuff measurement from becoming too wide.

+ This design features no body shaping; the hip and bust measurements are equal. A relaxed fit at the bust paired with a strained fit around the hips is neither attractive nor comfortable. Is your hip circumference larger than your bust? If so, consider working A-line shaping in the lower body. Working within the multiple of the rib pattern at the hem (multiple of 2 stitches + 3), cast on for your needed hip circumference. Then, starting several inches up from the cast on, gradually decrease to the stitch count for your bust size. This is a better solution than choosing a size based on the hip circumference, which would cause the garment to be far too large for you.

+ Before altering stitch counts for the sleeves, carefully review the materials on drop-shoulder construction earlier in this chapter. The sleeve width and armhole depth are fundamentally linked; changing one means changing the other (or you'll face a seaming nightmare when trying to fit the sleeve into the armhole).

back

With smaller needles, CO 85 (89, 95, 99, 105, 109, 115) sts.

ROW 1 (RS) Knit.
ROW 2 (WS) P2, *k1, p1; rep from * to last 3 sts, k1, p2.

Rep these 2 rows 4 more times—piece measures about 1½" (3.8 cm) from CO. Change to larger needles and work in St st (knit RS rows; purl WS rows) until piece measures 17 (17, 16½, 16, 15½, 15½, 15)" (43 [43, 42, 40.5, 39.5, 39.5, 38] cm) from CO (see Notes), ending with a WS row.

Shape Armholes

BO 6 (6, 7, 7, 7, 8, 8) sts at beg of next 2 rows—73 (77, 81, 85, 91, 93, 99) sts rem. Work even in St st until armholes measure 9¾ (10½, 11½, 12, 12½, 12½, 13)" (25 [26.5, 29, 30.5, 31.5, 31.5, 33] cm). Place sts on holder.

front

Work as for back until 2 rows before armhole shaping, ending with a WS row—85 (89, 95, 99, 105, 109, 115) sts; piece measures about 16½ (16½, 16, 15½, 15, 15, 14½)" (42 [42, 40.5, 39.5, 38, 38, 37] cm) from CO.

Shape Neck

NEXT ROW (RS) K42 (44, 47, 49, 52, 54, 57), BO center st, knit to end—42 (44, 47, 49, 52, 54, 57) sts rem each side.

Work neck and armhole shaping separately for each side as foll (sts for left front may rem on needle while working sts of right front).

RIGHT FRONT

NEXT ROW (WS) Purl to BO gap at center, turn.

DEC ROW (RS) Sl 1 pwise with yarn in back (wyb), k1, ssk, knit to end—1 st dec'd at neck edge.

NEXT ROW (WS) BO 6 (6, 7, 7, 7, 8, 8) sts for armhole, purl to end—35 (37, 39, 41, 44, 45, 48) sts rem.

Slipping the first st of every RS row, rep dec row on the next 1 (3, 5, 5, 6, 6, 7) RS row(s), then every other RS row (i.e., every 4th row) 10 times—24 (24, 24, 26, 28, 29, 31) sts rem. Work even in St st until armhole measures 9¾ (10½, 11½, 12, 12½, 12½, 13)" (25 [26.5, 29, 30.5, 31.5, 31.5, 33] cm). Place sts on holder.

LEFT FRONT

With WS facing, rejoin yarn to left front neck edge.

NEXT ROW (WS) Purl.

NEXT ROW (RS) BO 6 (6, 7, 7, 7, 8, 8) sts, knit to last 4 sts, k2tog, k2—35 (37, 39, 41, 44, 45, 48) sts rem.

NEXT ROW (WS) Sl 1 pwise with yarn in front (wyf), purl to end.

DEC ROW (RS) Knit to last 4 sts, k2tog, k2—1 st dec'd at neck edge.

Slipping the first st of WS rows, rep dec row on the next 0 (2, 4, 4, 5, 5, 6) RS rows, then every other RS row 10 times—24 (24, 24, 26, 28, 29, 31) sts rem. Work even in St st until armhole measures 9¾ (10½, 11½, 12, 12½, 12½, 13)" (25 [26.5, 29, 30.5, 31.5, 31.5, 33] cm). Place sts on holder.

sleeves

With smaller needles, CO 43 (43, 45, 45, 45, 47, 47) sts.

ROW 1 (RS) Knit.

ROW 2 (WS) P2, *k1, p1; rep from * to last 3 sts, k1, p2.

Rep these 2 rows 4 more times— piece measures about 1½" (3.8 cm) from CO. Change to larger needles and work 2 rows in St st, ending with a WS row.

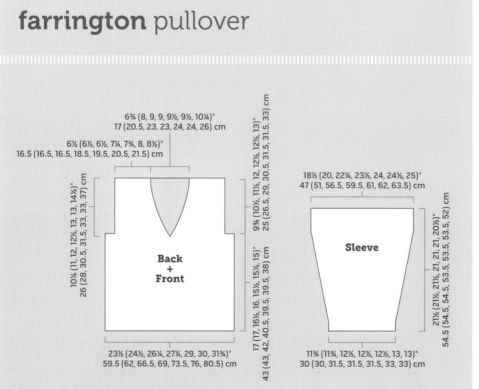

farrington pullover

6¾ (8, 9, 9, 9½, 9½, 10¼)"
17 (20.5, 23, 23, 24, 24, 26) cm

6½ (6½, 6½, 7¼, 7¾, 8, 8½)"
16.5 (16.5, 16.5, 18.5, 19.5, 20.5, 21.5) cm

9¾ (10½, 11½, 12, 12½, 12½, 13)"
25 (26.5, 29, 30.5, 31.5, 31.5, 33) cm

10¼ (11, 12, 12½, 13, 13, 14½)"
26 (28, 30.5, 31.5, 33, 33, 37) cm

Back + Front

17 (17, 16½, 16, 15½, 15½, 15)"
43 (43, 42, 40.5, 39.5, 39.5, 38) cm

23½ (24½, 26¼, 27¼, 29, 30, 31¾)"
59.5 (62, 66.5, 69, 73.5, 76, 80.5) cm

18½ (20, 22¼, 23½, 24, 24½, 25)"
47 (51, 56.5, 59.5, 61, 62, 63.5) cm

Sleeve

21½ (21½, 21½, 21, 21, 21, 20½)"
54.5 (54.5, 54.5, 53.5, 53.5, 53.5, 52) cm

11¾ (11¾, 12½, 12½, 12½, 13, 13)"
30 (30, 31.5, 31.5, 31.5, 33, 33) cm

INC ROW (RS) K2, M1 (see Glossary), knit to last 2 sts, M1, k2—2 sts inc'd.

[Work 7 (7, 5, 5, 3, 3, 1) row(s) even, then rep inc row] 5 (1, 4, 3, 20, 20, 4) time(s)—55 (47, 55, 53, 87, 89, 57) sts. Rep inc row every 6 (6, 4, 4, 0, 0, 4)th row 6 (13, 13, 16, 0, 0, 17) times—67 (73, 81, 85, 87, 89, 91) sts. Work even in St st until piece measures 21½ (21½, 21½, 21, 21, 21, 20½)" (54.5 [54.5, 54.5, 53.5, 53.5, 53.5, 52] cm) from CO (see Notes), ending with a WS row. BO all sts.

finishing

Block pieces to measurements. With RS touching and WS facing out, use the three-needle method (see Glossary) to BO 24 (24, 24, 26, 28, 29, 31) held back and right shoulder sts tog. Rep for left shoulder—25 (29, 33, 33, 35, 35, 37) center back sts rem on holder.

Collar

With 24" (60 cm) cir needle (see Notes) and RS facing, join yarn to beg of held center back sts. K25 (29, 33, 33, 35, 35, 37) back neck sts, pick up and knit 30 (32, 36, 36, 38, 38, 40) sts evenly spaced along left front neck to base of V-neck, pick up and knit 1 st from center front BO, then 30 (32, 36, 36, 38, 38, 40) sts evenly spaced along right front neck—86 (94, 106, 106, 112, 112, 118) sts total. Pm, and join for working in rnds; rnd beg at right shoulder.

INC RND [K1f&b (see Glossary), k1] 12 (14, 16, 16, 17, 17, 18) times, k1f&b, pm for left shoulder, [k1, k1f&b] 15 (16, 18, 18, 19, 19, 20) times, k1 (center front st) and place a removable marker in this st, [k1f&b, k1] 15 (16, 18, 18, 19, 19, 20) times—129 (141, 159, 159, 168, 168, 177) sts; 38 (44, 50, 50, 53, 53, 56) back neck sts; 45 (48, 54, 54, 57, 57, 60) sts each side of 1 marked center front st.

NOTE *The collar is worked in rev St st (purl on RS, knit on WS). Turn the work so the WS of the collar is facing so you can work the collar rnds by knitting each rnd instead of purling. Move the removable marker up as you work so you can always identify the center front st. Cont as foll with WS (knit side) of collar facing:*

RND 1 (dec rnd) K44 (47, 53, 53, 56, 56, 59) along right front neck to 1 st before marked st at center front, sl 2 tog kwise, k1, p2sso, knit to end—2 sts dec'd at center front.
RND 2 Knit.
RND 3 Knit to 1 st before marked st at center front, sl 2 tog kwise, k1, p2sso, knit to end—2 sts dec'd.
RND 4 Knit.

Rep the last 2 rnds 8 (9, 9, 9, 10, 10, 10) more times—109 (119, 137, 137, 144, 144, 153) sts rem; collar measures about 4¼ (4½, 4½, 4½, 5, 5, 5)" (11 [11.5, 11.5, 11.5, 12.5, 12.5, 12.5] cm) from pick-up rnd, measured straight up along a single column of sts (not along the mitered dec line at center front). Work short-rows (see Glossary) as foll:

SHORT-ROW 1 (knit side) Knit to 1 st before marked st at center front,
sl 2 tog kwise, k1, p2sso, knit to 6 sts beyond m at left shoulder (not beg-of-rnd m at right shoulder), wrap next st, turn.
SHORT-ROW 2 (purl side) Purl to 6 sts past beg-of-rnd m, wrap next st, turn.
SHORT-ROWS 3, 5, AND 7 Knit to 1 st before marked st at center front, sl 2 tog kwise, k1, p2sso, knit to 6 sts before previously wrapped st, wrap next st, turn.
SHORT-ROWS 4, 6, AND 8 Purl to 6 sts before previously wrapped st, wrap next st, turn.
NEXT ROW Knit to beg-of-rnd m at right shoulder; there is no need to work the wraps tog with the wrapped sts because the purl bumps will hide them—101 (111, 129, 129, 136, 136, 145) sts rem.

Beg working in rnds again and knit 1 rnd across all sts.

DEC RND K1 (1, 1, 1, 0, 0, 1), *k2tog; rep from *—51 (56, 65, 65, 68, 68, 73) sts rem.

Knit 1 rnd—collar measures about 6¾ (7, 7, 7, 7½, 7½, 7½)" (17 [18, 18, 18, 19, 19, 19] cm) from pick-up rnd in front and 4¾ (5, 5, 5, 5½, 5½, 5½)" (12 [12.5, 12.5, 12.5, 14, 14, 14] cm) in back, measured along a single column of sts. BO all sts kwise.

With yarn threaded on a tapestry needle, sew sleeve tops into armholes, matching midpoint of each sleeve with shoulder seam and easing to fit. Sew sleeve and side seams. Weave in loose ends. Block again if desired.

vauxhall tunic

DESIGNED BY **NANCY SHROYER**

A single color for the background and edging gives contemporary appeal to the stranded colorwork in this modified-drop pullover. Traditional Fair Isle patterns typically run in horizontal bands, but, for this tunic, Nancy Shroyer plotted snowflake motifs in vertical bands, then filled the interior sections with an allover lattice pattern. The A-line body, caftan-style neck placket, hemmed edges, and options for adjusting body and sleeve length are all friendly to plus-size curves. The armholes and neck openings are steeked; the sleeve stitches are picked up around the cut armhole edges and worked down—no seaming is required.

FINISHED SIZE
About 40½ (44¾, 47¾, 49, 52, 56¼, 59)" (103 [113.5, 121.5, 124.5, 132, 143, 150] cm) bust circumference. Tunic shown measures 44¾" (113.5 cm) with 19¾" (50 cm) sleeves.

YARN
Sportweight (#2 Fine).

Shown here: Brown Sheep Nature Spun Sport Weight (100% wool; 184 yd [168 m]/ 50 g): #114 storm (dark brown) 7 (8, 8, 9, 9, 10, 10) balls; #117 winter blue (medium blue), 1 (1, 1, 2, 2, 2, 2) skein(s); #N30 Nordic blue (dark blue), 1 (1, 1, 1, 2, 2, 2) skein(s); #115 bit of blue (light blue), 1 (1, 1, 1, 1, 1, 2) skein(s); #N21 mallard (dark green) and #N56 meadow green (medium green), 1 (1, 1, 1, 1, 2, 2) skein(s) each; #N20 arctic moss (light green), 1 (1, 2, 2, 2, 2, 2) skein(s); #N94 Bev's bear (dark gold), 1 skein for all sizes.

NEEDLES
Edging: size U.S. 2 (3 mm): 16" and 40" (40 and 100 cm) circular (cir) and set of 4 or 5 double-pointed (dpn).

Body and sleeves: size U.S. 5 (3.75 mm): 16" and 40 (40, 47, 47, 47, 47, 47)" (100 [100, 120, 120, 120, 120, 120] cm) cir and set of 4 or 5 dpn.

Adjust needle size if necessary to obtain the correct gauge.

NOTIONS
Markers (m), removable markers; stitch holders; tapestry needle; sewing machine or sharp-point sewing needle and matching thread for securing steeks.

GAUGE
28 stitches and 29 rounds = 4" (10 cm) in stockinette Fair Isle patterns from charts, worked in rounds.

notes

+ The tunic is worked in the round from the hemmed lower edge to the shoulder line. Steek stitches are cast-on at the base of the armholes and at the center of the front and back neck openings. These steeks are reinforced and cut open later in preparation for picking up sleeve stitches and finishing the neck edges.

+ The lower edge circumference is about 3" (7.5 cm) larger than the bust circumference, with side decreases to create an A-line silhouette.

+ If you would like to make the tunic longer, work the hem, then work one or more extra repeats of the entire 25-round pattern before continuing according to the directions. Every additional repeat will add about 3¼" (8.5 cm) to the lower body length. Plan on purchasing extra yarn for a longer garment.

+ Two sleeve length options are given: one with 5½ repeats of the chart patterns for a 19¾" (50 cm) sleeve and one with 6 repeats of the chart patterns for a 21½" (54.5 cm) sleeve. To determine sleeve length, try on the sweater, have someone else measure from the sweater armhole to your wrist, and compare this length to the available options. The sleeves given are planned to end after finishing a complete 25-round repeat above the hemmed cuff, so adjusting length by adding or subtracting a few rounds at the end of the sleeve is not recommended. Instead, make any changes by adding or removing half-repeats of the pattern, taking care to begin the sleeve patterns with either Rnd 1 (to begin with a whole repeat) or Rnd 13 (to begin with a half repeat) of the charts. Each half-repeat added or removed will lengthen or shorten the sleeve by about 1¾" (4.5 cm). The length can be further fine-tuned by working a deeper hem at the sleeve cuff.

body

With dark brown and longer cir needle in smaller size, use the knitted method (see Glossary) to CO 304 (334, 354, 364, 384, 414, 434) sts. Place marker (pm) and join for working in rnds, being careful not to twist sts; rnd begins at left side at start of front sts. Knit 3 rnds.

DEC RND *K8, k2tog; rep from * to last 4 sts, k4—274 (301, 319, 328, 346, 373, 391) sts rem.

Knit 3 rnds, then purl 1 rnd for fold line, then knit 3 rnds.

INC RND *K9, M1 (see Glossary); rep from * to last 4 sts, k4—304 (334, 354, 364, 384, 414, 434) sts.

Knit 3 rnds to complete hem—piece measures about ¾" (2 cm) from fold line.

Change to longer cir needle in larger size and knit 1 rnd. Join dark blue and establish patts from Rnd 1 of charts (page 39) as foll: *Work 25 (30, 35, 35, 40, 45, 50) sts according to Lattice chart, 31 sts according to Snowflake chart, 40 (45, 45, 50, 50, 55, 55) sts according to Lattice chart, 31 sts according to Snowflake chart, 25 (30, 35, 35, 40, 45, 50) sts according to Lattice chart, pm for right side; rep from * for back, omitting final pm because end-of-rnd m is already in place. Work in established patts until Rnd 20 of charts has been completed—piece measures about 3½" (9 cm) from fold line.

DEC RND (Rnd 21 of charts) Ssk, work in patt to 2 sts before next m, k2tog, slip marker (sl m), ssk, work in patt to last 2 sts, k2tog—4 sts dec'd.

Work 15 (14, 14, 13, 13, 12, 11) rnds even, then rep the dec rnd] 4 times—142 (157, 167, 172, 182, 197, 207) sts each for front and back. Work 27 (27, 27, 28, 28, 25, 25) rnds even—112 (108, 108, 105, 105, 98, 94) chart rnds completed; last chart rnd completed is Rnd 12 (8, 8, 5, 5, 23, 19); piece measures 16¼ (15¾, 15¾, 15¼, 15¼, 14¼, 13¾)" (41.5 [40, 40, 38.5, 38.5, 36, 35] cm) from fold line.

NOTE *All sizes are the same length to the shoulders; the larger sizes have increasingly shorter lower bodies because they have deeper armholes.*

Shape Armholes + Front Placket

NOTE *The steeks for the front placket opening are established on Rnd 13 of the 5th chart rep, or the 113th chart rnd from the beg. For the smallest size, this is the same rnd as the armhole steeks. For the remaining sizes, the front placket steek will be established while the armhole shaping is in progress.*

SIZE 40½" ONLY
ARMHOLE AND FRONT PLACKET STEEK RND (Rnd 13 of 5th chart rep) Use removable m to mark the center 14 front sts—64 front sts on each side of marked sts. Place the first 9 sts on a holder for the front half of left underarm, use the knitted method to CO 3 sts for steek, alternating background,

LATTICE

SNOWFLAKE

dark brown

dark blue

medium blue

light blue

dark green

medium green

light green

dark gold

pattern repeat

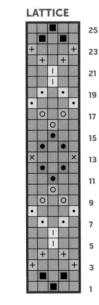

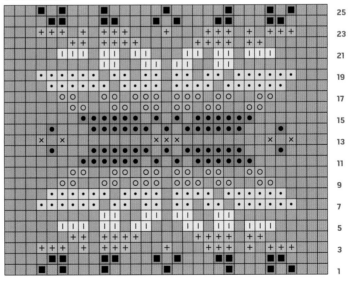

foreground, background (BFB) colors, pm, work in patt to marked center front sts, BO 14 sts in patt, work in patt to 9 sts before right side m, pm, place next 18 sts onto holder for right underarm (removing side m when you come to it), use the knitted method to CO 6 sts for steek (alternating colors as [BFB] 2 times), pm, work in patt to last 9 sts of back, place last 9 sts onto a holder for back half of left underarm, use the knitted method to CO 3 sts as BFB, pm for end-of-rnd—124 back sts; 55 front sts on each side of BO gap; 6 steek sts at each underarm; 11 sts in lattice patt outside snowflake patt at each side of front and back; rnd beg in center of left underarm steek.

Work each set of 6 steek sts in stripe patt of [BFB] 2 times throughout to create a visual guide for cutting and sewing the steeks later.

NEXT RND Work in patt to gap formed by center front BO sts, pm, use the knitted method to CO 6 steek sts as [BFB] 2 times, pm, work in patt to end—no change to back and front st counts; 6 steek sts at each underarm and center front.

SIZES (44¾, 47¾, 49, 52, 56¼, 59)" ONLY

ARMHOLE STEEK RND Place the first 9 sts on a holder for the front half of left underarm, use the knitted method to CO 3 sts for steek alternating background, foreground, background (BFB) colors, pm, work in patt to 9 sts before right side m, pm, place next 18 sts onto holder for right underarm (removing side m when you come to it), use the knitted method to CO 6 sts for steek (alternating colors as [BFB] 2 times), pm, work in patt to last 9 sts of back, place last 9 sts onto a holder for back half of left underarm, use the knitted method to CO 3 sts as BFB, pm for end of rnd—(139, 149, 154, 164, 179, 189) sts each for front and back; 6 steek sts at each underarm; (16, 21, 21, 26, 31, 36) sts in lattice patt outside snowflake patt at each side of front and back; rnd beg in center of left underarm steek.

NEXT RND Work 1 rnd even in patt, keeping steek sts in stripe patt of [BFB] 2 times to create a visual guide for cutting and sewing the steeks later.

ALL SIZES

NOTE *For the six largest sizes, the front placket BO and steek are worked while the armhole shaping is in progress; read all the way through the next sections before proceeding.*

ARMHOLE DEC RND Keeping in patt, work 3 steek sts, sl m, ssk, work to 2 sts before right armhole steek, k2tog, sl m, work 6 steek

vauxhall tunic

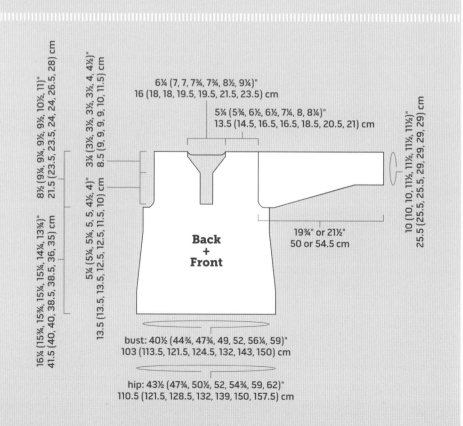

6¼ (7, 7, 7¾, 7¾, 8½, 9¼)"
16 (18, 18, 19.5, 19.5, 21.5, 23.5) cm

5¼ (5¾, 6½, 6½, 7¼, 8, 8¼)"
13.5 (14.5, 16.5, 16.5, 18.5, 20.5, 21) cm

8½ (9¼, 9¼, 9¼, 9½, 10½, 11)"
21.5 (23.5, 23.5, 24, 24, 26.5, 28) cm

3¼ (3¼, 3½, 3½, 3½, 4, 4½)"
8.5 (9, 9, 9, 9, 10, 11.5) cm

5¼ (5¼, 5¼, 5, 5, 4½, 4)"
13.5 (13.5, 13.5, 12.5, 12.5, 11.5, 10) cm

16¼ (15¾, 15¾, 15¾, 15¼, 14¼, 13¾)"
41.5 (40, 40, 38.5, 38.5, 36, 35) cm

10 (10, 10, 11½, 11½, 11½, 11½)"
25.5 (25.5, 25.5, 29, 29, 29, 29) cm

19¾" or 21½"
50 or 54.5 cm

Back + Front

bust: 40½ (44¾, 47¾, 49, 52, 56¼, 59)"
103 (113.5, 121.5, 124.5, 132, 143, 150) cm

hip: 43½ (47¾, 50½, 52, 54¾, 59, 62)"
110.5 (121.5, 128.5, 132, 139, 150, 157.5) cm

sts, sl m, ssk, work to 2 sts before left armhole steek, k2tog, sl m, work 3 steek sts—2 sts each dec'd from front and back.

[Work 1 rnd even in patt, then rep the dec rnd] 3 times—8 total sts each removed from front and back, including first dec rnd.

SIZES (44¾, 47¾, 49, 52, 56¼, 59)" ONLY

At the same time after completing Rnd 112 of the 5th chart rep (112th chart rnd from the beg), use removable m to mark the center (15, 15, 14, 14, 15, 15) front sts.

FRONT PLACKET STEEK RND (Rnd 13 of 5th chart rep) Work in patt to marked center front sts (including any required armhole shaping), BO (15, 15, 14, 14, 15, 15) sts in patt, work in patt to end.

NEXT RND Work in patt to gap formed by BO sts, pm, use the knitted method to CO 6 steek sts as BFBBFB, pm, work in patt to end—6 steek sts at each underarm and center front.

ALL SIZES

When all armhole and front placket shaping has been completed, there will rem 116 (131, 141, 146, 156, 171, 181) back sts; 51 (58, 63, 66, 71, 78, 83) front sts on each side of center front steek; three 6-st steeks; 7 (12, 17, 17, 22, 27, 32) sts in lattice patt outside snowflake patt at each side of front and back. Work even in patt until 150 (150, 150, 148, 148, 146, 142) chart rnds have been completed from the beg, ending with Rnd 25 (25, 25, 23, 23, 21, 17) of 6th

chart rep—armholes measure about 5¼ (5¾, 5¾, 6, 6, 6½, 6½)" (13.5 [14.5, 14.5, 15, 15, 16.5, 16.5] cm).

Shape Front Neck

NECK DEC RND (Rnd 1 [1, 1, 24, 24, 22, 18] of charts) Keeping in patt, work to 2 sts before front placket steek, ssk, sl m, work 6 steek sts, sl m, k2tog, work to end—2 sts dec'd; 1 st on each side of front steek.

Cont in patt, rep the neck dec rnd every rnd 14 (16, 16, 19, 19, 21, 24) more times—36 (41, 46, 46, 51, 56, 58) front sts rem on each side of center front steek; no change to other st counts. Work 4 (2, 2, 1, 1, 1, 2) rnd(s) even to end with Rnd 19 of the 7th patt rep—169 chart rnds total from beg; armholes measure 7¾ (8½, 8½, 8¾, 8¾, 9¾, 10¼)" (19.5 [21.5, 21.5, 22, 22, 25, 26] cm).

Shape Back Neck

Use removable m to mark the center 36 (41, 41, 46, 46, 51, 57) back sts—40 (45, 50, 50, 55, 60, 62) back sts each side of marked sts.

NEXT RND (Rnd 20 of charts) Keeping in patt, work to marked center back sts, place 36 (41, 41, 46, 46, 51, 57) marked sts on holder, pm, use the knitted method to CO 9 steek sts as [BFB] 3 times (a wider 9-st steek at back neck makes sewing easier later), pm, work in patt to end.

NECK DEC RND Keeping in patt, work to 2 sts before back neck steek, k2tog, sl m, work 9 steek sts, sl m, ssk, work to end—2 sts dec'd; 1 st on each side of back steek.

Cont in patt, rep the neck dec rnd every rnd 3 times, ending with Rnd 24 of charts—36 (41, 46, 46, 51, 56, 58) back sts rem on each side of center front steek; no change to other st counts.

NEXT RND (Rnd 25 of charts) Work in patt, BO all steek sts between m for all 4 steeks—175 chart rnds total from beg; armholes measure 8½ (9¼, 9¼, 9½, 9½, 10½, 11)" (21.5 [23.5, 23.5, 24, 24, 26.5, 28] cm).

Place 36 (41, 46, 46, 51, 56, 58) sts for each shoulder on separate holders.

sew + cut steeks

For the back neck steek, identify the center 5 sts. With sewing machine or by hand, sew a line of small straight stitches on each side of the center 5 sts. Sew 2 more lines of straight stitches, each 1 steek st farther out from center than the first 2 stitching lines; these 2 outer stitching lines should each be 1 st in from the end of the steek to leave a 1-st allowance at each side for picking up sts later. Carefully cut open the steek along its center st. For the 6-st front neck and armhole steeks, identify the center 2 sts. Sew a line of small straight stitches on each side of the center 2 sts, then sew 2 more lines of straight stitches, each 1 steek st farther out from center than the first 2 stitching lines. As for the back neck steek, these 2 outer stitching lines should each be 1 st in from the end of the steek to leave a 1-st allowance for picking up sts. Carefully cut between the center 2 steek sts to open the front and armhole steeks.

join shoulders

Place 36 (41, 46, 46, 51, 56, 58) right front shoulder sts on larger cir needle. Place corresponding right back shoulder sts on the other larger cir needle. Hold pieces tog with RS touching and WS facing out. With dark brown and dark blue, join the sts using the three-needle bind-off method (see Glossary), working each pair of sts with their matching color as you BO to mimic the patt from Rnd 25 of charts. Join the left shoulder in the same manner.

armhole facings

With dark brown and shorter cir needle in smaller size, use the knitted method to CO 143 (151, 151, 157, 157, 171, 177) sts. Pm and join for working in rnds, being

careful not to twist sts. Knit 7 rnds. Place sts on holder. Make a second facing in the same manner.

sleeves
Pick Up Sleeve Stitches + Join Armhole Facings

NOTE *For this step, you will pick up stitches around the armhole at the same time as joining the live stitches of the armhole facing. When the sleeve is complete, the facing will be folded over to conceal the raw edge of the steeked armhole.*

Place 143 (151, 151, 157, 157, 171, 177) held facing sts on longer cir needle in smaller size. With RS facing, place last 9 held underarm sts on shorter cir needle in smaller size and join dark brown in center of underarm at start of these sts. Hold needles tog with armhole facing needle in back of underarm needle, beg of armhole facing rnd aligned with center of underarm, and knit side of facing touching WS of garment. Using the other tip of the shorter cir needle, *insert the needle into the first st on underarm needle, then into the first st on facing needle, and knit these 2 sts tog; rep from * 8 more times—9 facing sts joined; first 9 sleeve sts on shorter cir needle. The next 62 (66, 66, 69, 69, 76, 79) sleeve sts are picked up along the steeked armhole edge between the underarm and the shoulder seam while joining to the live facing sts. The armhole is 63 (67, 67, 70, 70, 77, 81) rnds high, so you will need to skip 1 (1, 1, 1, 1, 1, 2) armhole rnd(s) when picking up sts. Pick

up the next section of armhole sts while joining to facing as foll: *Insert needle tip into armhole between the outer steek st and the first patt st, then into the next facing st, and draw through a loop onto the sleeve needle; rep from * until 62 (66, 66, 69, 69, 76, 79) sleeve sts have been picked up—71 (75, 75, 78, 78, 85, 88) sts on sleeve needle. Pick up 1 st from shoulder seam while joining to 1 facing st, then pick up 62 (66, 66, 69, 69, 76, 79) sleeve sts along other side of armhole while joining to facing sts—134 (142, 142, 148, 148, 162, 168) sts on sleeve needle. Place rem 9 held underarm sts on needle and knit them tog with 9 rem facing sts—143 (151, 151, 157, 157, 171, 177) sleeve sts; all facing sts have been joined. Work according to your chosen sleeve length as foll (see Notes).

Change to shorter cir needle in larger size. Join dark gold for 19¾" (50 cm) sleeve or dark blue for 21½" (54.5 cm) sleeve and establish patts from Rnd 13 of charts for the shorter sleeve or Rnd 1 for the longer sleeve as foll: Work last 1 (0, 0, 3, 3, 0, 3) st(s) of Lattice chart once, work entire 5-st patt 11 (12, 12, 12, 12, 14, 14) times, work 31 center sts in Snowflake patt, work entire 5-st lattice patt 11 (12, 12, 12, 12, 14, 14) times, work first 1 (0, 0, 3, 3, 0, 3) st(s) of lattice patt once, pm for beg of rnd. Cont for the sleeve length of your choice.

19¾" (50 cm) Sleeve

Cont in patt from charts, work 4 (0, 0, 0, 0, 0, 0) rnds even.

DEC RND Ssk, work in patt to last 2 sts, k2tog—2 sts dec'd.

Cont in patt, [work 2 rnds even, then rep dec rnd] 35 (39, 39, 37, 37, 21, 15) more times, changing to larger dpn when there are too few sts to fit on cir needle—71 (71, 71, 81, 81, 127, 145) sts rem. Cont in patt, rep the dec rnd every other rnd 0 (0, 0, 0, 0, 23, 32) times—71 (71, 71, 81, 81, 81, 81) sts rem. Work even until 138 chart rnds have been completed, ending with Rnd 25 of charts—5½ patt reps completed; piece measures 19" (48.5 cm) from pick-up rnd.

21½" (54.5 cm) Sleeve

Cont in patt from charts, work 0 (4, 4, 4, 4, 0, 0) rnds even.

DEC RND Ssk, work in patt to last 2 sts, k2tog—2 sts dec'd.

Cont in patt, [work 3 (2, 2, 2, 2, 2, 2) rnds even, then rep dec rnd] 17 (39, 39, 37, 37, 32, 29) times, changing to larger dpn when there are too few sts to fit on cir needle—107 (71, 71, 81, 81, 105, 117) sts rem. Cont in patt, [work 2 (0, 0, 0, 0, 1, 1) rnd(s) even, then rep dec rnd] 18 (0, 0, 0, 0, 12, 18) times—71 (71, 71, 81, 81, 81, 81) sts rem. Work even until 150 chart rnds have been completed, ending with Rnd 25 of charts—piece measures 20¾" (52.5 cm) from pick-up rnd.

Hemmed Cuff

Knit 1 rnd with dark brown. Change to smaller dpn. Knit 3 rnds.

DEC RND *K8, k2tog; rep from * to last st, k1—64 (64, 64, 73, 73, 73, 73) sts rem.

Knit 3 rnds, then purl 1 rnd for fold line—piece measures either 19¾" or 21½" (50 or 54.5 cm) from pick-up rnd, depending on your choice of sleeve length. Knit 3 rnds.

INC RND *K9, M1; rep from * to last st, k1—71 (71, 71, 81, 81, 81, 81) sts.

Knit 3 rnds to complete hem. Loosely BO all sts.

finishing

Placket

With dark brown, short cir needle in smaller size, and RS facing, pick up and knit 37 (37, 37, 35, 35, 33, 29) sts evenly spaced along selvedge of right front placket opening. Work back and forth in rows as foll:

ROWS 1–3 Work 3 rows in St st, beg and ending with a WS row.
ROW 4 (RS) Knit, dec 3 sts evenly spaced—34 (34, 34, 32, 32, 30, 26) sts.
ROWS 5–7 Work 3 rows in St st.
ROW 8 (RS) Purl 1 row for fold line.
ROWS 9–11 Work 3 rows in St st.
ROW 12 Knit, inc 3 sts evenly spaced—37 (37, 37, 35, 35, 33, 29) sts.
ROWS 13–15 Work 3 rows in St st, ending with a WS row.

BO all sts. Rep for left front placket opening.

Neckband

With dark brown, shorter cir needle in smaller size, RS facing, and beg at start of right front neck shaping, pick up and knit 25 (25, 25, 27, 27, 29, 32) sts along right neck to shoulder, 2 sts along right back neck, k36 (41, 41, 46, 46, 51, 57) held back neck sts, pick up and knit 2 sts along left back neck to shoulder, and 25 (25, 25, 27, 27, 29, 32) sts along left front neck to end at start of left front neck shaping; do not pick up any sts from plackets—90 (95, 95, 104, 104, 113, 125) sts total. The ends of the neckband are joined to the selvedges of the plackets by picking up 1 st at the end of each row.

ROWS 1 AND 3 (WS) Purl to end, pick up and purl (see Glossary) 1 st from edge of right front placket—1 st inc'd in each row.
ROW 2 (RS) Knit to end, pick up and knit 1 st from edge of left front placket—1 st inc'd.
ROW 4 (RS) Knit to end, dec 9 (9, 9, 10, 10, 11, 12) sts evenly spaced, pick up and knit 1 st from placket—85 (90, 90, 98, 98, 106, 117) sts rem.
ROWS 5–7 Work 3 rows in St st, picking up 1 st from placket at end of each row as established—3 sts inc'd.
ROW 8 (RS) Purl to last 4 sts for fold line, p3tog, p1, pick up and purl 1 st from placket fold line—87 (92, 92, 100, 100, 108, 119) sts.
ROWS 9 AND 11 Purl to last 4 sts, p3tog, p1, pick up and purl 1 st from placket—1 st dec'd in each row.

ROW 10 Knit to last 4 sts, sl 1 kwise, k2tog, pass slipped st over (psso), k1, pick up and knit 1 st from placket—1 st dec'd.

ROW 12 Knit, inc 9 (9, 9, 10, 10, 11, 12) sts evenly spaced to last 4 sts, sl 1, k2tog, psso, k1, pick up and knit 1 st from placket—92 (97, 97, 106, 106, 115, 127) sts.

ROWS 13 AND 14 Rep Rows 9 and 10—90 (95, 95, 104, 104, 113, 125) sts rem.

ROW 15 Purl to last 3 sts, ssp (see Glossary), p1, pick up and purl 1 st from placket—no change to st count.

BO all sts.

Weave in all loose ends. Fold lower body hem, sleeve cuffs, plackets, and neckband along fold lines and sew invisibly in place on WS, enclosing the raw edges of any steeks. Smooth the armhole facings so their knit side is showing on the inside of the garment to cover the cut armhole edges, then sew in place. Sew lower edges of plackets to BO sts at the bottom of the front opening. In preparation for blocking, temporarily baste the fold lines of the plackets tog so they just meet at center (without overlapping). Block sweater with a damp towel and hot iron. Remove the basting at center front when dry.

waltham cabled cardigan

DESIGNED BY **KATHY ZIMMERMAN**

Kathy Zimmerman combined modified-drop shaping with a V-neck and shawl collar for a casually classic look in this rugged cardigan. Panels of rope cables are flanked by ribs for a richly patterned non-bulky look that drapes nicely in a worsted-weight blend of alpaca and wool. This cardigan is finished with a one-piece short-row collar and front band that allows you to make as many buttonholes as you like. Kathy worked three buttons at the bust that allow the fronts to flow open at the lower edge. The combination of deep V-neck and wide shawl collar is attractive on most plus-size women.

FINISHED SIZE
About 40¼ (44¼, 48¼, 52¼, 56¼, 60¼)" (102 [112.5, 122.5, 132.5, 143, 153] cm) bust circumference, buttoned and including 1" (2.5 cm) front band. Sweater shown measures 48¼" (122.5 cm).

YARN
Worsted weight (#4 Medium).

Shown here: Louet Eastport Alpaca (70% alpaca, 30% merino; 150 yd [137 m]/75 g): #07 pagoda red (reddish brown), 10 (11, 12, 13, 14, 16) skeins.

NEEDLES
Body: size U.S. 7 (4.5 mm): straight.

Sleeve ribbing: size U.S. 5 (3.75 mm): straight.

Neckband: size U.S. 5 (3.75 mm): 40" (100 cm) circular (cir).

Adjust needle size if necessary to obtain the correct gauge.

NOTIONS
Two cable needles (cn); markers (m); tapestry needle; three ⅝" (1.5 cm) toggle-style buttons.

GAUGE
24 stitches and 26 rows = 4" (10 cm) in rib pattern from Charts A and D, worked on larger needles and slightly stretched after blocking.

35-stitch cable panels of Charts B and C measure 5¼" (13.5 cm) wide.

stitch guide +notes

2/1/2 RC (worked over 5 sts)
Sl 3 sts onto cn and hold in back, k2, sl st at left-hand end of cn to left needle and knit this st, k2 from cn; center st always stays in center.

2/1/2 LC (worked over 5 sts)
Sl 2 sts onto first cn and hold in front, sl next st onto second cn and hold in front, k2, k1 from second cn, k2 from first cn; center st always stays in center.

1/3/1 RPC (worked over 5 sts)
Sl 1 st onto first cn and hold in back, sl next 3 sts onto second cn and hold in back, k1, p3 from second cn, k1 from first cn; center 3 purl sts always stay in center.

1/3/1 LPC (worked over 5 sts)
Sl 1 st onto first cn and hold in front, sl next 3 sts onto second cn and hold in back, k1, p3 from second cn, k1 from first cn; center 3 purl sts always stay in center.

+ This cardigan is worked without body shaping. But because the side sections are worked in a fairly simple rib pattern (see Charts A and D), you could easily incorporate body shaping into the pattern.

+ The width of the sleeve at the top edge is exactly two times the depth of the armhole for each size. If you change the measurement of either piece, you will need to maintain this equivalence.

+ Work all increases and decreases 1 stitch in from the edge.

+ During shaping, if there are not enough stitches to work a complete cable crossing, work the stitches in reverse stockinette stitch (purl RS rows; knit WS rows) instead.

+ The final cross-back width measures 16¼ (18, 19¼, 20¾, 22, 23½)" (41.5 [45.5, 49, 52.5, 56, 59.5] cm). This is a fairly refined fit for a drop-shoulder sweater, especially relative to the largest sizes in the pattern. This narrower cross-back is achieved with dramatic underarm bind-offs—the total underarm span for each size measures about 3½ (4, 4¼, 5, 5½, 6¼)" (9 [10, 11, 12.5, 14, 16] cm). If you choose to bind off fewer stitches at the underarm to create a wider shoulder, you will need to reconfigure the shoulder shaping.

+ The sleeve is designed to have a specific depth worked even at the top edge. This depth corresponds to the width of the underarm bind-off; in finishing, you should seam the straight section of the sleeve perpendicularly to the inset of the underarm bind-off. If you change the underarm bind-off, keep this relationship in mind.

back

With larger straight needles, CO 128 (140, 152, 164, 176, 188) sts. Beg and ending as indicated for your size, establish patts from set-up rows of charts (pages 50 and 51) as foll (WS) Work 24 (30, 36, 42, 48, 54) sts of Chart D, place marker (pm), 35 sts of Chart C, pm, k4, p2, k4, pm, 35 sts of Chart B, pm, and 24 (30, 36, 42, 48, 54) sts of Chart A.

NOTE *From here, rep Rows 1 and 2 of Charts A and D for patts; do not rep the Set-up rows.*

Working the 10 center sts between the 35-st cable panels as they appear (knit the knits and purl the purls), work in established patts for 8 more rows, ending with WS Row 8 of Charts B and C.

NOTE *From here, rep Rows 9–26 of Charts B and C for patts; do not rep the Set-up rows or Rows 1–8.*

Cont in established patts until piece measures 14½ (15, 15½, 16, 16½, 17)" (37 [38, 39.5, 40.5, 42, 43] cm) from CO, ending with a WS row.

Shape Armholes

BO 12 (13, 14, 16, 18, 20) sts at beg of next 2 rows—104 (114, 124, 132, 140, 148) sts rem. Cont even in patts until armholes measure 7½ (8, 8½, 9, 9½, 10)" (19 [20.5, 21.5, 23, 24, 25.5 cm), ending with a WS row.

Shape Shoulders

BO 9 (10, 11, 12, 13, 14) sts at beg of next 4 rows, then BO 10 (11, 11, 12, 13, 13) sts at beg of next 2 rows—48 (52, 58, 60, 62, 66) back neck sts rem. BO all sts.

right front

With larger straight needles, CO 60 (66, 72, 78, 84, 90) sts. Beg and ending as indicated for your size, establish patts from set-up rows of charts as foll: (WS) Work 24 (30, 36, 42, 48, 54) sts of Chart D, pm, 35 sts of Chart C, pm, k1 (selvedge st; knit every row). Cont in established patts, working chart reps as for back, until piece measures 14½ (15, 15½, 16, 16½, 17)" (37 [38, 39.5, 40.5, 42, 43] cm) from CO, ending with a RS row.

Shape Armhole

BO 12 (13, 14, 16, 18, 20) sts at beg of next WS row—48 (53, 58, 62, 66, 70) sts rem. Work 4 (2, 4, 2, 4, 2) rows even, ending with a WS row—armhole measures ¾ (½, ¾, ½, ¾, ½)" (2 [1.3, 2, 1.3, 2, 1.3] cm).

Shape Neck

Dec 1 st at neck edge inside selvedge st at beg of RS rows (see Notes) every RS row 19 (20, 25, 25, 26, 28) times, then every 4th row 1 (2, 0, 1, 1, 1) time(s)—28 (31, 33, 36, 39, 41) sts rem. Cont even until armhole measures 7½ (8, 8½, 9, 9½, 10)" (19 [20.5, 21.5, 23, 24, 25.5] cm), ending with a RS row.

Shape Shoulder

BO 9 (10, 11, 12, 13, 14) sts at beg of next 2 WS rows, then BO 10 (11, 11, 12, 13, 13) sts at beg of foll WS row—no sts rem.

left front

With larger straight needles, CO 60 (66, 72, 78, 84, 90) sts. Beg and ending as indicated for your size, establish patts from set-up rows of charts as foll: (WS) K1 (selvedge st; knit every row), pm, work 35 sts of Chart B, pm, work 24 (30, 36, 42, 48, 54) sts of Chart A. Cont in established patts, working chart reps as for back, until piece measures 14½ (15, 15½, 16, 16½, 17)" (37 [38, 39.5, 40.5, 42, 43] cm) from CO, ending with a WS row.

Shape Armhole

BO 12 (13, 14, 16, 18, 20) sts at beg of next RS row—48 (53, 58, 62, 66, 70) sts rem. Work 3 (1, 3, 1, 3, 1) row(s) even, ending with a WS row.

Shape Neck

Dec 1 st at neck edge inside selvedge st at end of RS rows every RS row 19 (20, 25, 25, 26, 28) times, then every 4th row 1 (2, 0, 1, 1, 1) time(s)—28 (31, 33, 36, 39, 41) sts rem. Cont even until armhole measures 7½ (8, 8½, 9, 9½, 10)" (19 [20.5, 21.5, 23, 24, 25.5] cm), ending with a WS row.

Shape Shoulder

BO 9 (10, 11, 12, 13, 14) sts at beg of next 2 RS rows, then BO 10 (11, 11, 12, 13, 13) sts at beg of foll RS row—no sts rem.

sleeves

With smaller straight needles, CO 52 (58, 62, 62, 66, 70) sts. Beg and ending as indicated for your size, work WS set-up row of Chart E across all sts.

A

2

set-up

1

beg
all sizes

end
44¼"

end
48¼"

end
52¼"

end
56¼"

end
40¼", 60¼"

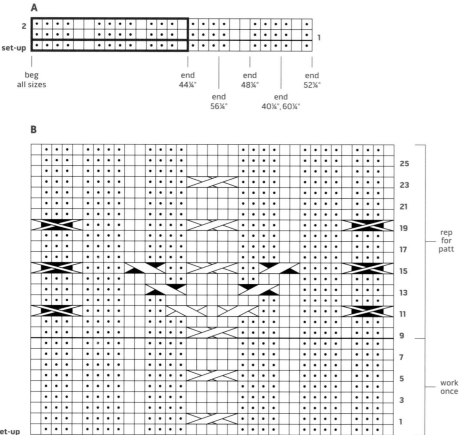

B

25
23
21
19
17
15
13
11
9
7
5
3
1

set-up

rep
for
patt

work
once

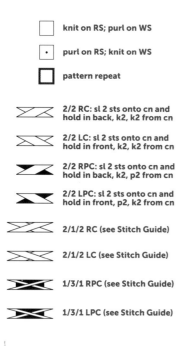

knit on RS; purl on WS

· purl on RS; knit on WS

pattern repeat

2/2 RC: sl 2 sts onto cn and
hold in back, k2, k2 from cn

2/2 LC: sl 2 sts onto cn and
hold in front, k2, k2 from cn

2/2 RPC: sl 2 sts onto cn and
hold in back, k2, p2 from cn

2/2 LPC: sl 2 sts onto cn and
hold in front, p2, k2 from cn

2/1/2 RC (see Stitch Guide)

2/1/2 LC (see Stitch Guide)

1/3/1 RPC (see Stitch Guide)

1/3/1 LPC (see Stitch Guide)

C

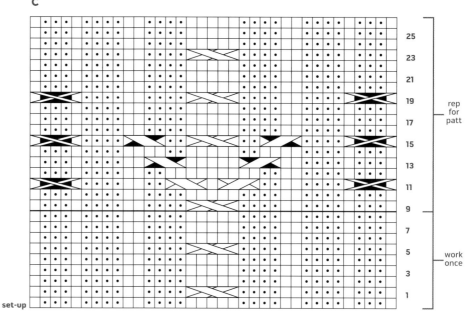

25
23
21
19
17
15
13
11
9
7
5
3
1

set-up

rep
for
patt

work
once

NOTE *From here, rep Rows 1 and 2 for chart patt; do not rep the Set-up row.*

Work in established patt until piece measures 1" (2.5 cm) from CO, ending with a WS row. Change to larger needles. Cont in patt as established and *at the same time* inc 1 st each end of needle inside edge sts on the next RS row, then every other row 0 (0, 0, 0, 0, 2) times, then every 4th row 6 (6, 9, 18, 22, 22) times, then every 6th row 12 (12, 10, 4, 1, 0) time(s), working new sts into rib patt—90 (96, 102, 108, 114, 120) sts. Cont even in patt until piece measures 18½ (18½, 18½, 18½, 18¼, 18)" (47 [47, 47, 47, 46.5, 45.5] cm) from CO, ending with a WS row.

NOTE *The largest sizes have deeper armhole notches and correspondingly taller sleeve caps, so their lower sleeves are slightly shorter to prevent the overall sleeve length from becoming too long.*

Mark each end of last row completed for beg of sleeve cap. Work even in patt for 2 (2¼, 2½, 2¾, 3, 3¼)" (5 [5.5, 6.5, 7, 7.5, 8.5] cm) beyond marked row—piece measures 20½ (20¾, 21, 21¼, 21¼, 21¼)" (52 [52.5, 53.5, 54, 54, 54] cm) from CO. BO all sts in patt.

Finishing

Block pieces to measurements. With yarn threaded on a tapestry needle, join fronts to back at shoulders. Sew sleeves into armholes. Sew sleeve and side seams.

Front Bands + Shawl Collar

With 40" (100 cm) cir needle in smaller size, RS facing, and beg at lower edge of right front, pick up and knit 76 (77, 80, 82, 84, 85) sts to start of neck shaping, pm, pick up and knit 1 st at base of V-neck, pm, pick up and knit 47 (48, 49, 51, 53, 55) sts along right front neck shoulder seam, pm, 47 (51, 57, 59, 61, 65) sts across back neck, pm, 47 (48, 49, 51, 53, 55) sts along left front neck to start of neck shaping, pm, pick up and knit 1 st at base of V-neck, pm, and 76 (77, 80, 82, 84, 85) sts along left front—295 (303, 317, 327, 337, 347) sts total.

ROW 1 (WS) Work in k1, p1 rib, beg and ending with p1, and *at the same time* inc 1 st on each side

of each marked V-neck sts as foll: *Work in rib to 1 st before marked st, work either [p1, k1] or [k1, p1] both in next st to maintain alternation of rib patt, sl m, work marked st in patt, sl m, work either [k1, p1] or [p1, k1] both in next st to maintain patt; rep from * once more, work in patt to end—1 st inc'd on each side of each marked V-neck st; 299 (307, 321, 331, 341, 351) sts total; 48 (49, 50, 52, 54, 56) sts at each front neck edge between V-neck st and shoulder m; 77 (78, 81, 83, 85, 86) sts along each center front edge below marked V-neck st.

ROW 2 (RS) Work sts as they appear.

Mark positions for buttonholes on right front as desired. For the

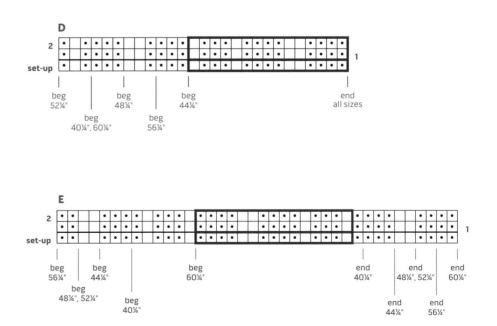

sweater shown, the 3 buttonholes are ½" (1.3 cm), 2½" (6.5 cm), and 4½" (11.5 cm) below start of neck shaping.

ROW 3 (WS) *Work to buttonhole position, [yo] 2 times, work either k2tog or p2tog to maintain rib patt; rep from * 2 more times, work to end of row.

ROW 4 *Work to double yo of buttonhole, drop 1 yo wrap, sl rem wrap to right needle pwise; rep from * 2 more times, work to end of row.

ROW 5 *Work to slipped buttonhole yo, work yo as either k1 or p1 to maintain rib patt; rep from * 2 times, work to end of row.

ROWS 6 AND 7 Work in rib patt as established, ending with a WS row.

SHAWL COLLAR

NOTE *Work inc'd sts of first collar short-row into established k1, p1 rib.*

Work short-rows (see Glossary) as foll:

SHORT-ROW 1 (RS) Work in patt to 2nd marker, sl m, work right front neck sts in patt to right shoulder m while inc 10 sts evenly spaced, sl m, work across back neck sts to left shoulder m while inc 14 sts evenly spaced, sl m, work left front neck sts in patt to next m while inc 10 sts evenly spaced, sl m, wrap next st (V-neck st), turn—333 (341, 355, 365, 375, 385) sts total; 58 (59, 60, 62, 64, 66) front neck sts

waltham cabled cardigan

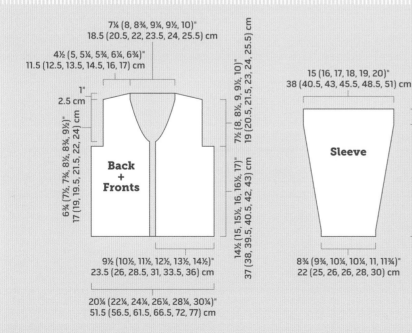

7¼ (8, 8¾, 9¼, 9½, 10)"
18.5 (20.5, 22, 23.5, 24, 25.5) cm

4½ (5, 5¼, 5¾, 6¼, 6¾)"
11.5 (12.5, 13.5, 14.5, 16, 17) cm

1"
2.5 cm

6¾ (7½, 7¾, 8½, 8¾, 9½)"
17 (19, 19.5, 21.5, 22, 24) cm

Back + Fronts

9½ (10½, 11½, 12½, 13½, 14½)"
23.5 (26, 28.5, 31, 33.5, 36) cm

20¼ (22¼, 24¼, 26¼, 28¼, 30¼)"
51.5 (56.5, 61.5, 66.5, 72, 77) cm

7½ (8, 9, 9½, 10)"
19 (20.5, 21.5, 23, 24, 25.5) cm

14½ (15, 15½, 16, 16½, 17)"
37 (38, 39.5, 40.5, 42, 43) cm

15 (16, 17, 18, 19, 20)"
38 (40.5, 43, 45.5, 48.5, 51) cm

Sleeve

2 (2¼, 2½, 2½, 3, 3¼)"
5 (5.5, 6.5, 6.5, 7.5, 8.5) cm

18½ (18½, 18½, 18¾, 18¼, 18)"
47 (47, 47, 46.5, 45.5) cm

8¾ (9¾, 10¼, 10¼, 11, 11¾)"
22 (25, 26, 26, 28, 30) cm

each side above marked V-neck st; 61 (65, 71, 73, 75, 79) back neck sts.

SHORT-ROW 2 (WS) Work in patt across left front neck, back neck, and right front neck to marked V-neck st of right front, sl m, wrap V-neck st, turn.

SHORT-ROWS 3 AND 4 Work in patt to 2 sts before previously wrapped st, wrap next st, turn.

SHORT-ROWS 5–40 Rep the last 2 rows 18 times—20 wrapped sts at each side.

SHORT-ROWS 41 AND 42 Work in patt to 4 sts before previously wrapped st, wrap next st, turn.

SHORT-ROWS 43–46 Rep the last 2 rows 2 times—23 wrapped sts at each side.

SHORT-ROWS 47 AND 48 Work in patt to 8 sts before previously wrapped st, wrap next st, turn—24 wrapped sts at each side.

NEXT ROW (RS) Work in patt to end, working wraps tog with wrapped sts as you come to them.

NEXT ROW Work in patt across all sts, working rem wraps tog with wrapped sts—collar measures about 7" (18 cm) from pick-up row at center back neck.

With larger needle, BO all sts in rib patt.

Weave in loose ends. Block lightly as needed. Sew buttons to left front band, opposite buttonholes.

the set-in
sweater

A set-in sweater features a tailored sleeve cap that is "set into" a correspondingly tailored armhole. The sleeve cap has a bell shape. The armhole of the body notches inward, then is worked straight to the shoulder. This style is known for its refined fit and clean appearance.

Set-in styling does not refer to just the sleeve shaping—it also refers to the upper body shaping. By decreasing stitches along the armholes of the yoke, the upper body gradually tapers from the wide bust to the narrower shoulder. This is extremely useful for plus-size knitters, whose lower bodies need greater expanse but whose cross-back widths don't increase in proportion. The set-in design provides a tidy vertical armhole line just outside the shoulder edge. The sleeve fits more closely than a drop-shoulder sleeve; you can make it as fitted as you like. In general, a set-in style allows for more customization than any other sweater construction.

who should wear the set-in style?

Women with narrow or petite frames should wear the set-in style, as should women with very large busts. Anyone can wear this style when designed with positive ease, but there's more chance that you'll need to customize the shaping for a fitted sweater or a sweater with negative ease on your problem areas. Women with large upper arms or wide shoulders need to be especially vigilant when choosing a size with set-in construction. Regardless of your

body type, always check the sleeve circumference and cross-back width for your chosen size, as these areas are second only to bust width for a good fit in this construction style.

set-in construction

When working a set-in sleeve sweater, the pieces can be worked flat or in the round. If the sleeves are worked in the round, they need to be split at the underarm and worked flat (back and forth in rows) for the caps, which can be shaped with decreases or short-rows to fit the armholes properly. The pieces can be worked separately from the bottom up or following more unusual constructions, such as in the Poppy Cardigan on page 66.

The set-in shape works well for vests (see the Cleveland Shell on page 76) as well as sleeved sweaters. It's also important to note that a set-in design can be a casual and loose-fitting sweater, while not as boxy as a drop-shoulder design.

The Yoke
Because the point of set-in construction (in a limited way) is to tailor the cross-back fit, you need to begin with your cross-back measurement. This is where the standard measurements, your own body and tape measure, and your favorite existing sweater all come in handy. The CYCA standards (page 19) give a cross-back width of 18½" (47 cm) for a woman with a 56" to 58" (142 to 147.5 cm) bust. What does it say for your bust size? Take your own cross-back measurement from shoulder bone

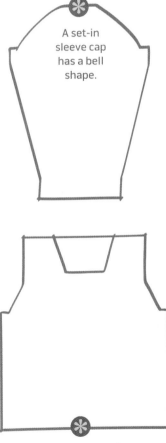

A set-in sleeve cap has a bell shape.

The armhole of the body is shaped at the base, then worked straight to the shoulder.

to shoulder bone across the back of your neck. Does it match the standards? If not, you may want to customize the armhole shaping to achieve a good fit across the shoulders.

Next, measure the cross-back width of one of your best-fitting sweaters or shirts (from armhole seam to armhole seam across the top of the yoke). How does this compare to your actual measurement? If the garment is fairly fitted, it should measure about 1" to 2" (2.5 to 5 cm) greater than your actual cross-back width. This is because a sweater's cross-back should always have some positive ease taken into account for layering and ease of wearing. If a set-in pattern achieves a cross-back width 1" to 2" (2.5 to 5 cm) greater than your actual cross-back measurement, that sweater should fit quite nicely.

You may not want a fitted sweater; instead you may want a looser garment for layering or aesthetic purposes. If this is the case, aim for 2" to 5" (5 to 12.5 cm) of positive ease across the shoulders in a set-in sweater (assuming the rest of the sweater has 2" or more positive ease). If the cross-back width has more than 5" (12.5 cm) of excess fabric, the shoulders will begin to overhang the upper arm excessively, ruining the fit of the set-in sleeve caps and making the sleeves appear too long.

If you need to alter the cross-back width of a pattern, you will need to determine the number of stitches to decrease from the underarm to the end of the armhole shaping to match your desired width, then reconfigure the rate of shaping. Remember that there should be a few inches of depth worked even at the top of the armhole—the shaping should not end close to the shoulder bind-off. If you change the number of stitches for the initial underarm bind-off, remember to change the initial bind-off at the base of the sleeve cap to match; those stitch counts should be identical.

The Sleeve

The length of the set-in sleeve from cuff to beginning of cap shaping should measure about the same length as your arm from wrist to underarm. The depth of the cap is determined by the width of the sleeve and depth of the armhole (see Sleeve Cap Formula on the following pages) and bears no obvious relation to your actual arm.

A set-in sleeve cap is shaped with a combination of bind-offs and decrease rows that are worked at varying intervals. The final bind-off at the top of the cap typically measures 2" to 5" (5 to 12.5 cm) and depends on the sweater size and the desired fit—the more fitted the sleeve,

notable effects of set-in construction

+ Bust width does not determine cross-back width.

+ Bust width does determine the amount of shaping required to achieve the desired cross-back width.

+ Sleeve circumference and sleeve cap shape are codependent.

+ Armhole circumference and cap shape are codependent.

+ The body has a bound-off underarm span.

+ The knitting (and pattern reading) is more complex than for a drop-shoulder style.

+ Sewing the sleeve into the armhole requires precision.

+ The standard armhole depth for set-ins is similar to that for raglans and seamless yokes.

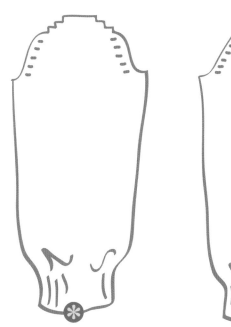

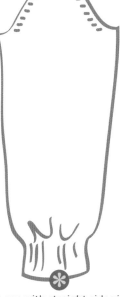

the narrower the final bind-off edge should be. The cap and armhole do not have a 1:1 row ratio as for raglans (page 84), nor a measurable equivalence like drop-shoulders (page 26).

The formula for calculating the shape of the sleeve cap is based on the armhole depth, upper sleeve circumference, and stitch and row gauge. It relies on the Pythagorean theorem and divides the cap into three segments—A, B, and C.

When planning the decreases and bind-offs in the cap, you have some creative leeway. You can work a rounded cap by utilizing short bind-offs for the last couple inches of shaping or work a straight-sided cap with decreases worked at each selvedge edge. A rounded cap is ideal for looser-fitting garments or if you have fleshy upper arms. Because the width of the sleeve at the underarm in plus-size sweaters is usually wide, there will be a lot of stitches to decrease for the cap. This often necessitates combining bind-offs and working decreases every right-side row. Conversely, sweaters in smaller sizes may have rows without any shaping at all. You don't want the cap to narrow too quickly, so, if possible, work decreases for the lower portion (about three-quarters) of the cap, then switch to bind-offs for the upper portion (about one-quarter of the cap).

If you change the upper arm width of a set-in sleeve, you will need to recalculate the sleeve cap shaping based on the formula on the following pages. If you change the armhole depth, you will also need to recalculate the sleeve cap. If you do not match the row gauge used to calculate the cap shaping, you will need to recalculate the sleeve cap. If the sleeve cap does not fit into the armhole, you will have trouble sewing in the sleeve; if the difference is drastic, the armhole seam will never look right.

If you change the width of the cross-back but the armhole depth remains the same, you will not need to recalculate the sleeve cap.

A set-in cap with a rounded top is shaped with a series of short bind-offs at each edge, which are worked over several rows before the final bind-off.

A cap with straight sides is shaped with decreases at each edge, usually worked every right-row in plus-size sweaters, before the final bind-off.

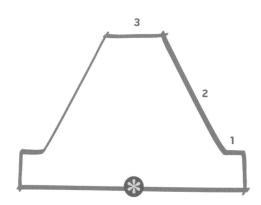

A sleeve cap is composed of three elements: the initial bind-off (1), the tapered sides (2), and the final bind-off (3) at the top.

calculating the cap

To calculate the cap shaping, divide the cap into a central rectangle flanked by two right-angle triangles, then use simple math and geometry to determine the final dimensions.

Step 1 | Calculate Side B

Side B is the length in inches that needs to be eliminated between the end of the first set of bound-off stitches and the beginning of the final bind-off stitches.

$$\frac{\text{one-half the number of stitches remaining on needle after the underarm bind-off}}{\text{stitch gauge}} - \frac{\text{one-half the width of the desired top bind-off edge}}{} = \text{the width of Side B}$$

For example, let's say we're working at a gauge of 4.5 stitches and 6 rows to the inch, and the sleeve measures 16" (40.5 cm) at the upper sleeve. We will have 72 stitches on the needle at the base of the cap. For the initial bind-off of 1" (2.5 cm) at each edge, we'll bind off 4 stitches at each end of needle, leaving us with 64 stitches. Let's also say that we want 4" (10 cm) of width remaining at the top of cap.

Side B is therefore:

$$\frac{32 \text{ sts}}{4.5 \text{ sts/in}} - \text{½ of } 4" = 7.11" - 2 = 5.11"$$

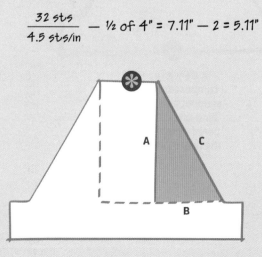

Use the Pythagorean theorem to determine the number of rows in the cap shaping.

Step 2 | Calculate Side C

Side C is the length of the tapered edge of the cap.

$$\text{The depth of the armhole on the sweater body} - \frac{\text{one-half the width of the top bind-off edge of the cap}}{} = \frac{\text{the length of Side C}}{}$$

For example, let's say the armhole depth of the sweater body is 9½" (24 cm).

Side C is therefore:

$$9.5" - \text{½ of } 4"$$
$$9.5" - 2" = 7.5"$$

Step 3 | Calculate Side A

Once you know the lengths for Sides B and C, you can use the Pythagorean Theorem to determine the length of Side A, which is the depth of the cap. You can then use this information to determine the number of rows in the cap and how to space the decreases.

The Pythagorean Theorem states that:

$$(A)^2 + (B)^2 = (C)^2$$

We can rearrange this formula to solve for A:

$$(A)^2 = (C)^2 - (B)^2$$

For our example, we have

$$A^2 = (7½")^2 - (5.11")^2$$
$$A^2 = 56.25" - 26.11"$$
$$A^2 = 30.14"$$

04

A is therefore the square root of 30.14", or 5.48". You'll want to use a calculator for this part!

We now know that the cap needs to be about 5½" (14 cm) deep to accommodate an upper sleeve width of 16" (40.5 cm), armhole depth of 9½" (24 cm), and final bind-off of 4" (10 cm).

Step 4 | Translate these Numbers into Directions for Working the Cap

To determine the number of rows in the cap, multiply Side A by the row gauge. For our example,

$$5.48" \times 6 \text{ rows/inch} = 32.88 \text{ rows}$$

Because we want to work rows in pairs (a right-side row followed by a wrong-side row), round this number to the nearest even number, which is 32 rows.

Next, add about ½" of rows for maneuverability in seaming. For our example,

$$½" \times (6 \text{ rows/inch}) = 3 \text{ rows}$$

Again, we want to work rows in pairs so we'll round this to 4 rows.

We now know that we'll work the cap over 32 rows plus 4 rows = 36 rows.

We also know that the final bind-off will be 4" (10 cm) wide. Multiply this width by the stitch gauge to determine how many stitches to bind off on the last row.

$$4" \times 4.5 \text{ stitches/inch} = 18 \text{ stitches}$$

If we begin the cap shaping with 64 stitches and end by binding off 18 stitches, we'll have a total of 46 stitches to decrease over those 36 rows.

$$\begin{array}{ccc} 64 \text{ stitches} & 18 \text{ stitches} & 46 \text{ stitches to} \\ \text{at the} & \text{at top} & \text{decrease} \\ \text{beginning} \quad - & \text{of cap} \quad = & \\ \text{of cap} & & \end{array}$$

Because we want to shape the two edges of the cap the same, we'll want to decrease 23 stitches at each edge of the piece. In other words, we'll decrease 2 stitches on every decrease row, 1 stitch at each end of the needle. For simplicity, we'll also want to work all of the decreases on right-side rows. Only half of the 36 rows are right-side rows, so we'll have only 18 rows over which to work the decreases.

$$36 \text{ rows in cap} \div \text{by } 2 = 18 \text{ right-side rows}$$

We now know that we need to decrease 23 stitches at each side over 18 right-side rows. If we decrease 2 stitches on each decrease row (1 at the right edge and 1 at the left edge), we'll only use up 18 of these 23 stitches. Therefore, we'll have to work some additional bind-offs, preferably at the top of the cap, to eliminate the remaining 5 stitches at each side. In general, we don't want to bind off more than 1" worth of stitches as we approach the top of the cap. This means that we won't bind off more than 4 stitches at a time. It's now time to play around with the numbers to figure out how many bind-off rows to work and how many stitches to bind off each row. In this scenario, I'd recommend working the cap like this:

After the underarm bind-off, decrease 1 stitch at each end of the needle every right-side row 16 times—32 stitches remain; 32 rows worked. Bind off 4 stitches at the beginning of the next 2 rows, then bind off 3 stitches at the beginning of the following 2 rows—18 stitches remain; 36 rows worked (and your goal is met!). Bind off remaining 18 stitches.

lystra pullover

DESIGNED BY **LISA SHROYER**

Worked at a fine gauge, this set-in pullover requires more knitting time but makes for a highly wearable and enduring wardrobe piece. The deep V-neck is framed with a welted band with little other adornment; just a seeded rib at cuff and hem. Work the body shaping and tweak the sleeve length as you like—the sleeves are shown with an extra-long fit, but you could substitute traditional full- or three-quarter length sleeves. A simple sweater like this will familiarize you with set-in construction and help you determine your shaping and size needs in this style, giving you knowledge that will help you knit successful set-in garments ever after.

FINISHED SIZE
About 41½ (44½, 47½, 50, 53, 56, 58½)" (105.5 [113, 120.5, 127, 134.5, 142, 148.5] cm) bust circumference. Sweater shown measures 41½" (105.5 cm).

YARN
DK weight (#3 Light).

Shown here: Yarn Rowan Pure Wool 4 Ply (100% superwash wool; 174 yd [160 m]/50 g): #428 raspberry, 9 (10, 11, 11, 12, 12, 13) balls.

NEEDLES
Body and sleeves: size U.S. 4 (3.5 mm): straight.

Edging: size U.S. 1 (2.25 mm): 24" (60 cm) circular (cir).

Adjust needle size if necessary to obtain the correct gauge.

NOTIONS
Markers (m); tapestry needle.

GAUGE
22½ stitches and 33 rows = 4" (10 cm) in stockinette stitch on larger needles, before blocking.

notes

+ The body of this pullover is worked without shaping. You could easily add waist shaping and/or short-row bust darts (see page 24). Work A-line shaping if you need greater circumference at the hips. Shorten or lengthen the lower body as needed.

+ The sleeves shown in the photographs are extra long—19¼" (49 cm) from CO to start of cap shaping—and fall below the wrist on a woman of average height. The pattern is written with conventional sleeve lengths that fall at the wrist. The yarn amounts given are sufficient for making longer sleeves.

+ The measurements shown on the schematic are the actual dimensions of the pieces (including selvedge stitches) for blocking purposes. The selvedge stitches lost in the seams do not count toward the finished size.

+ The underarm span in the finished, seamed garment measures about 1¾ (1¾, 2¼, 2¼, 2¼, 2¼, 2¼)" (4.5 [4.5, 5.5, 5.5, 5.5, 5.5, 5.5] cm) wide. If you need one size at the bust but find the cross-back width for that size is too wide for you, you can bind off more stitches at the underarm to reduce the cross-back even more before beginning the armhole shaping. Avoid working an underarm span that is too wide (see page 14 for tips). If you alter the body underarm, the underarm bind-off on the sleeves will need to match, which means you'll need to rework the sleeve cap shaping (see page 58 for tips on calculating cap shaping).

+ The front neck depth matches the yoke depth in this design, as the neck is split at the same level as the underarm bind-off. If you prefer a higher front neck, you can split the neck above the level of the underarms, but you will need to rework the frequency of neck decrease rows to ensure you end up with the final stitch counts needed for the shoulders. The number of stitches consumed by the front neck should equal the number of stitches across the back neck.

back

With larger needles, CO 119 (127, 135, 143, 151, 159, 167) sts.

ROW 1 (RS) Knit.
ROW 2 (WS) P2, *k1, p1; rep from * to last st, p1.

Rep these 2 rows 6 more times—14 rows total. Work even in St st (knit RS rows; purl WS rows) until piece measures 17" (43 cm) from CO or desired length, ending with a WS row.

Shape Armholes

BO 6 (6, 7, 7, 7, 7) sts at beg of next 2 rows—107 (115, 121, 129, 137, 145, 153) sts rem.

DEC ROW (RS) K2, ssk, knit to last 4 sts, k2tog, k2—2 sts dec'd.

Rep dec row every RS row 0 (4, 6, 8, 11, 21, 23) more times, then every other RS row (i.e., every 4th row) 8 (7, 7, 7, 7, 0, 0) times—89 (91, 93, 97, 99, 101, 105) sts rem. Work even in St st until armholes measure 9½ (9¾, 10, 10½, 10¾, 11, 11)" (24 [25, 25.5, 26.5, 27.5, 28, 28] cm), ending with a WS row.

Shape Neck + Shoulders

(RS) K27 (28, 28, 30, 30, 31, 32) for right back shoulder, join a second ball of yarn and BO center 35 (35, 37, 37, 39, 39, 41) sts, knit to last 5 (5, 5, 6, 6, 6, 6) sts, wrap next st, turn work. Work short-rows (see Glossary) separately for each side as foll, beginning with the left shoulder; the right shoulder sts rem unworked on needle while shaping left shoulder.

LEFT SHOULDER

SHORT-ROWS 1, 3, 5, AND 7 (WS) Purl to end of left shoulder sts, turn.
SHORT-ROW 2 (RS) BO 2 sts at neck edge, knit to 5 (5, 5, 6, 6, 6, 6) sts before previously wrapped st, wrap next st, turn.
SHORT-ROW 4 Dec 1 st at neck edge, knit to 5 (5, 5, 6, 6, 6, 6) sts before previously wrapped st, wrap next st, turn.
SHORT-ROW 6 Dec 1 st at neck edge, knit to 3 (4, 4, 3, 3, 4, 5) sts before previously wrapped st, wrap next st, turn.
SHORT-ROW 8 Dec 1 st at neck edge, knit to end, working wraps tog with wrapped sts when you come to them—22 (23, 23, 25, 25, 26, 27) shoulder sts rem.

Purl 1 WS row across all sts. Place sts on holder.

RIGHT SHOULDER

With WS facing and yarn attached to right shoulder, work short-rows as foll:

SHORT-ROW 1 (WS) BO 2 sts at neck edge, purl to last 5 (5, 5, 6, 6, 6, 6) sts, wrap next st, turn.
SHORT-ROW 2 (RS) Knit to end, turn.
SHORT-ROW 3 Purl to 5 (5, 5, 6, 6, 6) sts before previously wrapped st, wrap next st, turn.
SHORT-ROWS 4 AND 6 Knit to end, dec 1 st at neck edge at end of row, turn.
SHORT-ROW 5 Purl to 5 (5, 5, 6, 6, 6) sts before previously wrapped st, wrap next st, turn.
SHORT-ROW 7 Purl to 3 (4, 4, 3, 3, 4, 5) sts before previously wrapped st, wrap next st, turn.

SHORT-ROW 8 Knit to end, dec 1 st at neck edge at end of row, turn—22 (23, 23, 25, 25, 26, 27) shoulder sts rem.

Purl 1 WS row across all sts, working wraps tog with wrapped sts when you come to them. Place sts on holder.

front

CO and work as for back to start of armhole shaping, ending with a WS row—119 (127, 135, 143, 151, 159, 167) sts; piece measures 17" (43 cm) from CO.

Shape Armholes + Neck

With RS facing, BO 6 (6, 7, 7, 7, 7, 7) sts, knit until there are 52 (56, 59, 63, 67, 71, 75) sts on right needle, join a second ball of yarn and BO center 3 sts, knit to end.

NEXT ROW (WS) BO 6 (6, 7, 7, 7, 7, 7) sts at beg of first group of sts, purl to end of first group; purl across sts of second group—52 (56, 59, 63, 67, 71, 75) sts each side.

Work the right and left front neck and shoulder shaping separately, beginning with the right side; the left side sts rem unworked on needle while shaping the right side.

RIGHT SIDE

NOTE *Armhole and neck shaping are worked at the same time; read all the way through the next sections before proceeding.*

For armhole shaping, dec 1 st at armhole edge by working the last

4 sts as k2tog, k2 on the next 1 (5, 7, 9, 12, 22, 24) RS row(s), then every other RS row 8 (7, 7, 7, 7, 0, 0) times—9 (12, 14, 16, 19, 22, 24) sts total removed at armhole. *At the same time* dec 1 st at neck edge by working first 4 sts as k2, ssk on the next RS row, then every 4th row 2 times, then every RS row 18 (18, 19, 19, 20, 20, 21) times—21 (21, 22, 22, 23, 23, 24) sts removed from neck edge; 22 (23, 23, 25, 25, 26, 27) sts rem after all shaping is complete.

Work even until armhole measures same as back to shoulder, ending with a WS row. Shape shoulder as foll:

SHORT-ROW 1 (RS) Knit to last 5 (5, 5, 6, 6, 6, 6) sts, wrap next st, turn work.
SHORT-ROWS 2, 4, AND 6 (WS) Purl to end.
SHORT-ROWS 3 AND 5 Knit to 5 (5, 5, 6, 6, 6, 6) sts before previously wrapped st, wrap next st, turn work.

SHORT-ROW 7 Knit to 3 (4, 4, 3, 3, 4, 5) sts before previously wrapped st, wrap next st, turn work.

SHORT-ROW 8 Purl to end.

Knit 1 RS row across all sts, working wraps tog with wrapped sts when you come to them. Purl 1 WS row. Place sts on holder.

LEFT SIDE

NOTE *As for right side, armhole and neck shaping are worked at the same time; read all the way through the next sections before proceeding.*

For armhole shaping, dec 1 st at armhole edge by working the first 4 sts as k2, ssk on the next 1 (5, 7, 9, 12, 24) RS row(s), then every other RS row 8 (7, 7, 7, 7, 0, 0) times—9 (12, 14, 16, 19, 22, 24) sts total removed

at armhole. *At the same time* dec 1 st at neck edge by working last 4 sts as k2tog, k2 on the next RS row, then every 4th row 2 times, then every RS row 18 (18, 19, 19, 20, 20, 21) times—21 (21, 22, 22, 23, 23, 24) sts removed from neck edge; 22 (23, 23, 25, 25, 26, 27) sts rem after all shaping is complete.

Work even until armhole measures same as back to shoulder, ending with a RS row. Shape shoulder as foll:

SHORT-ROW 1 (WS) Purl to last 5 (5, 5, 6, 6, 6, 6) sts, wrap next st, turn work.

SHORT-ROWS 2, 4, AND 6 (RS) Knit to end.

SHORT-ROWS 3 AND 5 Purl to 5 (5, 5, 6, 6, 6, 6) sts before previously wrapped st, wrap next st, turn work.

SHORT-ROW 7 Purl to 3 (4, 4, 3, 3, 4, 5) sts before previously wrapped st, wrap next st, turn work.

SHORT-ROW 8 Knit to end.

Purl 1 WS row across all sts, working wraps tog with wrapped sts when you come to them. Place sts on holder.

sleeves

With larger needles, CO 59 (59, 63, 63, 65, 65, 67) sts.

ROW 1 (RS) Knit.
ROW 2 (WS) P2, *k1, p1; rep from * to last st, p1.

Rep these 2 rows 6 more times—14 rows total. Work 2 rows even in St st.

INC ROW (RS) K2, M1 (see Glossary), knit to last 2 sts, M1, k2—2 sts inc'd.

Cont in St st, rep inc row every 10 (10, 10, 10, 6, 4, 4)th row 4 (5, 5, 3, 3, 27, 28) more times, then every 6 (4, 4, 4, 4, 0, 0)th row 10 (12, 13, 19, 22, 0, 0) times, working new sts in St st—89 (95, 101, 109, 117, 121, 125) sts. Work even until piece measures 17 (17, 17, 17½, 18, 18, 18½)" (43 [43, 43, 44.5, 45.5, 45.5, 47] cm) from CO (see Notes about sleeve length of sample sweater), ending with a WS row.

Shape Cap

BO 6 (6, 7, 7, 7, 7, 7) sts at beg of next 2 rows—77 (83, 87, 95, 103, 107, 111) sts rem. BO 0 (3, 4, 5, 5, 6, 6) sts at beg of next 0 (2, 2, 2, 4, 4,

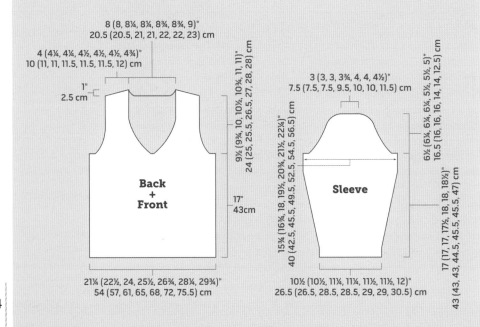

lystra pullover

8 (8, 8¼, 8¼, 8¾, 8¾, 9)"
20.5 (20.5, 21, 21, 22, 22, 23) cm

4 (4¼, 4¼, 4½, 4½, 4½, 4¾)"
10 (11, 11, 11.5, 11.5, 11.5, 12) cm

1"
2.5 cm

9½ (9¾, 10, 10½, 10¾, 11, 11)"
24 (25, 25.5, 26.5, 27, 28, 28) cm

Back + Front

17"
43cm

15¾ (16¾, 18, 19½, 20¾, 21½, 22¼)"
40 (42.5, 45.5, 49.5, 52.5, 54.5, 56.5) cm

21¼ (22½, 24, 25½, 26¾, 28¼, 29¾)"
54 (57, 61, 65, 68, 72, 75.5) cm

3 (3, 3¾, 4, 4, 4½)"
7.5 (7.5, 7.5, 9.5, 10, 10, 11.5) cm

6½ (6½, 6¼, 6¼, 6¼, 5½, 5½, 5)"
16.5 (16, 16, 16, 14, 14, 12.5) cm

Sleeve

10½ (10½, 11¼, 11¼, 11½, 11½, 12)"
26.5 (26.5, 28.5, 28.5, 29, 29, 30.5) cm

17 (17, 17, 17½, 18, 18, 18½)"
43 (43, 43, 44.5, 45.5, 45.5, 47) cm

4) rows, then 0 (0, 0, 0, 0, 0, 4) sts at beg of foll 0 (0, 0, 0, 0, 0, 2) rows—77 (77, 79, 85, 83, 83, 79) sts rem.

DEC ROW (RS) K2, ssk, knit to last 4 sts, k2tog, k2—2 sts dec'd.

Rep dec row every RS row 23 (21, 21, 19, 17, 17, 14) more times, ending with the final RS dec row—29 (33, 35, 45, 47, 47, 49) sts rem. Work 1 WS row. Bind off 3 (4, 5, 3, 6, 6, 6) sts at beg of next 4 (4, 2, 8, 4, 4, 4) rows, then BO 0 (0, 4, 0, 0, 0, 0) sts at beg of foll 0 (0, 2, 0, 0, 0, 0) rows—17 (17, 17, 21, 23, 23, 25) sts rem. With RS facing, BO all sts kwise.

finishing

Block pieces to measurements (see Notes) and allow to air-dry completely.

Seams

With WS facing tog, use the three-needle method (see Glossary) to join live sts of front and back at shoulders. With yarn threaded on a tapestry needle, sew side seams. Sew sleeve caps into armholes, matching midpoint of each cap to shoulder seam and easing cap to fit. Sew sleeve seams.

Neckband

With smaller cir needle, RS facing, and beg at right shoulder seam, pick up and knit 63 (63, 65, 65, 69, 69, 71) sts evenly across back neck, 81 (83, 85, 89, 91, 93, 93) sts along left front neck, place marker (pm), 2 sts at center front, pm, and 81 (83, 85, 89, 91, 93, 93) sts along right front neck edge—227 (231, 237, 245, 253, 257, 259) sts total. Pm and join for working in rnds. Work welting patt as foll:

RNDS 1 AND 3 Purl to 2 sts before m, p2tog, sl m, p2, sl m, ssp (see Glossary), purl to end—2 sts dec'd.

RND 2 Purl.

RND 4 Knit.

RND 5 Knit to 2 sts before m, k2tog, sl m, k2, sl m, ssk (see Glossary), knit to end—2 sts dec'd.

RNDS 6 AND 8 Purl.

RND 7 Purl to 2 sts before m, p2tog, sl m, p2, sl m, ssp, purl to end—2 sts dec'd.

RND 9 Knit to 2 sts before m, k2tog, sl m, k2, sl m, ssk, knit to end—2 sts dec'd.

RND 10 Knit.

RNDS 11–14 Rep Rnds 1–4—213 (217, 223, 231, 239, 243, 245) sts rem.

BO all sts pwise.

Block neckband and seams. Weave in loose ends.

poppy cardigan

DESIGNED BY **MANDY MOORE**

Mandy Moore's yoked cardigan features set-in shapes but is not worked like a traditional set-in sweater. The contrasting yoke is worked from its back edge up and over the shoulders to end at the front edges, using short-rows to shape the shoulder slope. The body and sleeve stitches are picked up along the yoke edges and worked downward in one piece with raglan-like increases to shape the body and sleeves. Short-row bust darts, knitted-in front bands, and gentle waist shaping all add up to make a visually simple but refined garment that just looks good on plus-size women.

FINISHED SIZE
39½ (42½, 47¼, 50½, 55, 58¾)" (100.5 [108, 120, 128.5, 139.5, 149] cm) bust circumference, buttoned. Cardigan shown measures 42½" (108 cm).

YARN
Worsted weight (#4 Medium).

Shown here: Cascade Yarns Cascade 200 Tweed (90% Peruvian highland wool, 10% Donegal tweed [9% acrylic, 1% viscose]; 220 yd [200 m]/100 g); #7617 dark grey tweed (MC), 6 (6, 7, 7, 8, 8) skeins.

Cascade Yarns Cascade 220 Wool (100% Peruvian highland wool; 220 yd [200 m]/100 g); #7804 coral pink, 1 (1, 1, 2, 2, 2) skein(s).

NEEDLES
Body and sleeves: size U.S. 7 (4.5 mm): 16" and 40" (40 and 100 cm) circular (cir) and set of 4 double-pointed (dpn).

Neckband: size U.S. 4 (3.5mm): 24" (60 cm) cir.

Adjust needle size if necessary to obtain the correct gauge.

NOTIONS
Markers (m); waste yarn for stitch holders; tapestry needle; eight ½" (1.3 cm) buttons.

GAUGE
20 stitches and 27 rows = 4" (10 cm) in stockinette stitch on larger needles.

20 stitches and 30 rows = 4" (10 cm) in garter rib on larger needles.

25 stitches and 27 rows = 4" (10 cm) in k1, p1 rib on larger needles.

stitch guide + notes

RIGHT LIFTED INCREASE (RLI)
Use the right needle to pick up the stitch below the next stitch on the left needle, then knit this picked-up st—1 st inc'd.

LEFT LIFTED INCREASE (LLI)
Use the left needle to pick up the stitch 2 rows below the last stitch on the right needle, then knit this picked-up st—1 st inc'd.

GARTER RIB
(odd number of sts)

ROW 1 (RS) Knit.
ROW 2 (WS) *P1, k1; rep from * to last st, p1.
Repeat Rows 1 and 2 for pattern.

+ The body of this top-down cardigan features hourglass shaping with a wider hip than bust. The narrow waist is achieved with decreases worked along internal darts; increases are worked along these same lines to widen for the hips. In addition to this shaping, short-rows are worked at the bust to provide more length over the fullest part of the bust. Once the lower body is established, the knitting is fairly straightforward, making it easy to customize the body shaping. This design lends itself to A-line shaping if you eliminate the waist decreases and then increase as needed to reach the final stitch counts for the lower edging.

+ Pay attention to the placement of the waist shaping. If you have a low bustline, you may want to lower the waist. As it is, the waist decreases begin 2 (2¼, 2½, 3, 3, 2¾)" (5 [5.5, 6.5, 7.5, 7.5, 7] cm below the underarm.

+ Because of its unusual top-down construction, this sweater does not mesh completely with the set-in guidelines provided earlier in this chapter. For one, the sleeve cap is worked as part of the upper body, more like a raglan than a set-in. Because of this, if you need to change the stitch count for the sleeve, it won't affect the cap in the same ways as for the Lystra Pullover on page 60. The stitches worked raglan-style for the cap are picked up later and, in conjunction with stitches picked up from the underarm, worked down to complete the sleeve. Making the sleeve larger with will be difficult. The depth of the yoke and the number of sleeve cap increase rows worked into that depth determine the number of stitches for the lower sleeve. One option is to pick up more stitches for the sleeve caps along the contrasting yoke piece. The instructed pick-up rate is about two stitches for every three rows along the yoke selvedge for the sleeve sections. Picking up too many stitches along an edge can lead to puckering, however. You could also work more increase rows on the sleeve caps as the yoke is worked, being careful not to disrupt the body and neck shaping.

yoke

With CC and longer cir needle in larger size, use the long-tail method (see Glossary) to CO 71 (75, 81, 85, 91, 95) sts. Purl 1 WS row. Work 2 rows in garter rib (see Stitch Guide), ending with a WS row.

Shape Shoulders

Continuing in garter rib as established, work short-rows (see Glossary) as foll:

SHORT-ROWS 1 (RS) AND 2 (WS) Work in patt to last 2 sts, wrap next st, turn work.

SHORT-ROWS 3 AND 4 Work in patt to 2 sts before previously wrapped st, wrap next st, turn work.

Repeat Short-rows 3 and 4 only 6 (6, 7, 7, 8, 9) more times—8 (8, 9, 9, 10, 11) wrapped sts at each side.

NEXT ROW (RS) Knit to end, working wraps tog with wrapped sts.

NEXT ROW (WS) Work across all sts in patt, working rem wraps tog with wrapped sts.

NEXT ROW (RS) K17 (17, 19, 19, 21, 23) for right shoulder, place next 37 (41, 43, 47, 49, 49) sts on a holder for back neck, place rem 17 (17, 19, 19, 21, 23) on a second holder for left shoulder —piece measures 3 (3, 3¼, 3¼, 3½, 3¾)" (7.5 (7.5, 8.5, 8.5, 9, 9.5) cm] from CO at center, and about ¾" (2 cm) at each selvedge.

RIGHT SHOULDER

Beg with a WS row, work 17 (17, 19, 19, 21, 23) right shoulder sts in garter rib for 30 (34, 36, 40, 42,

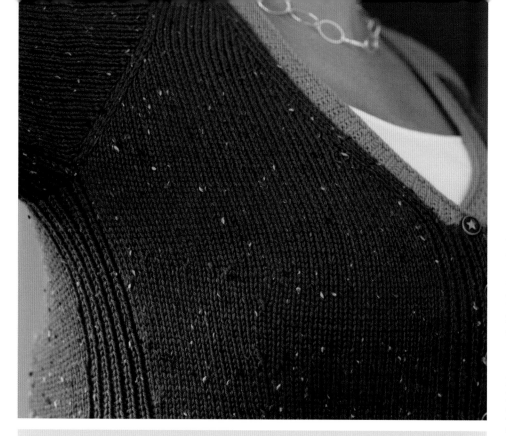

42) rows, ending with a RS row. Purl 1 WS row—piece measures 5 (5½, 5¾, 6¼, 6½, 6½)" (12.5 [14, 14.5, 16, 16.5, 16.5] cm) from CO at armhole edge (beg of RS rows) and 4¼ (4¾, 5, 5½, 5¾, 5¾)" (11 [12, 12.5, 14, 14.5, 14.5] cm] from where back sts were put on holder at neck edge (end of RS rows). Using the sewn method (see Glossary), BO all sts.

LEFT SHOULDER

Return 17 (17, 19, 19, 21, 23) left shoulder sts onto needle and join yarn with RS facing. Beg and ending with a RS row, work right shoulder sts in garter rib for 31 (35, 37, 41, 43, 43) rows—piece measures 5 (5½, 5¾, 6¼, 6½, 6½)" (12.5 [14, 14.5, 16, 16.5, 16.5] cm) from CO at armhole edge (end of RS rows) and 4¼ (4¾, 5, 5½, 5¾, 5¾)" (11 [12, 12.5, 14, 14.5, 14.5] cm) from where back sts were put on holder at neck edge (beg of RS rows). Using the sewn method, BO all sts.

upper body + sleeve caps

NOTES *When picking up sts along front BO edges and back CO edge of the yoke, do not pick up any sts in the corners. In addition, when picking up sts along front and back edges, roll the CO or BO edge slightly to the RS and pick up and knit sts from the WS purl bumps 1 row in from the edge; this will make the CO and BO edges form decorative ridges on RS of work. When picking up sts along armhole edges (yoke selvedges), pick up sts in*

poppy cardigan

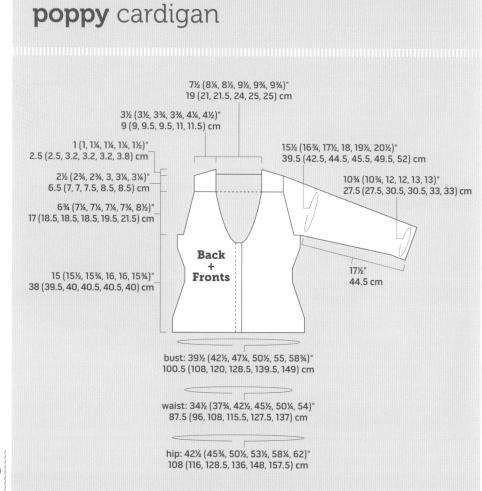

7½ (8¼, 8½, 9½, 9¾, 9¾)"
19 (21, 21.5, 24, 25, 25) cm

3½ (3½, 3¾, 3¾, 4¼, 4½)"
9 (9, 9.5, 9.5, 11, 11.5) cm

1 (1, 1¼, 1¼, 1¼, 1½)"
2.5 (2.5, 3.2, 3.2, 3.2, 3.8) cm

2½ (2¾, 2¾, 3, 3¼, 3¼)"
6.5 (7, 7, 7.5, 8.5, 8.5) cm

6¾ (7¼, 7¼, 7¼, 7¾, 8½)"
17 (18.5, 18.5, 18.5, 19.5, 21.5) cm

15 (15½, 15¾, 16, 16, 15¾)"
38 (39.5, 40, 40.5, 40.5, 40) cm

15½ (16¾, 17½, 18, 19½, 20½)"
39.5 (42.5, 44.5, 45.5, 49.5, 52) cm

10¾ (10¾, 12, 12, 13, 13)"
27.5 (27.5, 30.5, 30.5, 33, 33) cm

Back + Fronts

17½"
44.5 cm

bust: 39½ (42½, 47¼, 50½, 55, 58¾)"
100.5 (108, 120, 128.5, 139.5, 149) cm

waist: 34½ (37¾, 42½, 45½, 50¼, 54)"
87.5 (96, 108, 115.5, 127.5, 137) cm

hip: 42½ (45¾, 50½, 53½, 58¼, 62)"
108 (116, 128.5, 136, 148, 157.5) cm

the usual manner, beginning and end-ing the pick-up 1 to 2 rows from the BO or CO edges to avoid interfering with the decorative ridges.

Pick Up Stitches + Establish Front Edges

With MC, longer cir needle in larger size, RS facing, and beg at left front corner, pick up and knit 16 (16, 18, 18, 20, 22) left front sts along BO edge of left shoulder (see Note above), place marker (pm), 25 (27, 29, 31, 33, 33) left sleeve sts (about 2 sts for every 3 rows) along armhole selvedge, pm, 69 (73, 79, 83, 89, 93) back sts along CO edge of back, pm, 25 (27, 29, 31, 33, 33) right sleeve sts along armhole selvedge, pm, and 16 (16, 18, 18,

20, 22) right front sts along lower BO edge of right shoulder, ending at right front corner—151 (159, 173, 181, 195, 203) sts total.

NEXT ROW (WS) P2, k1, p1, k1, purl to last 5 sts, k1, p1, k1, p2.

NOTE *Throughout the foll shaping, maintain 5 sts at each end of row in rib as established (knit the knits and purl the purls as they appear) for neck edges.*

Shape Sleeve Caps + Begin Neck Shaping

ROW 1 (RS) Work 5 edge sts as established, *knit to m, sl m, RLI (see Stitch Guide), knit to m, LLI (see Stitch Guide), sl m; rep from *

once more, knit to last 5 sts , work 5 edge sts as established—4 sts inc'd: 2 sts inc'd each sleeve cap.

ROW 2 Work even in patt.

ROW 3 Work 5 edge sts, RLI, *knit to m, sl m, RLI, knit to m, LLI, sl m; rep from * once more, knit to last 5 sts , LLI, work 5 edge sts—6 sts inc'd: 1 st inc'd at each front neck inside edge sts and 2 sts inc'd each sleeve cap.

ROW 4 Work even in patt.

Rep the last 4 rows 4 (4, 3, 2, 2, 2) more times, then work Rows 1 and 2 once more—205 (213, 217, 215, 229, 237) sts total: 21 (21, 22, 21, 23, 25) sts each front; 69 (73, 79, 83, 89, 93) back sts; 47 (49, 47, 45, 47, 47) sts each sleeve.

Shape Raglans + Continue Neck Shaping

ROW 1 (RS) Work 5 edge sts, RLI, *knit to 1 st before m, LLI, k1, sl m, RLI, knit to m, LLI, sl m, k1, RLI; rep from * once more, knit to last 5 sts, LLI, work 5 edge sts—10 sts inc'd: 2 sts each front (1 st for both neck and raglan); 2 back sts; 2 sts each sleeve.

ROW 2 Work even in patt.

ROW 3 Work 5 edge sts, *knit to 1 st before m, LLI, k1, sl m, RLI, knit to m, LLI, sl m, k1, RLI; rep from * once more, knit to last 5 sts, work 5 edge sts—8 sts inc'd: 1 st each front (raglan only); 2 back sts; 2 sts each sleeve.

ROW 4 Work even in patt.

Rep the last 4 rows 4 (5, 6, 7, 8, 9) more times, then work Rows 1 and 2 once more—305 (331, 353, 369, 401, 427) sts total: 38 (41, 45, 47,

52, 57) sts each front; 91 (99, 109, 117, 127, 135) back sts; 69 (75, 77, 79, 85, 89) sts each sleeve; piece measures 6¾ (7¼, 7¼, 7¼, 7¾, 8½)" (17 [18.5, 18.5, 18.5, 19.5, 21.5] cm) from pick-up row.

lower body

DIVIDING ROW (RS) Work 5 edge sts, RLI, *knit to m, sl m, place next 69 (75, 77, 79, 85, 89) left sleeve sts on waste yarn holder, use the backward-loop method to CO 11 (11, 13, 13, 15, 17) sts for left underarm, sl m; rep from * once more for right sleeve and underarm, knit to last 5 sts, LLI, work 5 edge sts—191 (205, 227, 239, 263, 285) sts rem: 39 (42, 46, 48, 53, 58) sts each front; 91 (99, 109, 117, 127, 135) back sts; 11 (11, 13, 13, 15, 17) sts between m at each underarm.

NEXT ROW (WS) Work 5 edge sts, *purl to m, sl m, k1, [p1, k1] 5 (5, 6, 6, 7, 8) times, sl m; rep from * once more, purl to last 5 sts, work 5 edge sts.

Working underarm sts between m as they appear, cont in patt and *at the same time* inc 1 st at each front neck inside edge sts every RS row 3 (4, 5, 7, 7, 6) times, then work 1 WS row even—197 (213, 237, 253, 277, 297) sts; 42 (46, 51, 55, 60, 64) sts each front; 91 (99, 109, 117, 127, 135) back sts, 11 (11, 13, 13, 15, 17) sts each underarm; lower body measures 1¼ (1½, 1¾, 2¼, 2¼, 2)" (3.2 [3.8, 4.5, 5.5, 5.5, 5] cm) from underarm.

Set Up Front Bands

SHORT-ROW 1 (RS) Work 4 sts in patt at left front edge, wrap next st, turn work.

SHORT-ROW 2 (WS) Work 4 sts in patt, turn work.

SHORT-ROW 3 Work across all sts in patt, working wrap tog with wrapped st.

SHORT-ROW 4 (WS) Work 4 sts in patt for right front edge, wrap next st, turn work.

SHORT-ROW 5 Work 4 sts in patt, turn work.

NEXT ROW (WS) Use the cable method (see Glossary) to CO 8 sts, p2, [k1, p1] 5 times, k1, work in patt to end, working rem wrap tog with wrapped st—8 sts added at right front edge.

NEXT ROW (RS) Use the cable method to CO 8 sts, k2, [p1, k1] 5 times, p1, work in patt to last 13 sts, work sts as they appear—213 (229, 253, 269, 293, 313) sts: 50 (54, 59, 63, 68, 72) sts each front; no change to other st counts.

NOTE *Throughout the foll shaping, maintain 13 sts at each end of row as established for front edges.*

Work 1 WS row even in patt—lower body measures 1¾ (2, 2¼, 2¾, 2¾, 2½)" (4.5 [5, 5.5, 7, 7, 6.5] cm) from underarm at sides.

Short-Row Bust Shaping

NOTES *The following short-row sequence will add about 1¼" (3.2 cm) to the length at center front to accommodate a large bust. If more length is desired, this sequence can be* worked a second time after working 2 rows even across all sts. If you repeat the short-row sequence, be sure to take the additional rows into account when spacing buttonholes (worked every 12th row).

SHORT-ROW 1 (RS) Work in patt to 5 (5, 6, 6, 7, 7) sts before first m at left underarm, wrap next st, turn work.

SHORT-ROWS 2, 4, 6, AND 8 (WS) Work in patt to left front edge, turn work.

SHORT-ROWS 3, 5, AND 7 Work in patt to 5 (5, 6, 6, 7, 7) sts before previously wrapped st, wrap next st, turn work.

SHORT-ROW 9 (RS; buttonhole row) Working wraps tog with wrapped sts, work in patt to last 7 sts, yo, k2tog, work 5 sts in patt.

SHORT-ROW 10 (WS) Work in patt to 5 (5, 6, 6, 7, 7) sts before first m at right underarm, wrap next st, turn work.

SHORT-ROWS 11, 13, 15, AND 17 Work in patt to right front edge, turn work.

SHORT-ROWS 12, 14, AND 16 Work in patt to 5 (5, 6, 6, 7, 7) sts before previously wrapped st, wrap next st, turn work.

NEXT ROW (WS) Work all sts in patt, working wraps tog with wrapped sts—lower body measures 2 (2¼, 2½, 3, 3, 2¾)" (5 [5.5, 6.5, 7.5, 7.5, 7] cm) at sides.

Shape Waist

BUTTONHOLE NOTES *Work 6 more buttonholes during waist shaping for a total of 7 buttonholes on the front band; the 8th buttonhole is worked later as part of the neckband. Work*

229, 245, 269, 289) sts rem: 44
(48, 53, 57, 62, 66) sts each front;
79 (87, 97, 105, 115, 123) back
sts; 11 (11, 13, 13, 15, 17) sts each
underarm. Work even in patt until
lower body measures 7¼ (7½, 7¾,
8¼, 8¼, 8)" (18.5 [19, 19.5, 21, 21,
20.5] cm) at sides, beg and ending
with a WS row (about 13 rows).

INC ROW (RS) *Work in patt to dart
m, sl m, RLI, knit to underarm m,
LLI, sl m, work underarm rib sts,
sl m, RLI, knit to dart m, LLI,
sl m; rep from * once more, work
in patt to end—8 sts inc'd.

[Work 7 rows even in patt, then
rep the inc row] 4 times—229
(245, 269, 285, 309, 329) sts: 54
(58, 63, 67, 72, 76) sts each front;
99 (107, 117, 125, 135, 143) back
sts; 11 (11, 13, 13, 15, 17) sts each
underarm. Work even in patt until
lower body measures 12¾ (13¼,
13½, 13¾, 13¾, 13½)" (32.5 [33.5,
34.5, 35, 35, 34.5] cm) at sides
(about 5 rows), or 2¼" (5.5 cm) less
than desired length, ending with a
WS row.

Lower Edge Ribbing

SET-UP ROW (RS) Removing markers
as you come to them, work 13 edge
sts, k3 (5, 5, 7, 2, 4), M1, [k5, M1]
7 (7, 8, 8, 11, 11) times, k3 (5, 5,
7, 2, 4), work underarm sts in rib
patt to next m, k7 (6, 6, 5, 5, 4),
M1, [k5, M1] 17 (19, 21, 23, 25,
27) times, k7 (6, 6, 5, 5, 4), work
in rib patt to next m, k3 (5, 5, 7,
2, 4), M1, [k5, M1] 7 (7, 8, 8, 11,
11) times, k3 (5, 5, 7, 2, 4), work
rem 13 edge sts in patt—263 (281,
309, 327, 359, 381) sts.

*the next front band buttonhole on the
12th row after the buttonhole from
Short-row 9 of the bust shaping, then
work the next 5 buttonholes every
12th row thereafter. Buttonholes are
worked on the last 7 sts of RS rows
as "yo, k2tog, work 5 sts in patt."
Count rows frequently to ensure that
you do not accidentally work past a
buttonhole position.*

SET-UP ROW (RS) *Work in patt
to 20 (20, 25, 25, 30, 30) sts
before first underarm m, pm
for dart, work in patt to 20 (20,
25, 25, 30, 30) sts after second
underarm m, pm for dart; rep
from * once more, work in patt to
end—8 m total: 4 new dart m; 2
underarm m at each side.

NEXT ROW (WS) Work even in patt.

DEC ROW (RS) *Work in patt to dart
m, sl m, k2tog, knit to 2 sts before
underarm m, ssk, sl m, work
underarm rib sts, sl m, k2tog, knit
to 2 sts before dart m, ssk, sl m; rep
from * once more, work in patt to
end—8 sts dec'd.

[Work 9 rows even in patt, then rep
the dec row] 2 times—189 (205,

ROW 1 (RS) K2, *p1, k1; rep from * to last st, k1.

ROW 2 (WS) P2, *k1, p1; rep from * to last st, p1.

Rep the last 2 rows 5 more times, then work Row 1 once more.

NEXT ROW (RS) K2tog, *sl 1 pwise with yarn in front (wyf), k1; rep from * to last 3 sts, sl 1 wyf, ssk—261 (279, 307, 325 357, 379) sts rem.

NEXT ROW *Sl 1 pwise wyf, k1; rep from * to last st, sl 1 pwise wyf—lower body measures about 15 (15½, 15¾, 16, 16, 15¾)" (38 [39.5, 40, 40.5, 40.5, 40] cm) at sides.

Using the tubular method (see Glossary), BO all sts.

sleeves

With RS facing, join yarn to center st of sts CO at underarm. Using shorter cir needle in larger size, pick up and knit 6 (6, 6, 6, 8, 8) sts along CO, knit across 69 (75, 77, 79, 85, 89) held sleeve sts, then pick up and knit 5 (5, 7, 7, 7, 9) sts along CO to end at center, pm for beg of rnd—80 (86, 90, 92, 100, 106) sts total.

SET-UP RND [K1, p1] 3 (3, 3, 3, 4, 4) times, pm, knit to last 5 (5, 7, 7, 7, 9) sts, pm, [p1, k1] 2 (2, 3, 3, 3, 4) times, p1—11 (11, 13, 13, 15, 17) marked rib sts at underarm with beg-of-rnd m near center of marked sts. Work sts as they appear for 7 (5, 6, 5, 5, 4) rnds.

DEC RND Work in patt to first m, sl m, k2tog, knit to 2 sts before next m, ssk, sl m, work in patt to end of rnd—2 sts dec'd.

[Work 7 (5, 6, 5, 5, 4) rnds even, then rep dec rnd] 11 (14, 13, 14, 15, 18) times, changing to double-pointed needles when there are too few sts to fit comfortably on cir needle—56 (56, 62, 62, 68, 68) sts rem. Cont even in patt until sleeve measures 15¼" (38.5 cm) from underarm or 2¼" (5.5 cm) less than desired total length.

NEXT RND *K1, p1; rep from *. Work in rib as established for 12 more rnds.

NEXT RND *K1, sl 1 pwise wyf; rep from *.

NEXT RND *Sl 1 pwise with yarn in back (wyb), p1; rep from *— sleeve measures 17½" (44.5 cm) or desired length.

Using the tubular method, BO all sts.

finishing
Neckband

With CC, smaller needle, RS facing, and beg at lower corner of right front neck (where front band joins body), pick up and knit 36 (40, 41, 43, 45, 47) sts along right neck edge to yoke (about 2 sts for every 3 rows), 20 (24, 25, 27, 29, 29) sts along yoke selvedge to back neck corner, pm, k37 (41, 43, 45, 49, 49) held back neck sts, pm, pick up and knit 20 (24, 25, 27, 29, 29) sts along yoke selvedge, and 36 (40, 41, 43, 45, 47) sts along left neck edge

to end at lower corner of left front neck—149 (169, 175, 185, 197, 201) sts total.

ROW 1 (WS) P2, *k1, p1; rep from * to last st, p1.

ROW 2 K1, M1, *knit to 2 sts before m, ssk, sl m, k2tog; rep from * once, knit to last st, M1, k1—2 sts dec'd; 1 st dec'd each side of each m (4 decs total); 1 st inc'd at each end (2 incs total).

ROW 3 P2, work sts as they appear (purl the garter st columns; knit the St st columns) to last 2 sts, p2.

ROW 4 Rep Row 2—2 sts dec'd. Repeat Rows 3 and 4 three times—139 (159, 165, 175, 187, 191) sts rem.

Using the sewn method, BO all sts. With MC threaded on a tapestry needle, sew one neckband selvedge to top of left front buttonband. Sew the other neckband selvedge to top of right front buttonhole band, leaving a gap in the center of the seam to form the top buttonhole.

Weave in loose ends. Block to measurements.

NOTE *The lower body lengths shown on the schematic are measured straight down at sides and do not follow the curve of the waist. The center front edges will be slightly longer because of the short-row bust shaping. Insert a rolled-up towel into the bust area to pad out the front contours and align the lower edges of the fronts with the lower back edge.*

Sew buttons to buttonband opposite buttonholes.

cleveland shell

DESIGNED BY **LOU SCHIELA**

Summer knits can be tough for plus-size women—often designed as skimpy bits of fabric, they just don't translate into our sizes well. Lou Schiela gives us this ladylike alternative in cotton and linen with A-line shaping courtesy of an inserted lace gusset. The straps and princess neckline provide plenty of upper-body coverage—you could wear this without an underlayer—while the extra-long lower body emphasizes vertical lines. The set-in shaping of the armholes, combined with shoulder shaping, makes for a refined fit across the cross-back. This tank illustrates the fact that set-in construction isn't just about sleeve shape; the tailored armhole is really the most important aspect of this construction style.

FINISHED SIZE
About 36 (40, 44, 48, 52, 56, 60)" (91.5 [101.5, 112, 122, 132, 142, 152.5] cm) bust circumference. Garment shown measures 44" (112 cm).

YARN
Sportweight (#2 Fine).

Shown here: Classic Elite Allegoro (70% organic cotton, 30% linen; 152 yd [139 m]/ 50 g): #5636 linen, 7 (8, 9, 9, 10, 10, 11) balls.

NEEDLES
Body: size U.S. 5 (3.75 mm); 32" (80 cm) circular (cir).

Neckband and armhole edgings: size U.S. 5 (3.75 mm): 16" (40 cm) cir.

Adjust needle size if necessary to obtain the correct gauge.

NOTIONS
Markers (m); stitch holders; tapestry needle.

GAUGE
26 stitches and 32 rows = 4" (10 cm) in textured rib pattern from chart.

41 sts at lower edge of lace inset chart = 6¼" (16 cm) wide.

notes

+ The schematic shows the width of the back lower edge; the front lower edge measures about 5¾" (14.5 cm) wider than the back, but the front lace inset will form a pleat at center front when worn. Both the back and front measure the same across the bustline.

+ The A-line shape of the lower body is central to this design. The back and front both feature side shaping to achieve this line, plus the lace insert on the front also creates additional A-line shaping.

+ The cross-back width (after all armhole shaping) should measure about 1" (2.5 cm) to 1½" (3.8 cm) more than your actual cross-back measurement. Tweak the armhole shaping to achieve your needed cross-back width but leave the back neck width and neck shaping as they are to limit the amount of reworking. If you alter the stitch count for the shoulders, you will need to rework the short-row shoulder shaping to accommodate your stitch counts.

+ Because there are no sleeves to this design, changing the armhole depth doesn't create (as many) problems as it would in other set-in designs. The front neck shaping is tied to the position of the underarms, so you need to consider neck depth (and the required number of decrease rows) when changing the beginning of the armholes. The overall length of the garment would also be affected by changing the armhole depth; consider how the lower body length might need to change to accommodate a shorter or deeper armhole.

back

With longer cir needle, CO 143 (157, 169, 175, 195, 201, 221) sts. Do not join. Knit 2 rows, ending with a RS row.

SET-UP ROW (WS) Work set-up row of Textured Rib chart (page 81) beg and ending where indicated for your size as foll: Work 9 (1, 7, 10, 5, 8, 3) sts before patt rep box once, work 30-st rep 4 (5, 5, 5, 6, 6, 7) times, work 14 (6, 12, 15, 10, 13, 8) sts after patt rep box once.

NOTE *As you work the foll instructions, rep Rows 1–24 of chart for patt; do not rep the set-up row.*

Cont in patt from chart until piece measures 1" (2.5 cm) from CO, ending with a WS row.

Shape sides

DEC ROW (RS) K1, k2tog, work as established to last 3 sts, ssk, k1—2 sts dec'd.

Work 9 (9, 9, 13, 9, 13, 9) rows even in patt. Cont in patt, rep the shaping of the last 10 (10, 10, 14, 10, 14, 10) rows 12 (12, 12, 8, 12, 8, 12) more times—117 (131, 143, 157, 169, 183, 195) sts rem. Cont even in patt until piece measures 17½ (17½, 18, 18, 18, 18½, 18½)" (44.5 [44.5, 45.5, 45.5, 45.5, 47, 47] cm) from CO, ending with a WS row.

Shape Armholes

BO 3 (5, 7, 8, 10, 12, 13) sts at beg of next 2 rows—111 (121, 129, 141, 149, 159, 169) sts rem. Dec 1 st each end of needle every row 0 (0, 0, 9, 11, 21, 26) times, then every other row 4 (8, 13, 8, 8, 2, 0) times, then every 4th row 3 (2, 0, 0, 0, 0, 0) times—97 (101, 103, 107, 111, 113, 117) sts rem. Work even in patt until armholes measure 8½ (9, 9, 9, 9½, 9½, 10)" (21.5 [23, 23, 23, 24, 24, 25.5] cm), ending with a WS row.

Shape Shoulders

Work short-rows (see Glossary) as foll:

SHORT-ROWS 1 (RS) AND 2 (WS) Work in patt to last 10 (11, 11, 11, 12, 11, 12) sts, wrap next st, turn work.

SHORT-ROWS 3 AND 4 Work in patt to 10 (10, 11, 11, 11, 11, 12) sts before previously wrapped st, wrap next st, turn work.

SHORT-ROW 5 Work in patt to end of row, working wraps tog with wrapped sts, turn.

NEXT ROW (WS) Work 29 (31, 32, 32, 34, 33, 35) sts in patt, BO center 39 (39, 39, 43, 43, 47, 47) sts for back neck, work to end of row, working wraps tog with wrapped sts—29 (31, 32, 32, 34, 33, 35) sts at each side.

Place sts on holders.

front

With longer cir needle, CO 179 (193, 205, 211, 231, 237, 257) sts.

SET-UP ROW (WS) K69 (76, 82, 85, 95, 98, 108), place marker (pm), work set-up row of Lace Inset chart (page 82) over center 41 sts, pm, k69 (76, 82, 85, 95, 98, 108).

NEXT ROW (RS) Knit to first m, sl m, work Row 1 of Lace Inset chart over center 41 sts, sl m, knit to end.

NEXT ROW (WS) Beg and ending where indicated for your size, establish patt from set-up row of Textured Rib chart on each side of marked center sts as foll: For right front, work 9 (1, 7, 10, 5, 8, 3) sts before patt rep box once, work 30-st rep 2 (2, 2, 2, 3, 3, 3) times, work first 0 (15, 15, 15, 0, 0, 15) sts of patt rep once; sl m, work Row 2 of Lace Inset chart over center 41 sts, sl m; for left front, work last 25 (10, 10, 10, 25, 25, 10) sts of patt rep once, work 30-st rep 1 (2, 2, 2, 2, 2, 3) time(s), work 14 (6, 12, 15, 10, 13, 8) sts after patt rep once.

Cont in established patts, until piece measures 1" (2.5 cm) from CO, ending with a WS row.

Shape Sides

DEC ROW (RS) K1, k2tog, work as established to last 3 sts, ssk, k1—2 sts dec'd.

Work 9 (9, 9, 13, 9, 13, 9) rows even in patt. Cont in patt, rep the shaping of the last 10 (10, 10, 14, 10, 14, 10) rows 12 (12, 12, 8, 12, 8, 12) more times and *at the same time* dec sts from lace inset section as shown on chart—117 (131, 143, 157, 169, 183, 195) sts rem after all shaping.

NOTE *After completing Row 103 of Lace Inset chart, remove m on each side of rem 5 center sts and work these sts into established Textured Rib patt.*

Cont even in patt until piece measures same as back to armhole, ending with a WS row.

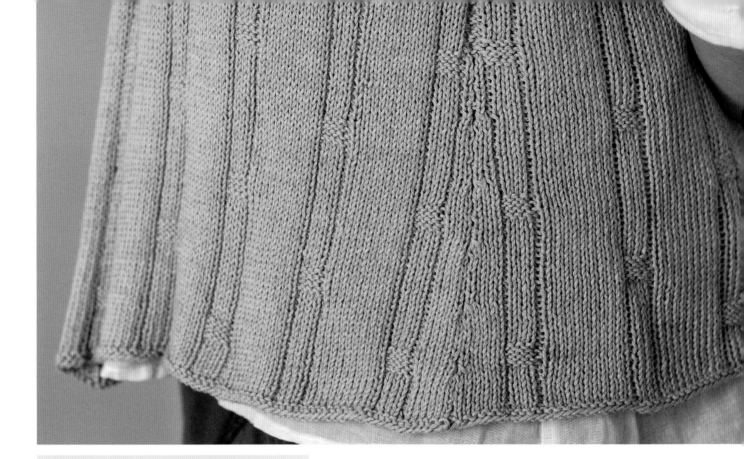

cleveland shell

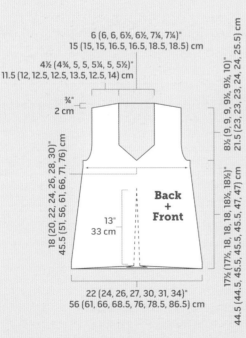

6 (6, 6, 6½, 6½, 7¼, 7¼)"
15 (15, 15, 16.5, 16.5, 18.5, 18.5) cm

4½ (4¾, 5, 5, 5¼, 5, 5½)"
11.5 (12, 12.5, 12.5, 13.5, 12.5, 14) cm

¾"
2 cm

8½ (9, 9, 9, 9½, 9½, 10)"
21.5 (23, 23, 23, 24, 24, 25.5) cm

18 (20, 22, 24, 26, 28, 30)"
45.5 (51, 56, 61, 66, 71, 76) cm

13"
33 cm

Back + Front

17½ (17½, 18, 18, 18, 18½, 18½)"
44.5 (44.5, 45.5, 45.5, 45.5, 47, 47) cm

22 (24, 26, 27, 30, 31, 34)"
56 (61, 66, 68.5, 76, 78.5, 86.5) cm

Shape Armholes + Neck

Mark center st—58 (65, 71, 78, 84, 91, 97) sts each side of marked st.

NEXT ROW (RS) BO 3 (5, 7, 8, 10, 12, 13) sts, work in patt to marked st, join a second ball of yarn, k2tog (marked st with st after it), work in patt to end.

NEXT ROW BO 3 (5, 7, 8, 10, 12, 13) sts at beg of first group of sts, work to end of first group, then work in patt to end of second group—55 (60, 64, 70, 74, 79, 84) sts each side.

NOTE *Neck and armholes are shaped at the same time; read all the way through the next section before proceeding.*

Working each side separately, dec 1 st at each armhole edge every row 0 (0, 0, 9, 11, 21, 26) times, then every other row 4 (8, 13, 8, 8, 2, 0) times, then every 4th row 3 (2, 0, 0, 0, 0, 0)

times—7 (10, 13, 17, 19, 23, 26) sts total removed from each armhole edge. *At the same time* dec 1 st at each neck edge every row 19 (19, 19, 21, 21, 23, 23) times—29 (31, 32, 32, 34, 33, 35) sts rem each side after all shaping. Cont even until armholes measure 8½ (9, 9, 9, 9½, 9½, 10)" (21.5 [23, 23, 23, 24, 24, 25.5] cm), ending with a WS row.

Shape Shoulders

Work short-rows as foll:

SHORT-ROW 1 (RS) Work left shoulder sts; work in patt to last 10 (11, 11, 11, 12, 11, 12) right shoulder sts, wrap next st, turn work.

SHORT-ROW 2 (WS) Work right shoulder sts; work in patt to last 10 (11, 11, 11, 12, 11, 12) left shoulder sts, wrap next st, turn work.

SHORT-ROW 3 Work left shoulder sts; work right shoulder sts in patt to 10 (10, 11, 11, 11, 11, 12) sts

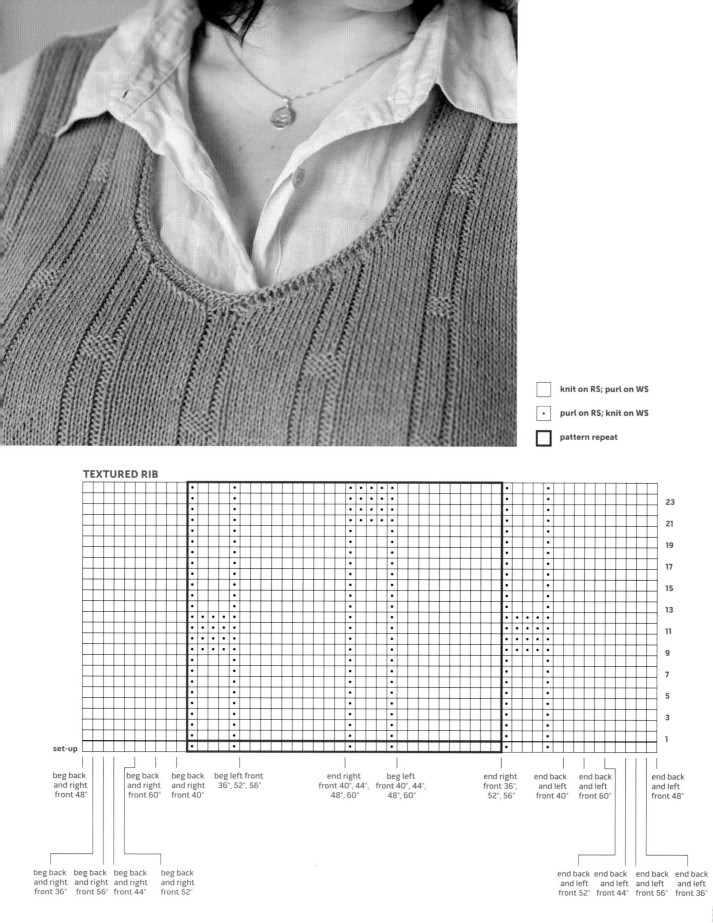

knit on RS; purl on WS

· purl on RS; knit on WS

pattern repeat

TEXTURED RIB

set-up

23
21
19
17
15
13
11
9
7
5
3
1

beg back and right front 48"

beg back and right front 60"

beg back and right front 40"

beg left front 36", 52", 56"

end right front 40", 44", 48", 60"

beg left front 40", 44", 48", 60"

end right front 36", 52", 56"

end back and left front 40"

end back and left front 60"

end back and left front 48"

beg back and right front 36"

beg back and right front 56"

beg back and right front 44"

beg back and right front 52"

end back and left front 52"

end back and left front 44"

end back and left front 56"

end back and left front 36"

LACE INSET ROWS SET-UP to 52

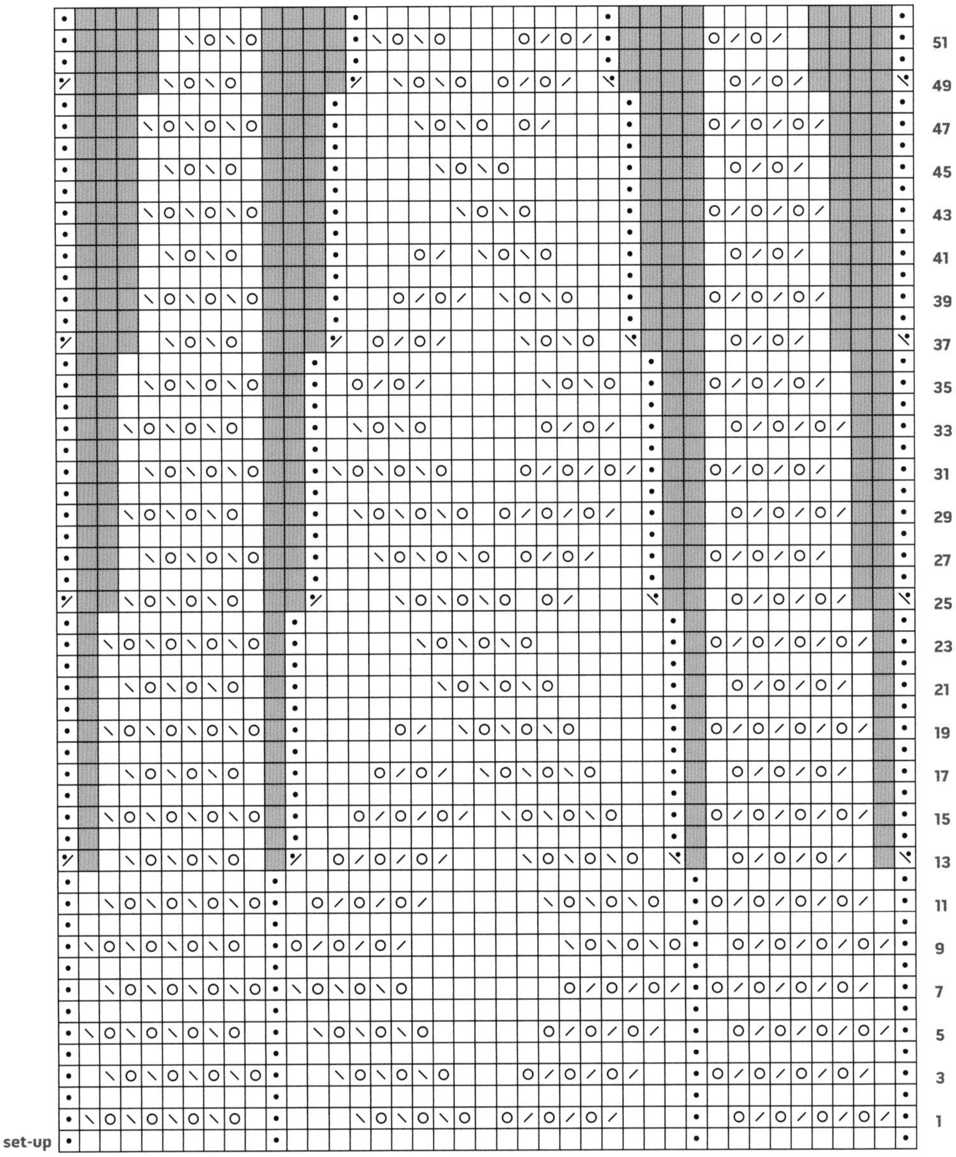

before previously wrapped st, wrap next st, turn work.

SHORT-ROW 4 Work right shoulder sts; work left shoulder sts in patt to 10 (10, 11, 11, 11, 11, 12) sts before previously wrapped st, wrap next st, turn work.

SHORT-ROW 5 Work left shoulder sts; work right shoulder sts to end, working wraps tog with wrapped sts.

NEXT ROW Work all sts, working wraps tog with wrapped sts on left shoulder.

Place sts on holders.

LACE INSET ROWS 53 to 103

knit on RS; purl on WS

• purl on RS; knit on WS

O yo

/ k2tog

\ ssk (see Glossary)

⁄ p2tog

⟍ ssp (see Glossary)

no stitch

58 (61, 61, 61, 65, 64, 68) sts along
right neck edge—156 (162, 162, 166,
174, 176, 184) sts total. Pm and join
for working in rnds. Knit 1 rnd, purl
1 rnd. BO all sts.

Armhole Edgings

With shorter cir needle, RS facing,
and beg at underarm seam, pick up
and knit 3 (5, 7, 8, 10, 12, 13) sts
along BO edge, 58 (62, 62, 62, 65,
65, 69) sts to shoulder seam, 58 (62,
62, 62, 65, 65, 69) sts to underarm,
and 3 (5, 7, 8, 10, 12, 13) sts along
BO edge—122 (134, 138, 140, 150,
154, 164) sts total. Pm and join for
working in rnds. Knit 1 rnd, purl 1
rnd. BO all sts.

Weave in loose ends.

finishing

Block pieces to measurements.
Using the three-needle method (see
Glossary), join shoulder sts tog. With
yarn threaded on a tapestry needle,
sew side seams.

Neckband

With shorter cir needle, RS facing,
and beg at right shoulder seam, pick
up and knit 39 (39, 39, 43, 43, 47,
47) sts across back neck edge, 58 (61,
61, 61, 65, 64, 68) sts along left front
neck edge, 1 st at center front, and

the raglan
sweater

The raglan is characterized by diagonal shaping along the join between the sleeve cap and upper body. These diagonal seams are created by regular decreases that gradually taper the yoke from the underarm width to the neck width. Both sleeve cap and yoke are truncated triangles. The sleeve cap extends all the way to the neck edge. A raglan has a true yoke, often worked in one piece, and is particularly suited to working in the round. The casual, sporty look of raglans gives them a somewhat youthful look that has long made them a favorite in knitwear.

Raglans can be attractive on plus-size women, but it's an issue of individual shape. Because the raglan lines draw the eye in from the curves of the bust, they're quite flattering on curvy women—emphasizing the bust while creating a look of feminine narrowness across the shoulders. On small-busted women, especially those with large upper arms or lower bodies, these same lines can serve to emphasize that disproportion. The extended sleeve cap, which matches the yoke in depth and number of rows, has a diagonal tension (a line of stress in the fabric) that cuts across the outer arm and shoulder and can be uncomfortable for women with larger upper arms or broad shoulders. The sleeve cap has to stretch over the outer joint of the shoulder and across the top of the shoulder to the neckline, requiring a flat plane of fabric to curve over an angled area. For some women, this construction can result in sleeves appearing too short and too tight, and can create discomfort at the underarm and armhole. If a raglan is worked with plenty of positive ease, however, these problems are alleviated.

who should wear the raglan style?

Raglan shaping isn't preferable for any particular body type, although it can produce strain on the sleeve caps for women with broad shoulders and fleshy arms. This problem can be alleviated with custom shaping, but if you don't want to customize, either avoid raglan shaping altogether or allow plenty of positive ease. In general, raglan shaping offers strong design qualities and creates a unique canvas for yoke patterns—whether you adorn the raglan lines themselves or work concentric patterning around a one-piece yoke.

raglan construction

When working a raglan sweater, each piece can be worked bottom-up or top-down. The body and sleeves can be worked separately in pieces that are seamed together or the body and sleeves can be worked in the round to the armholes, then joined and worked in a single piece to the neck. The sleeve cap is a triangle that mirrors the shape of the armhole, with the top of the sleeve (the neck edge) measuring 0" to 4" (0 to 10 cm); plus sizes fit best with at least 1" (2.5 cm) remaining at the top of the sleeve. Because the top of the sleeve forms the neck edge, the front neck shaping can be included in the final rows of the sleeves—angle the top of the cap by working more shaping on the side that will correspond with the front of the body. The sleeve cap and body can be shaped at different rates or at the same rate; just remember that in most cases, the sleeve and

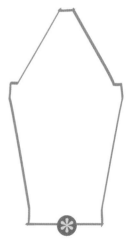

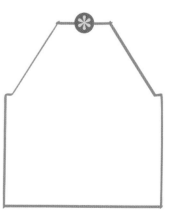

The typical shape of a raglan sleeve and body when the pieces are worked separately.

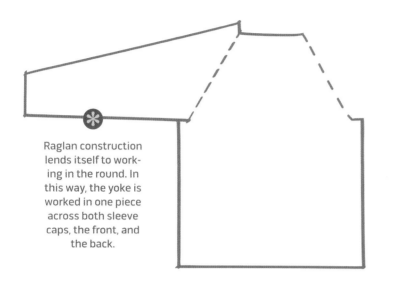

Raglan construction lends itself to working in the round. In this way, the yoke is worked in one piece across both sleeve caps, the front, and the back.

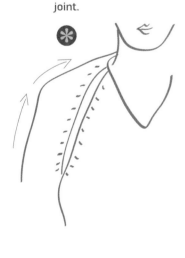

The flat plane of a raglan sleeve cap has to curve over the outer arm and shoulder joint.

body need to have the same number of rows or rounds between the armhole and the neck.

All three of the raglan designs in this book are worked from the bottom up, which means that the raglan shaping is achieved with decreases. To work a raglan from the top down, you would begin at the neck edge and achieve the raglan shaping with increases. This is a useful construction that allows you to try on the sweater as you go.

The Yoke

Working a raglan yoke in the round makes it easy to ensure that the sleeve and body decreases are worked on the same rounds. You can work the decreases adjacent to each other—decrease over the first two and last two stitches of each body section and decrease over the first two and last two stitches of each sleeve section. For a more pronounced raglan line, you can place buffer stitches (typically 1 to 4) between the decreases. These buffer stitches allow for creative elements such as narrow cables and lace patterns. Although the one-piece yoke is worked in one piece, be sure to keep the sleeves and body conceptually separate—think of the raglan decreases as shaping the sleeve cap and armhole edges, respectively. Placing markers on the first yoke

+ The sleeve cap and yoke/armhole have a 1:1 relationship—they are worked over the same number of rows and the selvedge edges match exactly.

+ If the yoke is worked in one piece, the sleeves are worked simultaneously with the body, which reduces the amount of finishing and the bulk of seams.

+ The yoke has a cone shape that is wide at the armholes and narrow at the neck.

+ There is no measurable cross-back in raglan construction.

+ Because there is no defined shoulder, there are no shoulder seams and shoulder shaping is not an option.

+ In one-piece yokes, short-rows can be used to raise the back neck (effectively dropping the front neck).

+ There is almost always an underarm span.

+ If more than 1" (2.5 cm) of stitches remain at the top of the sleeve (where the sleeve top becomes the neck edge), the neck opening will have straight sides (as in the Banstead Pullover on page 88).

+ If few or no stitches remain at the top of the sleeve, the neck opening will have a round shape (excluding the front neck depth shaping).

+ To create a better fit at the upper arm/shoulder joint, short-rows can be worked across the center of the cap shortly after the underarm bind-off (see section on short-rows in Chapter 02).

round will visually separate the sections and help you align the decreases (or increases, if working top-down) from round to round.

If the sleeves and body are worked completely separate, use a mattress stitch (see Glossary) to seam the caps into the armholes. Because the pieces meet selvedge to selvedge with the same number of rows the entire length, seaming is straightforward—there is no need to ease fabric or transition from bind-off edge to selvedge edge, as for a set-in sleeve (see Chapter 04).

For large sizes, the yoke shaping may need to slow down so as not to narrow too quickly, as compared to smaller sizes of the same pattern. Many raglan patterns call for decreases every other row throughout the yoke. If this brings you to the desired neck width too soon, work the decreases every fourth row as needed to achieve the proper length (i.e., decrease every other row for the first few inches, then every fourth row until you reach the desired yoke depth and neck width). Keep in mind that both the yoke depth and neck width (or circumference, if working in rounds) are important in raglan shaping. For a traditional look, the decreases should begin at the armhole and end at the neck edge—there shouldn't be any significant depth worked even between the last decrease and the neck edge.

The Sleeve

As for set-in sleeves, the length of the sleeve from the cuff to the beginning of the armhole shaping should closely match the actual length of your arm from wrist to underarm. But what if you want to alter the width of the sleeve?

If you alter the sleeve width at the upper arm and follow the raglan yoke shaping instructions as set, you will end up with a different number of stitches at the top of the sleeve than the pattern calls for. If, for example, you added stitches to the upper arm, you will end up with

more stitches (greater width) at the top of the sleeve. This will result in a wider neck (a greater distance between the front and back at the sides of the neck). To fix this, you can increase the rate of raglan shaping on the sleeves to eliminate these extra stitches while working the raglan shaping on the body as instructed. Or, you can eliminate the extra stitches by working internal decreases at the center of the sleeve cap—which will produce a line of shaping at the center of the cap near the neck edge—while working the raglan shaping on both the body and sleeves as instructed. If, on the other hand, you subtracted stitches from the upper arm, there will be fewer stitches at the top of the sleeve, which will result in a narrower neck. To fix this, you can cease working raglan decreases on the sleeve when you reach the target stitch count and work the last bit of the sleeve cap without any raglan shaping. Or, you can slow down the rate of sleeve decreases so that you end up with exactly the desired number of sleeve stitches when the cap measures the desired length.

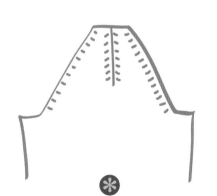

✴

If you widen the sleeve and need to eliminate those extra stitches within the cap, work a line of central decreases (in addition to the regular raglan decreases) as the cap approaches the neck edge.

✴

If more than 1" (2.5 cm) of fabric remains at the top of the sleeve cap, the neck opening will have square sides (top).

If 1" (2.5 cm) or less remains, this sliver of fabric joins the front and back neck edges to create more of round neck opening (center). If you add a neckband to this neck, it will force the opening into a true round shape.

Neck shaping can angle into the top of the sleeve cap (bottom), which is a subtle way to help make room for neckline treatments such as shawl collars.

banstead pullover

DESIGNED BY **LISA SHROYER**

This simple raglan pullover is worked in pieces from the bottom up, then joined for a one-piece yoke. A slightly ruched slip-stitch panel at the center front results in a bit of vertical compression that causes the neckline to dip into a subtle V shape. The yoke is fairly shallow and the neck somewhat wide for a youthful look that pairs well with halter-top underlayers or camisoles. The rolled edges are finished with an applied reverse stockinette trim. This basic project allows for easy customization and design tweaks; once you've mastered the raglan style with a simple design like this, you can apply your knowledge to more involved projects.

FINISHED SIZE
About 42 (46, 50, 54, 58, 62, 66)" (106.5 [117, 127, 137, 147.5, 157.5, 167.5] cm) bust circumference, to be worn with negative to zero ease at bust. Sweater shown measures 42" (106.5 cm).

YARN
Worsted weight (#4 Medium).

Shown here: Blue Sky Alpacas Suri Merino (60% baby suri alpaca; 40% merino; 164 yd [150 m]/100 g): #418 dusk, 6 (7, 7, 8, 9, 9, 10) skeins.

NEEDLES
Size U.S 7 (4.5 mm): 24" (60 cm) circular (cir; see Notes) and set of double-pointed (dpn).

Adjust needle size if necessary to obtain the correct gauge.

NOTIONS
Markers (m); stitch holders; tapestry needle.

GAUGE
16 stitches and 23 rows/rounds = 4" (10 cm) in stockinette stitch.

stitch guide + notes

SLIP-STITCH PATTERN IN ROWS (panel of 6 sts)

ROWS 1 AND 3 (RS) Sl 1 pwise with yarn in back (wyb), k1, sl 2 pwise wyb, k1, sl 1 pwise wyb.

ROWS 2 AND 4 (WS) Sl 1 pwise with yarn in front (wyf), p1, sl 2 pwise wyf, p1, sl 1 pwise wyf.

ROW 5 K6.

ROW 6 P6.

Rep Rows 1–6 for pattern.

SLIP-STITCH PATTERN IN ROUNDS (panel of 6 sts)

RNDS 1–4 Sl 1 pwise with yarn in back wyb, k1, sl 2 pwise wyb, k1, sl 1 pwise wyb.

RNDS 5 AND 6 Knit.

Rep Rnds 1–6 for pattern.

+ A 24" (60 cm) circular needle is required to work the yoke and is also used for the body. If desired, the body can also be worked on straight needles or a different length circular.

+ The lower body and sleeves are worked flat (back and forth in rows), then joined for working the yoke in the round to the neck edge with decreases along the raglan lines. I recommend working this sweater flat and seaming it during finishing because it helps prevent the singles yarn from biasing, but you could choose to work the lower body in the round to the underarms.

+ This garment should fit with little to no ease at the bust but with some positive ease over the belly and hips. Choose a size based on your needed bust circumference, then determine if the corresponding lower body measurements (see schematic on page 92) will work for you.

+ The body of this pullover features gentle A-line shaping from hip to bust; the stitch count at the bust determines yoke height and back neck width. You can change the hip and waist stitch counts to achieve a custom fit, but before starting the yoke, you should adjust the bust stitch count

to match the instructions for your size to avoid having to recalculate the yoke shaping.

+ If you alter the width of the hips and waist, the stitch gauge is 4 stitches to 1" (2.5 cm). The front and back both require an even number of stitches, so add or decrease stitches in sets of two. Remember that 1 stitch from each selvedge edge will be lost in the seams, leading to a total reduction of 1" (2.5 cm) in the finished circumference. For example, if you want to work the 42" (106.5 cm) bust with a hip measurement of about 48" (122 cm), cast on 98 stitches at the hips for the front and back pieces (98 sts – 2 selvedge sts ÷ 4 = 24" [61 cm]), then decrease until there are 86 stitches at the bust as given in the directions.

+ The stitches that remain at the tops of the sleeves create the side edges of the neck opening. If you alter the sleeve stitch counts, consider the effect on that edge—more stitches than directed will lead to a larger neck opening; fewer stitches will lead to a smaller opening (shallower between front and back necklines). The schematic shows this edge (the fabric jutting up from the neckline at the right-hand side); the measurements given reflect the width of that edge when the garment is laid flat and this width of fabric is folded in half. The total width of the fabric at the top of the sleeve is therefore two times the schematic measurements for this element.

+ The front slip-stitch panel begins when the piece measures 13½" (34.5 cm) from the cast-on edge for all sizes. This panel is longer for the larger sizes because they have progressively deeper yokes. The panel should start just below the breasts; the longer panel length will accommodate lower and larger bustlines as the sizes increase.

+ The measurements shown on the schematic are the actual dimensions of the pieces (including selvedge stitches) for blocking purposes. The selvedge stitches lost in the seams do not count toward the finished size. The rolled edgings of the lower body and sleeves are also not shown on the schematic and will add about ½" (1.3 cm) to the finished lengths. The neckband is not shown on the schematic for clarity.

back

CO 94 (102, 110, 118, 126, 134, 142) sts. Beg with a purl row, work in St st (knit RS rows; purl WS rows) until piece measures 7 (7½, 7½, 8, 8½, 8½, 8½)" (18 [19, 19, 20.5, 21.5, 21.5, 21.5] cm) from CO, ending with a WS row.

Shape Sides

DEC ROW (RS) K2, ssk, knit to last 4 sts, k2tog, k2—2 sts dec'd.

[Work 11 rows even in St st, then rep the dec row] 3 times—86 (94, 102, 110, 118, 126, 134) sts rem. Work even in St st until piece measures 16½ (17, 17, 17½, 18, 18, 18)" (42 [43, 43, 44.5, 45.5, 45.5, 45.5] cm) from CO, ending with a WS row.

Shape Armholes

BO 5 (5, 6, 6, 7, 7, 8) sts at beg of next 2 rows—76 (84, 90, 98, 104, 112, 118) sts rem. Place sts on holder.

front

CO 94 (102, 110, 118, 126, 134, 142) sts. Beg with a purl row, work in St st until piece measures 7 (7½, 7½, 8, 8½, 8½, 8½)" (18 [19, 19, 20.5, 21.5, 21.5, 21.5] cm) from CO, ending with a WS row. Mark the center 6 sts—44 (48, 52, 56, 60, 64, 68) sts each side of marked sts.

Shape Sides + Establish Slip-stitch Pattern

NOTE *For the six largest sizes, the side shaping will still be in progress when the slip-stitch patt is introduced; read the foll sections all the way through before proceeding.*

banstead pullover

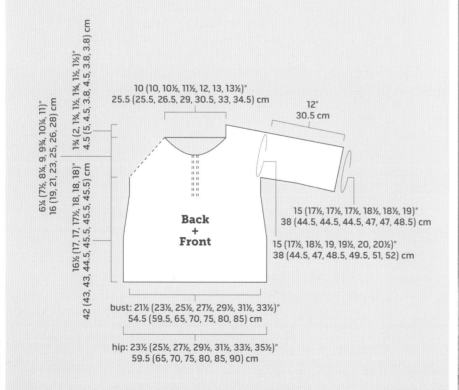

10 (10, 10½, 11½, 12, 13, 13½)"
25.5 (25.5, 26.5, 29, 30.5, 33, 34.5) cm

12"
30.5 cm

1¾ (2, 1¾, 1¾, 1¾, 1½, 1½)"
4.5 (5, 4.5, 3.8, 4.5, 3.8, 3.8) cm

6¼ (7½, 8¼, 9, 9¾, 10¼, 11)"
16 (19, 21, 23, 25, 26, 28) cm

16½ (17, 17, 17½, 18, 18, 18)"
42 (43, 43, 44.5, 45.5, 45.5, 45.5) cm

Back + Front

15 (17½, 17½, 17½, 18½, 18½, 19)"
38 (44.5, 44.5, 44.5, 47, 47, 48.5) cm

15 (17½, 18½, 19, 19½, 20, 20½)"
38 (44.5, 47, 48.5, 49.5, 51, 52) cm

bust: 21½ (23½, 25½, 27½, 29½, 31½, 33½)"
54.5 (59.5, 65, 70, 75, 80, 85) cm

hip: 23½ (25½, 27½, 29½, 31½, 33½, 35½)"
59.5 (65, 70, 75, 80, 85, 90) cm

Shape sides as for back and *at the same time* when piece measures 13½" (34.5 cm) from CO, beg working slip-stitch patt (see Stitch Guide) in rows over center 6 sts—86 (94, 102, 110, 118, 126, 134) sts when side shaping complete; 40 (44, 48, 52, 56, 60, 64) sts each side of marked center sts. Work even in St st until piece measures same as back to armholes, ending with a WS row.

Shape Armholes

BO 5 (5, 6, 6, 7, 7, 8) sts at beg of next 2 rows—76 (84, 90, 98, 104, 112, 118) sts rem. Note last row of slip-stitch patt worked so you can resume working the patt on the yoke with the correct rnd. Place sts on holder.

sleeves

CO 60 (70, 70, 70, 74, 74, 76) sts. Beg with a purl (WS) row, work in St st until piece measures 12 (12, 6, 6, 6, 6, 6)" (30.5 [30.5, 15, 15, 15, 15, 15] cm) from CO, ending with a WS row.

SIZES (50, 54, 58, 62, 66)" ONLY

Inc 1 st each end of needle on next RS row, then every (8, 6, 8, 6, 6)th row (1, 2, 1, 2, 2) time(s)—(74, 76, 78, 80, 82) sts. Work even in St st until piece measures 12" (30.5 cm) from CO for all sizes, ending with a WS row.

ALL SIZES

BO 5 (5, 6, 6, 7, 7, 8) sts at beg of foll 2 rows—50 (60, 62, 64, 64, 66, 66) sts rem. Place sts on holder. Work a second sleeve the same as the first, but leave sts on needle.

yoke

JOINING RND With cir needle and RS facing, k50 (60, 62, 64, 64, 66, 66) sts of one sleeve, pm, work 76 (84, 90, 98, 104, 112, 118) front sts with marked center sts worked according to slip-stitch patt in rnds, pm, k50 (60, 62, 64, 64, 66, 66) sts of other sleeve, pm, k76 (84, 90, 98, 104, 112, 118) back sts—252 (288, 304, 324, 336, 356, 368) sts total.

Pm and join for working in rnds; rnd begs at start of left sleeve. Cont slip-stitch patt on front sts, dec for yoke as foll:

DEC RND *Ssk, work in patt to 2 sts before raglan m, k2tog; rep from * 3 more times—8 sts dec'd.

[Work 1 rnd even, then rep the dec rnd] 17 (21, 23, 25, 24, 26, 26) times—108 (112, 112, 116, 136, 140, 152) sts rem; 14 (16, 14, 12, 14, 12, 12) sts each sleeve; 40 (40, 42, 46, 54, 58, 64) sts each for front and back; yoke measures about 6¼ (7½, 8¼, 9, 8¾, 9¼, 9¼)" (16 [19, 21, 23, 22, 23.5, 23.5] cm), measured straight up at center back (do not measure along diagonal raglan lines).

SIZES (58, 62, 66)" ONLY

Work 1 rnd even in patt.

NEXT RND *Knit to m at end of sleeve, slip marker (sl m), ssk, knit to next raglan m, k2tog, sl m; rep from * once more—4 sts dec'd; 2 sts each from front and back; no change to sleeve st counts.

Cont in patt, rep the last 2 rnds (2, 2, 4) more times—(124, 128, 132) sts rem; (14, 12, 12) sts each sleeve; (48, 52, 54) sts each for front and back; yoke measures about (9¾, 10¼, 11)" ([25, 26, 28] cm), measured straight up at center back.

Neckband

For all sizes, work 1 rnd even across all sts. Purl 1 rnd, dec 6 sts evenly spaced—102 (106, 106, 110, 118, 122, 126) sts rem. Purl 2 rnds—neckband measures about ¾" (2 cm). BO all sts pwise.

finishing

Lay flat to block, spritz with water, and allow to air-dry (see Notes). With yarn threaded on a tapestry needle, sew sleeve and side seams. Sew underarm seams.

Lower Edging

With cir needle and RS facing, pick up and knit 1 st for every CO st around lower edge of body, not including selvedge sts in the seams—184 (200, 216, 232, 248, 264, 280) sts total. Pm and join for working in rnds. Purl 3 rnds. BO all sts pwise.

Sleeve Edgings

With dpn and RS facing, pick up and knit 1 st for every CO st around lower edge of sleeve, not including selvedge sts in the seams—58 (68, 68, 68, 72, 72, 74) sts total. Pm and join for working in rnds. Purl 3 rnds. BO all sts pwise.

Weave in loose ends. Block again, if desired.

cheviot henley

DESIGNED BY **LISA SHROYER**

A large-footprint chevron lace pattern is worked on the front and back of this two-tone raglan pullover. The sleeve caps decrease at a slower rate than the body, which creates more fabric for the rounded upper arm/shoulder area and allows the caps to extend to the neckline. The front is worked for only about half the depth of the back raglan and includes a placket opening that begins below the armholes. The front raglan edges of the sleeves and the top edge of the front create a princess neckline that is finished with contrasting trim.

FINISHED SIZE
About 40½ (43½, 48, 50, 53, 58, 59½, 62½)" (103 [110.5, 122, 127, 134.5, 147.5, 151, 159] cm) bust circumference. Sweater shown measures 50" (127 cm).

YARN
Worsted weight (#4 Medium) and DK weight (#3 Light).

Shown here: Classic Elite Princess (40% merino, 28% viscose, 10% cashmere, 7% angora, 15% nylon; 150 yd [137 m]/50 g): #3409 proud peacock (MC), 8 (8, 9, 10, 10, 11, 11, 12) balls.

Classic Elite Fresco (60% wool, 30% baby alpaca, 10% angora; 164 yd [150 m]/50 g): #5346 mallard blue (CC), 1 skein for all sizes.

NEEDLES
Body and sleeves: size U.S. 7 (4.5 mm): 16" and 32" (40 and 80 cm) circular (cir) and set of 4 or 5 double-pointed (dpn).

Edging: size U.S. 5 (3.5 mm): any length cir.

Adjust needle size if necessary to obtain the correct gauge.

NOTIONS
Markers (m); waste yarn; tapestry needle; four (four, four, five, five, five, five, six) ¾" (2 cm) buttons.

GAUGE
16¾ stitches and 27 rows = 4" (10 cm) in pattern from Chevron chart on larger needle.

19½ stitches and 26 rounds = 4" (10 cm) in stockinette stitch on larger needle, worked in rounds.

notes

+ The back and front are worked back and forth in rows beginning with a provisional cast-on. The front raglan is about half the depth of the back raglan to form a lowered front neckline. After sewing the side seams, the lower edging is worked in the round downward from the provisional cast-on.

+ The sleeves are worked in the round to the underarm, then worked back and forth in rows for the cap shaping.

+ The raglan sleeve caps decrease at a slower rate than the body raglans, which creates more fabric in the shoulder area and allows for the caps to extend to the neckline. The sleeve caps are mirror images of one another, with the front and back raglans containing a different number of decreases.

+ Although the yoke is not deep, the diagonal measurement along the raglan lines (and the depth of the sleeve caps) is quite generous and creates plenty of room for the plus-size wearer.

+ The bound-off stitches across the bottom of each armhole have about a 2¼ (2¾, 4¾, 4¾, 4¾, 5¼, 5¼, 4¾)" (5.5 [7, 12, 12, 12, 13.5, 13.5, 12] cm) span.

+ For a bombshell fit, choose a size with zero positive ease to 2" (5 cm) negative ease or work waist shaping in pattern on the front and back.

+ When working shaping in the chevron pattern, maintain the pattern for as long as possible. If there are not enough stitches to work a corresponding decrease and its companion yarnover, work those stitches in stockinette instead.

+ Before applying the bands at the neck and placket, the neck opening will look large and floppy. The garter bands will draw in the neckline and give it structure.

+ The sleeves in this pullover are designed for a close fit with little to no positive ease. Carefully review the schematic measurements for your size. If the upper sleeve is too small for your size and you need to increase the stitch count below the cap, you can then place a line of decreases along the center of the raglan cap to be worked in addition to the raglan shaping already provided. Plan these numbers and decrease rows carefully; you don't want the stitch count to decrease too rapidly and create puckering nor do you want to disrupt the planned raglan shaping. The ending stitch counts for the caps in all sizes are already fairly wide, so you should try to reach the final instructed stitch counts as much as possible.

+ If you need a little more room in the shoulder or along the outer part of your upper arm, you can work short-rows across the center of the raglan cap just above the underarm bind-off (see page 24 for tips on short-rows).

+ Remember that the length of raglan sleeves to the cap should closely match the length of your actual arm from wrist to underarm. This pattern calls for an 18" (45.5 cm) sleeve in all sizes; adjust this length as needed.

back

With MC and longer cir needle in larger size, use the invisible-provisional method (see Glossary) and waste yarn to CO 85 (91, 101, 105, 111, 121, 125, 131) sts. Do not join.

SET-UP ROWS Purl 1 WS row, knit 1 RS row, purl 1 WS row.

NEXT ROW (RS) K1 (edge st), work Row 1 of Chevron chart (pages 100 and 101) for your size to last st, k1 (edge st).

Working edge sts in St st (knit on RS rows; purl on WS rows), cont in patt until piece measures 15¼" (38.5 cm) from CO, ending with a WS row.

Shape Armholes

Keeping in patt, BO 5 (6, 10, 10, 10, 11, 11, 10) sts at beg of next 2 rows—75 (79, 81, 85, 91, 99, 103, 111) sts rem.

RAGLAN DEC ROW (RS) K2, k2tog, work in patt to last 4 sts, ssk, k2—2 sts dec'd.

Work 1 WS row even. Keeping in patt as much as possible (see Notes), rep the last 2 rows 19 (23, 23, 27, 27, 31, 31, 35) more times, ending with a RS row—35 (31, 33, 29, 35, 35, 39, 39) sts rem; armholes measure about 6¼ (7½, 7½, 8½, 8½, 9¾, 9¾, 11)" (16 [19, 19, 21.5, 21.5, 25, 25, 28] cm), measured straight up at center back. Purl 1 WS row. With RS facing, BO all sts kwise.

cheviot henley

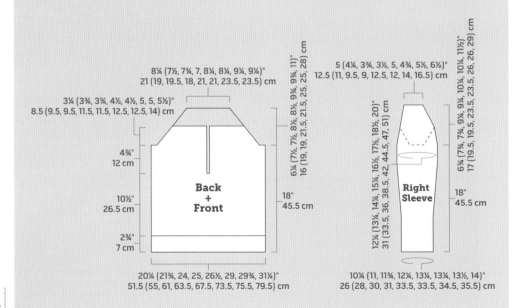

8¼ (7½, 7¾, 7, 8¼, 8¼, 9¼, 9¼)"
21 (19, 19.5, 18, 21, 21, 23.5, 23.5) cm

3¼ (3¾, 3¾, 4½, 4½, 5, 5, 5½)"
8.5 (9.5, 9.5, 11.5, 11.5, 12.5, 12.5, 14) cm

6¼ (7½, 7½, 8½, 8½, 9¾, 9¾, 11)"
16 (19, 19, 21.5, 21.5, 25, 25, 28) cm

4¾"
12 cm

Back + Front

10½"
26.5 cm

18"
45.5 cm

2¾"
7 cm

20¼ (21¾, 24, 25, 26½, 29, 29¾, 31¼)"
51.5 (55, 61, 63.5, 67.5, 73.5, 75.5, 79.5) cm

5 (4¼, 3¾, 3½, 5, 4¾, 5½, 6½)"
12.5 (11, 9.5, 9, 12.5, 12, 14, 16.5) cm

6¾ (7¾, 7¾, 9¼, 9¼, 10¼, 10¼, 11½)"
17 (19.5, 19.5, 23.5, 23.5, 26, 26, 29) cm

12¼ (13¾, 14¼, 15¼, 16½, 17½, 18½, 20)"
31 (33.5, 36, 38.5, 42, 44.5, 47, 51) cm

Right Sleeve

18"
45.5 cm

10¼ (11, 11¾, 12¼, 13¼, 13¼, 13½, 14)"
26 (28, 30, 31, 33.5, 33.5, 34.5, 35.5) cm

front

Work as for back until Rows 1–34 of chart have been worked 2 times—68 lace patt rows and 3 St st set-up rows; piece measures about 10½" (26.5 cm) from CO.

Divide for Placket

Mark 3 center sts—41 (44, 49, 51, 54, 59, 61, 64) sts each side of marked sts.

NEXT ROW (RS) Keeping in patt, work to center 3 sts, join a second ball of yarn and BO 3 sts, work to end—41 (44, 49, 51, 54, 59, 61, 64) sts rem each side.

Working each side separately, work charted patt as close to the placket edges as possible (see Notes) until piece measures 15¼" (38.5 cm) from CO, ending with same WS row as for back.

Shape Armholes

Keeping in patt, BO 5 (6, 10, 10, 10, 11, 11, 10) sts at each armhole once—36 (38, 39, 41, 44, 48, 50, 54) sts rem each side.

RAGLAN DEC ROW (RS) For left front, k2, k2tog, work in patt to placket opening; for right front, work in patt to last 4 sts, ssk, k2—2 sts dec'd; 1 st at each armhole edge.

Keeping in patt as much as possible, rep the raglan dec row on the next 9 (11, 11, 13, 13, 15, 15, 17) RS rows, ending with a RS dec row—26 (26, 27, 27, 30, 32, 34, 36) sts rem each side; armholes measure about 3¼ (3¾, 3¾, 4½, 4½, 5, 5, 5½)" (8.5 [9.5, 9.5, 11.5, 11.5, 12.5,

12.5, 14] cm) measured straight up at center front; placket measures about 8 (8½, 8½, 9¼, 9¼, 9¾, 9¾, 10¼)" (20.5 [21.5, 21.5, 23.5, 23.5, 25, 25, 26] cm. Purl 1 WS row. With RS facing, BO all sts kwise.

lower body section

With MC threaded on a tapestry needle, use the mattress st with a 1-st selvedge (see Glossary) to sew side seams. Remove waste yarn from provisional CO and carefully place live sts on cir needle—170 (182, 202, 210, 222, 242, 250, 262) sts total. Arrange sts on longer cir needle in larger size so the first 2 sts of the rnd are the edge sts from the front and back at one side seam. Place marker (pm) and join for working in rnds.

JOINING RND With MC, k2tog to join front and back at side "seam," knit to next 2 seam sts, k2tog to join sts of second seam, knit to end—168 (180, 200, 208, 220, 240, 248, 260) sts rem.

Work even in St st (knit every rnd) until piece measures 2¼" (5.5 cm) from joining rnd—body measures about 17½" (44.5 cm) from underarm. Purl 4 rnds for rolled edge—body measures about 18" (45.5 cm). BO all sts pwise.

right sleeve

With MC and dpn, CO 50 (54, 58, 60, 64, 64, 66, 68) sts. Pm and join for working in rnds, being careful not to twist sts. Purl 4 rnds. Cont in St st until piece measures 10 (10, 8,

7½, 7, 3, 3, 2)" (25.5 [25.5, 20.5, 19, 18, 7.5, 7.5, 5] cm) from CO.

INC RND K1, M1 (see Glossary), knit to last st, M1, k1—2 sts inc'd.

Inc 1 st each end of rnd in this manner every 4th rnd 0 (0, 0, 0, 0, 0, 0, 5) times, then every 8th rnd 4 (4, 3, 5, 5, 7, 8, 9) times, then every 10th rnd 0 (0, 2, 1, 2, 3, 3, 0) time(s), working new sts in St st, and changing to shorter cir needle in larger size when there are too many sts to fit comfortably on dpn—60 (64, 70, 74, 80, 86, 90, 98) sts. Work even until piece measures 18" (45.5 cm) from CO.

Shape Raglan Cap

BO 4 (5, 9, 9, 9, 10, 10, 9) sts, knit to end. Turn work so WS is facing, BO 4 (5, 9, 9, 9, 10, 10, 9) sts, purl to end—52 (54, 52, 56, 62, 66, 70, 80) sts rem. Working back and forth in rows, shape raglan as foll:

DEC ROW 1 (RS) K2, k2tog, knit to last 4 sts, ssk, k2—2 sts dec'd.

Work 3 rows even in St st. Rep the last 4 rows 3 (4, 4, 5, 5, 6, 6, 7) more times, then rep Dec Row 1 once more—42 (42, 40, 42, 48, 50, 54, 62) sts rem. Purl 1 WS row.

DEC ROW 2 (RS) K2, k2tog, knit to end—1 st dec'd only at front raglan (beg of RS rows).

Purl 1 WS row.

DEC ROW 3 (RS) K2, k2tog, knit to last 4 sts, ssk, k2—2 sts dec'd.

SIZES 40½", 50", and 59½"
(multiple of 20 sts + 3)

SIZES 43½", 53", and 62½"
(multiple of 20 sts + 29)

SIZES 48" and 58"
(multiple of 20 sts + 19)

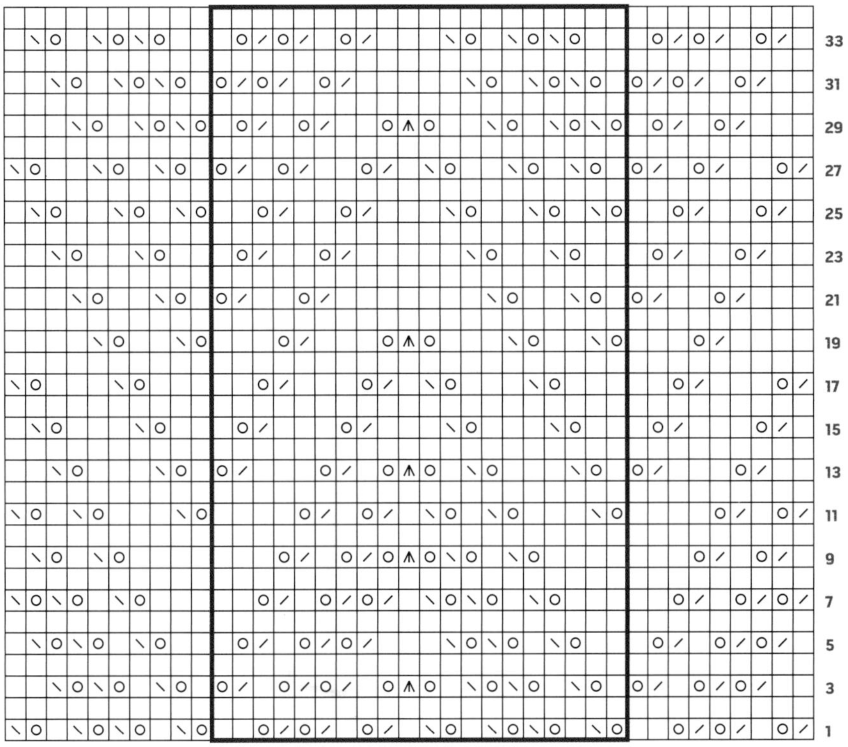

The chart below is read from right to left on odd (RS) rows. Column 1 is the rightmost stitch. Symbols: blank = knit on RS/purl on WS; O = yo; ╱ = k2tog; ╲ = ssk; Λ = sl 2 as if to k2tog, k1, p2sso. The pattern repeat is the boxed section (columns 17–36, counting from the right). Row numbers are printed at the right edge (odd rows only, 1–33).

Row	c1	c2	c3	c4	c5	c6	c7	c8	c9	c10	c11	c12	c13	c14	c15	c16	c17	c18	c19	c20	c21	c22	c23	c24	c25	c26	c27	c28	c29	c30	c31	c32	c33	c34	c35	c36	c37	c38	c39	c40	c41	c42	c43	c44	c45	c46	c47	c48
33		╲	O		╲	O	╲	O			O	╱	O	╱		O	╱			╲	O		╲	O	╲	O	╲	O		O	╱	O	╱		O	╱												
31			╲	O		╲	O	╲	O	O	╱	O	╱		O	╱					╲	O		╲	O	╲	O	╲	O	O	╱	O	╱		O	╱												
29				╲	O		╲	O	╲	O	O	╱		O	╱		O	Λ	O			╲	O		╲	O	╲	O	╲	O	O	╱		O	╱													
27	╲	O			╲	O		╲	O	O	╱		O	╱			O	╱		╲	O			╲	O		╲	O	O	╱		O	╱			O	╱											
25		╲	O			╲	O		╲	O		O	╱		O	╱			╲	O			╲	O		╲	O		O	╱		O	╱		O	╱												
23			╲	O			╲	O			O	╱		O	╱			╲	O			╲	O		╲	O		O	╱		O	╱																
21				╲	O			╲	O	O	╱		O	╱			╲	O			╲	O		O	╱		O	╱																				
19					╲	O			╲	O		O	╱		O	Λ	O			╲	O		O	╱																								
17	╲	O				╲	O			O	╱			O	╱		╲	O			O	╱		O	╱			╲	O		O	╱																
15		╲	O				╲	O		O	╱			O	╱			O	╱	╲	O		O	╱																								
13			╲	O				╲	O	O	╱				O	╱		O	╱	O	Λ	O	╲	O		O	╱		O	╱																		
11	╲	O		╲	O				╲	O			O	╱		O	╱		╲	O		O	╱		O	╱																						
9		╲	O		╲	O				O	╱		O	╱	O	╱	O	Λ	O	╲	O		╲	O		O	╱		O	╱																		
7	╲	O	╲	O		╲	O			O	╱		O	╱	O	╱	O	╱	╲	O	╲	O		╲	O		O	╱		O	╱	O	╱															
5		╲	O	╲	O		╲	O		O	╱		O	╱	O	╱			╲	O	╲	O		╲	O		O	╱		O	╱	O	╱															
3			╲	O	╲	O		╲	O	O	╱		O	╱	O	╱		O	Λ	O	╲	O	╲	O		╲	O		O	╱		O	╱	O	╱														
1	╲	O		╲	O	╲	O			O	╱	O	╱		O	╱		╲	O		╲	O	╲	O	╲	O		O	╱	O	╱		O	╱															

Chart key:

□	knit on RS; purl on WS
O	yo
╱	k2tog
╲	ssk (see Glossary)
Λ	sl 2 as if to k2tog, k1, p2sso
▭ (bold box)	pattern repeat

Purl 1 WS row. Rep the last 4 rows 4 (5, 5, 6, 6, 7, 7, 8) more times, then work the first 3 of these 4 rows once more, ending with Dec Row 3—24 (21, 19, 18, 24, 23, 27, 32) sts rem; cap measures about 6¾ (7¾, 7¾, 9¼, 9¼, 10¼, 10¼, 11½)" (17 [19.5, 19.5, 23.5, 23.5, 26, 26, 29] cm), measured straight up at center. With WS facing, BO all sts pwise.

left sleeve

Work as for right sleeve to start of raglan cap shaping—60 (64, 70, 74, 80, 86, 90, 98) sts; piece measures 18" (45.5 cm) from CO.

Shape Raglan Cap

Work as for right sleeve cap until 42 (42, 40, 42, 48, 50, 54, 62) sts rem, ending with Dec Row 1. Purl 1 WS row.

DEC ROW 2 (RS) Knit to last 4 sts, ssk, k2—1 st dec'd at front raglan (end of RS rows).

Purl 1 WS row.

DEC ROW 3 (RS) K2, k2tog, knit to last 4 sts, ssk, k2—2 sts dec'd.

Purl 1 WS row. Rep the last 4 rows 4 (5, 5, 6, 6, 7, 7, 8) more times, then work the first 3 of these 4 rows once more, ending with Dec Row 3—24 (21, 19, 18, 24, 23, 27, 32) sts rem; cap measures about 6¾ (7¾, 7¾, 9¼, 9¼, 10¼, 10¼, 11½)" (17 [19.5, 19.5, 23.5, 23.5, 26, 26, 29] cm), measured straight up at center. With WS facing, BO all sts pwise.

finishing

Sew Raglan Seams

Pin back sleeve raglans to back, matching the center of each underarm, aligning the BO back neck edge with the BO top edges of sleeve caps, and easing to fit. Pin front sleeve raglans to front along the first 22 (26, 26, 30, 30, 34, 38) rows of cap shaping, matching row-for-row with the front, and leaving the upper 21 (25, 25, 29, 29, 33, 33, 37) rows of front sleeve raglan unattached to form the sides of the front neck. With MC threaded on a tapestry needle, sew sleeves to body using mattress st with 1-st selvedge. Reinforce the end of each seam at the front neck corners on WS.

Back Neckband

With CC, smaller cir needle, RS facing, and beg at BO edge of right sleeve, pick up and knit 24 (21, 19,

18, 24, 23, 27, 32) sts across top of right sleeve cap, pm, 35 (31, 33, 29, 35, 35, 39, 39) sts across back neck, pm, and 24 (21, 19, 18, 24, 23, 27, 32) sts across BO edge at top of left sleeve cap—83 (73, 71, 65, 83, 81, 93, 103) sts total. Knit 1 WS row.

DEC ROW (RS) K2, ssk, [knit to 2 sts before m, ssk, slip marker (sl m), k2tog] 2 times, knit to last 4 sts, k2tog, k2—6 sts dec'd.

Working in garter st (knit all sts every row), rep dec row on the next 4 RS rows, ending with a RS row—53 (43, 41, 35, 53, 51, 63, 73) sts rem. With WS facing, BO all sts kwise—6 garter ridges on RS, including ridge formed by BO.

Left Front Band

With CC, smaller cir needle, RS facing, and beg at BO edge of back neckband, pick up and knit 6 sts (1 st for each garter ridge) along left selvedge of back neckband, 21 (25, 25, 29, 29, 33, 33, 37) sts along left sleeve raglan to front neck corner (about 1 st for every sleeve raglan row), pm, and 26 (26, 27, 27, 30, 32, 34, 36) sts across BO edge of left front—53 (57, 58, 62, 65, 71, 73, 79) sts total.

NEXT ROW (WS) Knit to m at neck corner, sl m, knit across sts picked-up along sleeve raglan and *at the same time* dec 4 (5, 5, 6, 6, 7, 7, 8) sts evenly spaced over these sts, knit last 6 sts—49 (52, 53, 56, 59, 64, 66, 71) sts rem.
DEC ROW (RS) K2, ssk, knit to 2 sts before corner m, ssk, sl m, k2tog, knit to end—3 sts dec'd.

Knit 1 WS row. Rep the last 2 rows 3 more times, then work Dec row once more—34 (37, 38, 41, 44, 49, 51, 56) sts rem. With WS facing, BO all sts kwise—6 garter ridges.

Right Front Band

With CC, smaller cir needle, RS facing, and beg right front placket opening, pick up and knit 26 (26, 27, 27, 30, 32, 34, 36) sts across BO edge of right front, pm, 21 (25, 25, 29, 29, 33, 33, 37) sts along right sleeve raglan (1 st for each sleeve raglan row), and 6 sts along right selvedge of back neckband—53 (57, 58, 62, 65, 71, 73, 79) sts total.

NEXT ROW (WS) K6, knit across sts picked-up along sleeve raglan and *at the same time* dec 4 (5, 5, 6, 6, 7, 7, 8) sts evenly spaced over these sts, sl m, knit to end—49 (52, 53, 56, 59, 64, 66, 71) sts rem.
DEC ROW (RS) Knit to 2 sts before corner m, ssk, sl m, k2tog, knit to last 4 sts, k2tog, k2—3 sts dec'd.

Knit 1 WS row. Rep the last 2 rows 3 more times, then work Dec row once more—34 (37, 38, 41, 44, 49, 51, 56) sts rem. With WS facing, BO all sts kwise—6 garter ridges.

Placket Bands

With CC, smaller cir needle, RS facing, and beg at BO edge of left front neckband, pick up and knit 6 sts along selvedge of neckband (1 st for each garter ridge), then 35 (37, 37, 41, 41, 43, 43, 47) sts evenly spaced along left front to base of placket opening—41 (43, 43, 47, 47, 49, 49, 53) buttonband sts.

NOTE *If desired, you can pick up 1 st for every row along the side of the placket opening, then dec to the indicated number of sts on the foll row so the band will lie flat.*

Knit 10 rows, ending with a RS row. With WS facing, BO all sts kwise—6 garter ridges.

With CC, smaller cir needle, and beg at base of placket opening on right front, pick up and knit 35 (37, 37, 41, 41, 43, 43, 47) sts evenly spaced along right front to neckband, then 6 sts from neckband selvedge—41 (43, 43, 47, 47, 49, 49, 53) sts total. Knit 5 rows, beg and ending with a WS row—3 garter ridges.

BUTTONHOLE ROW (RS) K8 (10, 10, 5, 5, 7, 7, 2), [work 3-st one-row buttonhole (see Glossary), k6] 3 (3, 3, 4, 4, 4, 4, 5) times, work 3-st one-row buttonhole, k3—4 (4, 4, 5, 5, 5, 5, 6) buttonholes.

Knit 4 rows, ending with a RS row. With WS facing, BO all sts kwise—6 garter ridges. Sew selvedges of placket bands to BO at base of placket, with buttonhole band overlapping buttonband.

Weave in all loose ends. Block as desired. Sew buttons to buttonband, opposite buttonholes.

audubon shrug

DESIGNED BY **LISA SHROYER**

Shrugs make great layering pieces, they don't take much time or yarn, and they're adorable. But for women with large upper arms or fleshy upper backs, the shallow shrug back can distort into a concave curve along the back hem that tends to resemble football garb. The product of much experimentation, Audubon Shrug is ideal for plus-size women in three ways: the longer, fuller sleeves draw the eye down from the shoulder; the back is worked for several inches below the armholes to provide more coverage; and the center back decrease line adds vertical emphasis and creates a pointed hemline that suggests a nipped-in waist while preventing hem creep-up.

FINISHED SIZE
About 18¾ (21, 23¼, 25½, 28)" (47.5 [53.5, 59, 65, 71] cm) back width between underarm centers. Shrug shown measures 18¾" (47.5 cm).

YARN
DK weight (#3 Light).

Shown here: Filatura di Crosa Zara (100% merino; 137 yd [125 m]/50 g): #1503 olive green, 7 (8, 8, 9, 10) balls.

NEEDLES
Body and sleeves: size U.S. 7 (4.5 mm): 24" (60 cm) or longer circular (cir).

Collar and front edging: size 5 (3.5 mm): 24" (60 cm) or longer cir.

Adjust needle size if necessary to obtain the correct gauge.

NOTIONS
Markers (m); stitch holders or spare cir needles; tapestry needle.

GAUGE
18 stitches and 26 rows = 4" (10 cm) in stockinette stitch on larger needle.

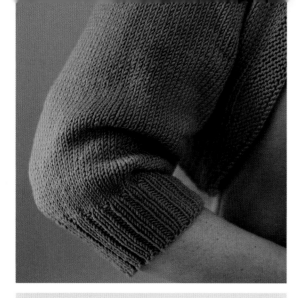

notes

+ Because there is no complete front to this garment, bust circumference does not determine the size. The shrug's back needs to fit across your back from underarm to underarm but not across the bust in front. Choose a back width as close to your actual back width as possible, with little or no ease, for a close fit along the lower edge, as shown in the photographs. The pointed back hemline should lie snugly against your back and not hang away from the body like a coat tail. The sleeve circumference at the upper arm should have some positive ease.

+ If you have a lot of flesh along your back bra line, repeat Rows 19 and 20 of the lower body section more times to increase the body length 1" to 3" (2.5 to 7.5 cm) before binding off for the armholes. This will create extra fabric to accommodate the outward curvature of your body in this area.

+ The yarn shown here is deliberately worked at a looser gauge than is typical for DK weight in order to produce a softly draping fabric.

+ Short-rows are worked in the garter-stitch trim to fill in the uneven contours of the front edges and create a smooth finish. This trim is not meant to cover the bust; it should recede to the outside of the bust and under the arms. If you think you need more coverage or a firmer edge, the finishing instructions point out where to add more rows in the trim.

lower body

With larger cir needle, CO 122 (134, 146, 158, 170) sts. Do not join.

ROW 1 (RS) [K2, p1] 6 times, k2, place marker (pm) for inc, [p1, k2] 10 (12, 14, 16, 18) times, pm, k11, pm for center back, k11, pm, [k2, p1] 10 (12, 14, 16, 18) times, pm for inc, [k2, p1] 6 times, k2.

ROW 2 (WS) Work sts as they appear (knit the knits, and purl the purls) to second m, slip marker (sl m), k11, sl center m, k11, sl m, work sts as they appear to end.

ROWS 3–6 Rep Rows 1 and 2 two more times—3 garter ridges at center back on RS.

ROW 7 (inc/dec row) Work in established rib to first m (inc m), sl m, M1 (see Glossary), work in rib to next m, sl m, knit to 3 sts before center m, ssk, k1, sl m, k1, k2tog, knit to next m, sl m, work in rib to next m (inc m), M1, sl m, work in rib to end—2 sts dec'd at center back; 1 st inc'd at each side; no change to st count.

ROW 8 Work in rib to second m, sl m, purl to center m, sl m, purl to next m, work in rib to end.

ROWS 9–14 Rep Rows 7 and 8 three more times, working inc'd sts in St st.

ROW 15 (inc/dec row) [K2, p1] 3 times, knit to first m (inc m), sl m, M1, knit to next m, remove m, knit to 3 sts before center m, ssk, k1, sl m, k1, k2tog, knit to next m, remove m, knit to next m (inc m), M1, sl m, knit to last 9 sts, [p1, k2] 3 times—no change to st count.

ROW 16 Work 9 sts in established rib, purl to last 9 sts, work 9 sts in established rib.

ROW 17 (inc/dec row) Work 9 sts in rib, knit to first m (inc m), sl m, M1, knit to 3 sts before center m, ssk, k1, sl m, k1, k2tog, knit to next m (inc m), M1, sl m, knit to last 9 sts, work 9 sts in rib—no change to st count.

ROW 18 Rep Row 16.

ROWS 19–32 Rep Rows 17 and 18 seven more times—13 inc/dec rows completed; piece measures about 5" (12.5 cm) from CO measured straight up at selvedges; do not measure along the diagonal shaping lines.

NEXT ROW (RS; inc/dec row) Work 9 sts in rib, BO 8 sts, knit to next m, M1, sl m, knit to 3 sts before center m, ssk, k1, sl m, k1, k2tog, knit to next m, M1, sl m, knit to last 17 sts, BO 8 sts, work to end in rib—106 (118, 130, 142, 154) sts rem; 82 (94, 106, 118, 130) back sts in bias St st between inc m, 3 sts in regular St st on each side of back between BO gap and inc m; 9 front sts at each side.

Place sts on holder, but do not cut yarn—back measures about 15¾ (18, 20¼, 22¾, 25)" (40 [45.5, 51.5, 58, 63.5] cm) between inc m and about 18¾ (21, 23¼, 25½, 28)" (47.5 [53.5, 59, 65, 71] cm) between centers of underarm BO gaps. Remove all markers except for the center back m.

sleeves

With larger cir needle, CO 56 (62, 68, 71, 74) sts. Do not join.

NEXT ROW (RS) K2, *p1, k2; rep from *.

NEXT ROW (WS) P2, *k1, p2; rep
  from *.

Rep the last 2 rows until piece
measures 3" (7.5 cm) from CO,
ending with a WS row.

NEXT ROW (RS) K5, *k1f&b (see
  Glossary), k2; rep from * to last 3
  sts, k3—72 (80, 88, 92, 96) sts.

Work even in St st until piece
measures 4¾" (12 cm) from CO,
ending with a WS row.

INC ROW (RS) K2, M1, knit to last 2
  sts, M1, k2—2 sts inc'd.

[Work 5 rows even, then rep inc
row] 2 (1, 0, 1, 2) time(s)—78 (84,
90, 96, 102) sts. Work even until
piece measures 11¼" (28.5 cm)

from CO for all sizes, ending with
a WS row. BO 5 sts at beg of next 2
rows—68 (74, 80, 86, 92) sts rem.
Place sts on holder.

yoke

JOINING ROW With WS of pieces
  facing and working yarn attached
  to left front edge, work 9 left
  front sts in rib, pm, purl 68 (74,

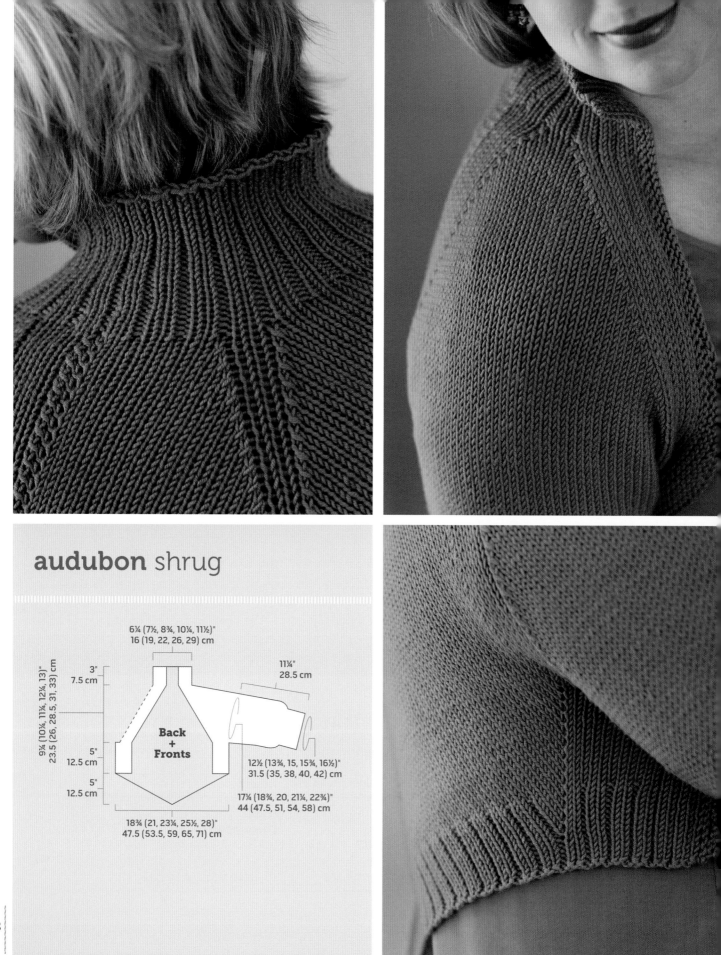

audubon shrug

6¼ (7½, 8¾, 10¼, 11½)"
16 (19, 22, 26, 29) cm

3"
7.5 cm

11¼"
28.5 cm

9¼ (10¼, 11¼, 12¼, 13)" cm
23.5 (26, 28.5, 31, 33) cm

Back + Fronts

12½ (13¾, 15, 15¾, 16½)"
31.5 (35, 38, 40, 42) cm

5"
12.5 cm

17¼ (18¾, 20, 21¼, 22¾)"
44 (47.5, 51, 54, 58) cm

5"
12.5 cm

18¾ (21, 23¼, 25½, 28)"
47.5 (53.5, 59, 65, 71) cm

80, 86, 92) left sleeve sts, pm, purl 88 (100, 112, 124, 136) back sts, pm, purl 68 (74, 80, 86, 92) right sleeve sts, pm, work 9 right front sts in rib—242 (266, 290, 314, 338) sts total.

ROW 1 (RS) Work 9 sts in rib, sl m, k2, k2tog, knit to 4 sts before next m, ssk, k2, sl m, k2, k2tog, M1, knit to 3 sts before center m, ssk, k1, sl m, k1, k2tog, knit to 4 sts before next m, M1, ssk, k2, sl m, k2, k2tog, knit to 4 sts before next m, ssk, k2, sl m, work 9 sts in rib—6 sts dec'd; 2 sts from each sleeve; 2 sts at center back.

ROW 2 (WS) Work 9 sts in rib, purl to last 9 sts, work 9 sts in rib.

Rep the last 2 rows 29 (32, 35, 38, 41) more times—62 (68, 74, 80, 86) sts rem; 28 (34, 40, 46, 52) back sts, 8 sts each sleeve, 9 sts each front; yoke measures about 9¼ (10¼, 11¼, 12¼, 13)" (23.5 [26, 28.5, 31, 33] cm), measured straight up along center of sleeve cap.

collar

Change to smaller cir needle.

NEXT ROW (RS) *K2, p1; rep from to last 2 sts, k2.

NEXT ROW (WS) *P2, k1; rep from * to last 2 sts, p2.

Shape back neck with short-rows (see Glossary) as foll:

SHORT-ROW 1 (RS) Work 44 (50, 56, 62, 68) sts in rib to 1 st before left back raglan m, wrap next st (a purl st), turn.

SHORT-ROW 2 (WS) Work 26 (32, 38, 44, 50) sts in rib to 1 st before right back raglan m, wrap next st (a knit st as viewed from WS), turn.

SHORT-ROWS 3 AND 4 Work in rib to 3 sts before previously wrapped st, wrap next st, turn.

NEXT ROW (RS) Work in established rib to end of row; wraps do not need to be worked tog with wrapped sts because they will be hidden by the purl bumps.

Cont in rib across all sts until collar measures about 3" (7.5 cm), measured straight up from center of sleeve, and 3½" (9 cm), measured straight up at center back. BO all sts in rib.

finishing

With yarn threaded on a tapestry needle, sew sleeve seams. Sew underarm seams.

Front Edgings

NOTE *For both front edgings, you can add more width to each front by working extra rows in garter st across all sts before beginning the short-rows. The edgings are not shown on the schematic.*

LEFT FRONT

With smaller cir needle, RS facing, and beg at BO edge of collar, pick up and knit 82 (86, 90, 96, 100) sts evenly spaced along left front edge. Knit 2 rows, ending with a RS row. Shape with short-rows as foll:

SHORT-ROW 1 (WS) K46, turn.
SHORT-ROW 2 (RS) K41, turn.
SHORT-ROW 3 K36, turn.
SHORT-ROW 4 Knit to 3 sts before previous turn, turn.
SHORT-ROWS 5–11 Rep Short-row 4 seven more times, ending with a WS row (last row is worked as k12, turn).
NEXT ROW (RS) Knit to end of row.

With WS facing, BO all sts kwise.

RIGHT FRONT

With smaller cir needle, RS facing, and beg at CO edge of right front, pick up and knit 82 (86, 90, 96, 100) sts evenly spaced along right front edge, ending at BO of collar. Knit 1 WS row. Shape with short-rows as foll:

SHORT-ROW 1 (RS) K46, turn work.
SHORT-ROW 2 (WS) Knit to end.
SHORT-ROW 3 (RS) K41, turn.
SHORT-ROW 4 (WS) K36, turn.
SHORT-ROWS 5–11 Rep Short-row 4 seven more times, ending with a RS row (last row is worked as k12, turn).
NEXT ROW (WS) Knit to end of row.

Knit 1 RS row. With WS facing, BO all sts kwise.

Weave in loose ends. Lay shrug flat, pin out center point at lower back edge, and block in place. Block other sections as desired.

the seamless yoke
sweater

The yoke of the seamless yoke sweater is worked simultaneously over the sleeves and body, just as for some raglans (Chapter 05). In addition, the seamless yoke is continuous between the sleeves and body—there are no seams or shaping lines. The upper body is a tube of fabric with concentric shaping instead of aligned decreases. The effect of seamless shaping is that the yoke has less structure and visual definition than other styles, which makes it tougher to achieve a close fit. In general, it's best to wear seamless yokes with some positive ease. For plus-size women, the yoke can become very deep, and the result of joining of wide sleeves to a wide body makes for a large circumference at the beginning of the yoke—and therefore a lot of stitches on the needle. Typically, the decreases don't begin until the yoke is a few inches deep, then the circumference is drastically decreased in a series of vertically spaced rounds to produce a shape much like a stepped pyramid, instead of the straight sides produced by raglan shaping.

Seamless yoke construction is common to many ethnic traditions and has distinct benefits—the yoke provides an uninterrupted canvas (except for the shaping rows or rounds) for colorwork and stitch patterns. The shape has a universal fit and is more forgiving of broad shoulders than raglans. Except for cardigans and sweaters with deep necklines, you'll find most seamless yoke sweaters are worked in the round, which is appealing to those who don't like to sew seams (or purl).

who should wear the seamless yoke style?

The seamless yoke is one of the more universal styles in terms of fit. It offers one-piece construction that is appealingly uncluttered and drapes to fit most women quite nicely. Women who are petite or short from neck to underarm may find the yoke too deep and too voluminous without customization. You'll know this is a problem if the fabric along the neckline tends to fold forward on itself instead of lying smooth.

seamless yoke construction

The seamless yoke can be worked bottom-up or top-down. In bottom-up construction, the body and sleeves are typically worked separately to the armholes, then they are joined and the yoke is shaped with decreases to the neck. Neckbands and collars can be worked directly on the stitches remaining at the neck—there are no bound-off or shaped edges along which to pick up stitches.

In top-down construction, you can use a provisional cast-on at the neck edge, then use those live stitches later for the neckband treatment. Or, you can use a regular cast-on and simply pick up stitches along the cast-on edge.

All the seamless yoke patterns in this book are worked in the round from the bottom up. However, the Barton Cardigan (page 128) is worked with a steek that is cut open during the finishing stage.

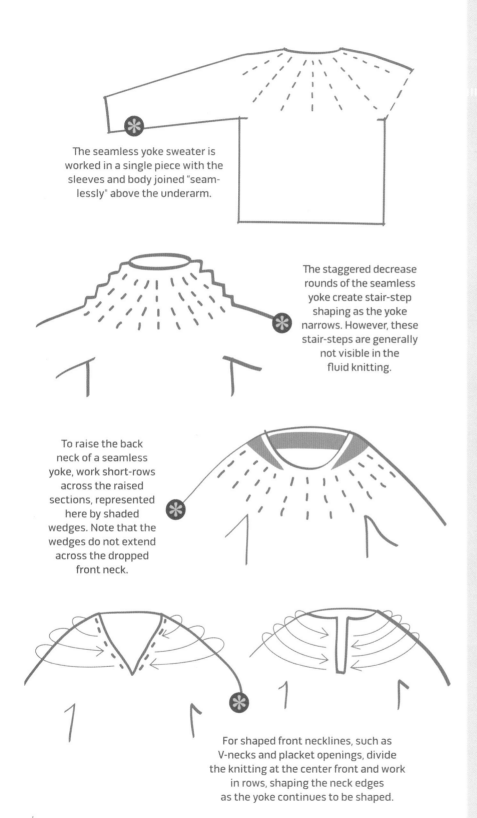

The seamless yoke sweater is worked in a single piece with the sleeves and body joined "seamlessly" above the underarm.

The staggered decrease rounds of the seamless yoke create stair-step shaping as the yoke narrows. However, these stair-steps are generally not visible in the fluid knitting.

To raise the back neck of a seamless yoke, work short-rows across the raised sections, represented here by shaded wedges. Note that the wedges do not extend across the dropped front neck.

For shaped front necklines, such as V-necks and placket openings, divide the knitting at the center front and work in rows, shaping the neck edges as the yoke continues to be shaped.

notable effects
of seamless yoke construction

+ There is usually an underarm span similar in width to other construction types.

+ There is no shoulder or shoulder seam.

+ The sleeve and body stitch counts need to be planned to accommodate the decrease shaping multiple in the yoke. For example, to work a shaping round as "*k5, k2tog; rep from *," there must be a multiple of 7 stitches in the yoke.

+ The neck opening is circular.

+ Any type of neck shaping requires adding short-rows or working the neck back and forth in rows, which will interrupt the yoke shaping.

+ To tailor the final neck circumference, you may need to break the regularity of the yoke shaping. For example, to get a smaller neck opening for the Haviland Pullover on page 114, you would not be able to work a fifth decrease round in line with the decreases in first four rounds—doing so would result in a stitch count that would be too narrow to fit over the head. To get a smaller neck circumference, that isn't too small, you would need to work a fifth decrease round of the pattern from the rest of the yoke shaping, working fewer decreases on this round.

+ If you have a large bust, the yoke joining round may cut horizontally across the middle of your breasts. To minimize this effect, do not change stitch patterns or colors at this point (see The Yoke at right).

+ Seamless yoke cardigans look best when fastened. When worn unbuttoned, the front edges tend to meet at the neck and flare outward at the hem.

The Yoke

The number of stitches in the front, back, and two sleeves must add up to a multiple of the number of stitches in the yoke shaping. It is therefore common for adjustments to be made in the first yoke round after the pieces are joined at the armhole. The Haviland Pullover on page 114 uses this type of adjustment so that the yoke is a multiple of 11 stitches for all sizes. You can work any kind of decrease for the yoke shaping—single decreases should have smaller stitch repeats (fewer stitches between individual decreases) while double decreases should be worked in larger stitch repeats (more stitches between individual decreases).

If the decrease rounds are too closely spaced, begin too early in the yoke, or decrease too many stitches at a time, the yoke will narrow too quickly. In general, you should work 2" to 3" (5 to 7.5 cm) even before working the first decrease round and there should be a total of three to four decrease rounds to the neck, ending with about 25% of the original yoke stitches for a crewneck. In traditional yoke construction, the first decrease round removes 20% of the stitches, the second removes 25% of the remaining stitches, and the third and fourth each remove 33% of the remaining stitches, respectively. The yoke depth, and therefore the distance between each decrease round, depends on your size. The distance between decrease rounds is usually equal to the depth worked even at the beginning of the yoke.

Because the yoke is worked in rounds, the neck opening will be round, without any specialized shape. To drop the front neck, you need to raise the back neck with short-rows worked back and forth across the back and tops of the sleeves. To make a placket or give the front neck a defined shape, such as a V-neck, bind off a couple stitches at the center front, then work the yoke back and forth in rows, incorporating any neck shaping at the beginning and

end of the rows. At the same time, continue to work the shaping rounds as necessary.

To alleviate the bisecting effect of changing patterns at the yoke joining round (common in patterned yoke sweaters), begin the patterning a few inches below the underarm or a few inches after the yoke has been joined.

The Sleeve

The sleeve length in circular yoke construction is similar to the raglan or set-in because the yoke encompasses the upper arm, acting like a kind of sleeve cap. Aim for a sleeve that matches your arm length from wrist to underarm, adding a little extra length to ensure full coverage.

If you alter the circumference of a seamless sleeve, you will directly affect the placement and multiple of decreases in the yoke. You can adjust a few stitches to achieve a stitch count that has the correct multiple after joining the pieces for the yoke (adjusting the stitch count by 2 to 8 stitches is acceptable), but this becomes problematic if it involves increasing or decreasing a lot of stitches. If you end up with a lot of extra sleeve stitches, the best option is to work raglan-style decreases for the sleeves from the joining round at the armhole until the sleeves reach the stitch count called for in the pattern—this will bring the yoke stitch count in line before the first seamless decrease round is worked. If you do add stitches to the upper sleeve, be sure to add an even number of stitches so that they can be decreased in pairs raglan-style at the base of the yoke. In general, if a pattern calls for large-scale stitch multiples for the yoke shaping or for the stitch pattern, it might be more trouble than it's worth to change the stitch count on the sleeves. The more restrictive the multiple, the harder it will be to customize the shape. You might be better off choosing a different construction type.

If you change colors or patterns at the yoke joining round, the contrast between yoke and lower body will create a horizontal, bisecting line across the widest part of the bust. Drawing lines across wide areas is generally not advised for plus-size women. To alleviate this effect and accentuate the bust in a flattering way, place the change in color/pattern a couple inches below or a couple inches above the joining round.

haviland pullover

DESIGNED BY **LISA SHROYER**

Concentric yoke decreases provide the "pattern" in this stockinette pullover. The body and sleeves are worked in the round from the bottom up, then joined for a seamless yoke that features evenly spaced vertical double decreases. The plain styling allows you to showcase unusual yarns, but be beware of yarns that have long runs of color with this one-piece construction—the variations in round length could cause unattractive color pooling. This project provides easy practice for round-yoke knitting and will help you determine the yoke depth that works best for your shape. Never be afraid to rip out and add or remove depth—you'll learn much in the process, and you'll end up with a perfect fit.

FINISHED SIZE
About 41 (44¼, 46½, 49¾, 53, 55½, 58¾)" (104 [112.5, 118, 126.5, 134.5, 141, 149] cm) bust circumference. Sweater shown measures 44¼" (112.5 cm).

YARN
Worsted weight (#4 Medium).

Shown here: Cascade Eco Alpaca (100% alpaca; 220 yd [201 m]/100 g): #1511 natural tan, 6 (6, 7, 7, 8, 8, 9) skeins.

NEEDLES
Body: size U.S. 6 (4 mm): 32" (81.5 cm) or longer (depending on size) circular (cir).

Sleeves: size U.S. 6 (4 mm): set of 4 or 5 double-pointed (dpn) and 16" (40 cm) cir.

Yoke: size U.S. 6: (4 mm) 16" and 24" (40 and 60 cm) cir.

Adjust needle size if necessary to obtain the correct gauge.

NOTIONS
Markers (m); stitch holders or waste yarn; tapestry needle.

GAUGE
19¾ stitches and 26 rounds = 4" (10 cm) in stockinette stitch worked in rounds.

notes

+ The body and sleeves are worked separately in the round to the underarms, then joined for working the yoke in the round to the neck edge.

+ At the start of the yoke, the beginning of the round falls at the beginning of the left sleeve stitches. After working even for a few inches, the yoke's stitch count is adjusted to be a multiple of 11 stitches for all sizes, then the beginning of the round is moved to the center of the left sleeve. This ensures that the decreases are placed symmetrically around the yoke, with a decrease at the center of each sleeve and the remaining decreases evenly spaced in between.

+ If you modify the body and sleeve stitch counts to create a custom fit, make sure to adjust the stitch count of the yoke before starting the yoke decreases so the total number is a multiple of 11 stitches, with an odd number of stitches in each sleeve, the front, and the back.

+ The length measurements for all sizes in this pattern are based on women of average height. If you are petite, you may need to work a shallower yoke and shorter sleeves. If you are tall, the given directions should work for you, as

seamless yokes tend to err on the side of roomy and long (in the yoke itself).

+ If you'd like to experiment with yoke depth before working the lower body and sleeves, use a provisional method to cast on for the body about 2" (5 cm) below the underarms. Work in the round in pattern to the underarm split. Separately, use a provisional method to cast on for two sleeves and work each of those to the underarm split. Join and work the yoke as directed, then try on the yoke. Does it fold forward on itself below the neckline in front? Then it's too deep for you. Is the fabric strained horizontally across the collarbones and shoulders? Then it's too shallow for you. The effects will probably be more subtle, but if you're not totally happy with the yoke depth, you can rework the directions to increase or decrease rounds in the yoke. Then either reknit the sweater completely, or if you're happy with your yoke, work the lower body and sleeves separately as directed and then graft the provisional yoke to those pieces; or place the live stitches of the body on a circular needle and work the body down to the hem and likewise with the sleeves.

body

With longest cir needle, CO 202 (218, 230, 246, 262, 274, 290) sts. Place marker (pm) and join for working in rnds, being careful not to twist sts.

RND 1 *K1, p1; rep from *.
RND 2 Knit.

Rep these 2 rnds 5 more times and *at the same time* pm in the last rnd after the first 101 (109, 115, 123, 131, 137, 145) sts to mark side of body—piece measures about 1½" (3.2 cm) from CO. Work in St st (knit every rnd) until piece measures 15" (38 cm) from CO for all sizes.

NEXT RND *Knit to 5 (5, 5, 6, 6, 6, 7) sts before m, place next 10 (10, 10, 12, 12, 12, 14) sts on holder, removing m in center; rep from * once more—182 (198, 210, 222, 238, 250, 262) sts rem; 91 (99, 105, 111, 119, 125, 131) sts each for front and back. Break yarn and set aside.

sleeves

With dpn, CO 50 (50, 50, 56, 56, 60, 60) sts. Divide sts as evenly as possible on 3 or 4 dpn, pm, and join for working in rnds, being careful not to twist sts.

RND 1 *K1, p1; rep from *.
RND 2 Knit.

Rep these 2 rnds 8 more times, then rep Rnd 1 once more—piece measures about 2" (5 cm) from CO.

NEXT RND [K4 (4, 4, 6, 6, 5, 5), k1f&b (see Glossary)] 10 (10, 10, 8, 8, 10, 10) times—60 (60, 60, 64, 64, 70, 70) sts.

Work even in St st until piece measures 6 (5, 4¾, 4¾, 4¾, 4¾, 4)" (15 [12.5, 12, 12, 12, 12, 10] cm) from CO.

INC RND K1, M1 (see Glossary), knit to last st, M1, k1—2 sts inc'd.

[Work 8 rnds even, then rep the inc rnd] 6 (8, 4, 3, 2, 2, 0) times—74 (78, 70, 72, 70, 76, 72) sts. [Work 4 rnds even, then rep the inc rnd] 0 (0, 7, 9, 12, 11, 17) times, changing to shortest cir needle when there are too many sts to fit comfortably on dpn—74 (78, 84, 90, 94, 98, 106) sts. Work even until piece measures 18½ (19, 19½, 19½, 19½, 20, 20)" (47 [48.5, 49.5, 49.5, 49.5, 51, 51] cm) from CO. Place 5 (5, 5, 6, 6, 6, 7) sts on each side of end-of-rnd m on holder—64 (68, 74, 78, 82, 86, 92) sts rem. Break yarn and set aside. Make another sleeve in the same manner.

yoke

JOINING RND Rejoin yarn with RS facing to beg of sleeve sts and with longest cir needle, knit across 64 (68, 74, 78, 82, 86, 92) left sleeve sts, 91 (99, 105, 111, 119, 125, 131) front sts, 64 (68, 74, 78, 82, 86, 92) right sleeve sts, then 91 (99, 105, 111, 119, 125, 131) back sts—310 (334, 358, 378, 402, 422, 446) sts total.

haviland pullover

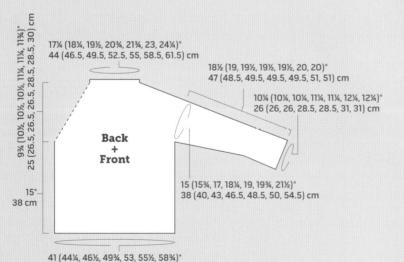

9¾ (10½, 10½, 10½, 11¼, 11¼, 11¾)"
25 (26.5, 26.5, 26.5, 28.5, 28.5, 30) cm

17¼ (18¼, 19½, 20¾, 21¾, 23, 24¼)"
44 (46.5, 49.5, 52.5, 55, 58.5, 61.5) cm

18½ (19, 19½, 19½, 19½, 20, 20)"
47 (48.5, 49.5, 49.5, 49.5, 51, 51) cm

10¼ (10¼, 10¼, 11¼, 11¼, 12¼, 12¼)"
26 (26, 26, 28.5, 28.5, 31, 31) cm

Back + Front

15"
38 cm

15 (15¾, 17, 18¼, 19, 19¾, 21½)"
38 (40, 43, 46.5, 48.5, 50, 54.5) cm

41 (44¼, 46½, 49¾, 53, 55½, 58¾)"
104 (112.5, 118, 126.5, 134.5, 141, 149) cm

Pm and join for working in rnds; rnd beg at start of left sleeve. Work even in St st until piece measures 2 (2¼, 2¼, 2¼, 2½, 2½, 2½)" (5 [5.5, 5.5, 5.5, 6.5, 6.5, 6.5] cm) from joining rnd. Adjust st count for your size as foll.

SIZE 41" ONLY

K31, k2tog (center of sleeve), k153, k2tog (center of sleeve), k122—308 sts rem; 2 sts dec'd, 1 st from each sleeve.

SIZE 44¼" ONLY

K33, k2tog (center of sleeve), k35, k2tog, k91, k2tog, k35, k2tog (center of sleeve), k132—330 sts rem; 4 sts dec'd, 2 sts from front, 1 st from each sleeve.

SIZE 46½" ONLY

K36, k2tog (center of sleeve), k38, k2tog, k97, k2tog, k38, k2tog (center of sleeve), k38, k2tog, k97, k2tog, k2—352 sts rem; 6 sts dec'd, 2 sts each from front and back, 1 st from each sleeve.

SIZE 49¾" ONLY

K38, k2tog (center of sleeve), k40, k2tog, k103, k2tog, k40, k2tog (center of sleeve), k149—374 sts rem; 4 sts dec'd, 2 sts from front, 1 st from each sleeve.

SIZE 53" ONLY

K40, k2tog (center of sleeve), k42, k2tog, k111, k2tog, k42, k2tog (center of sleeve), k42, k2tog, k111, k2tog, k2—396 sts rem; 6 sts dec'd, 2 sts each from front and back, 1 st from each sleeve.

SIZE 55½" ONLY

K42, k2tog (center of sleeve), k44, k2tog, k117, k2tog, k44, k2tog (center of sleeve), k167—418 sts rem; 4 sts dec'd, 2 sts from front, 1 st from each sleeve.

SIZE 58¾" ONLY

K45, k2tog (center of sleeve), k47, k2tog, k123, k2tog, k47, k2tog (center of sleeve), k47, k2tog, k123, k2tog, k2—440 sts rem; 6 sts dec'd, 2 sts each from front and back, 1 st from each sleeve.

ALL SIZES

Knit 1 rnd.

NEXT RND Knit to end of rnd, remove m, k33 (35, 38, 40, 42, 44, 47) to end 1 st past center st of left sleeve, pm for new beg of rnd—yoke measures 2½ (2¾, 2¾, 3, 3, 3)" (6.5 [7, 7, 7, 7.5, 7.5, 7.5] cm) from joining rnd.

Shape Yoke

NOTE *Change to shorter cir needle when there are too few sts to fit comfortably on long cir needle.*

DEC RND 1 *K8, sl 2 tog kwise, k1, p2sso; rep from *—252 (270, 288, 306, 324, 342, 360) sts rem.

Work 13 (14, 14, 14, 15, 15, 16) rnds even, moving end-of-rnd m 1 st to the left in last rnd as foll: Knit to end, remove m, k1, replace m.

DEC RND 2 *K6, sl 2 tog kwise, k1, p2sso; rep from *—196 (210, 224, 238, 252, 266, 280) sts rem.

Work 13 (14, 14, 14, 15, 15, 16) rnds even, moving end-of rnd m 1 st to the left in last rnd.

DEC RND 3 *K4, sl 2 tog kwise, k1, p2sso; rep from *—140 (150, 160, 170, 180, 190, 200) sts rem.

Work 13 (14, 14, 14, 15, 15, 16) rnds even, moving end-of-rnd m 1 st to the left in last rnd.

DEC RND 4 *K2, sl 2 tog kwise, k1, p2sso; rep from *—84 (90, 96, 102, 108, 114, 120) sts rem.

Work 5 rnds even—yoke measures about 9¾ (10½, 10½, 10½, 11¼, 11¼, 11¾)" (25 [26.5, 26.5, 26.5, 28.5, 28.5, 30] cm) from joining rnd.

Neckband

NOTE *The three largest sizes have very wide neck openings; to narrow the neck for these sizes, dec 6 to 18 sts evenly spaced in the first rib rnd.*

Work in k1, p1 rib for 2 rnds, then purl 4 rnds. BO all sts pwise—neckband measures about ½" (3.2 cm) high with BO edge allowed to roll.

finishing

With yarn threaded on a tapestry needle, use the Kitchener st (see Glossary) to graft underarm sts tog. Use yarn tails to close up any holes at underarms. Weave in loose ends. Block as desired.

passyunk pullover

DESIGNED BY **LISA R. MYERS**

In this seamless yoke design, Lisa R. Myers keeps the viewer's eye moving around the garment by changing stitch patterns at strategic points. The gradual and irregular transitions from one pattern to the next eliminate the potentially unflattering horizontal lines that more abrupt changes would create. Lisa came up with this plan in response to the challenge: "How can you design a seamless yoke pullover with design elements that don't depend on a graphic shift at the yoke joining round?" As mentioned earlier in this chapter, changing patterns on the joining round creates a horizontal line that cuts across the widest part of the bust. The Passyunk Pullover deftly skirts this problem.

FINISHED SIZE
About 40½ (44½, 48½, 52½, 56½, 60½)" (103 [113, 123, 133.5, 143.5, 153.5] cm) bust circumference. Sweater shown measures 44½" (113 cm).

YARN
Worsted weight (#4 Medium).

Shown here: Manos del Uruguay Rittenhouse Merino 5-Ply (100% merino; 240 yd [220 m]/100 g): #512 cinnamon, 5 (6, 6, 7, 8, 8) skeins.

NEEDLES
Size U.S. 7 (4.5 mm): 16" and 32" (40 and 60 cm) circular (cir).

Adjust needle size if necessary to obtain correct gauge.

NOTIONS
Markers (m); stitch holders; tapestry needle.

GAUGE
20 stitches and 30 rows = 4" (10 cm) in leaf pattern from Rows 1–12 of charts.

notes

+ This pullover is worked from the bottom up in pieces that are joined and worked seamlessly for the yoke.

+ The charted pattern limits the ways in which you can alter the lower body length. If you need to add length to the body, you can either repeat the last two rows of the chart, working purl columns and twisted knit ribs, until you reach your desired length, or you can repeat Rows 1–12 more than the directed two times. Every repeat of Rows 1–12 will add about 1½" (3.8 cm) in length. Likewise, if you need to shorten the body, you can work Rows 1–12 only once, shortening the body by about 1½" (3.8 cm). Otherwise, you will need to rework the pattern and decrease the amount of chart rows worked above Row 95 (the plainest section of the patterning).

+ The yoke begins with raglan-style decreases, tailoring the shape of the upper body. This leads to a more refined fit than often found in seamless yoke designs. After short-rows are worked to raise the back neck, the shaping transitions to traditional concentric yoke shaping.

+ The yoke is fairly shallow for all sizes in this design. This yoke depth, paired with the above-mentioned raglan shaping at the beginning of the yoke, leads to a more form-fitting yoke. Compare the Passyunk schematic on page 126 to the Haviland schematic on page 118. For similar sizes with similar neck circumferences, there is quite a difference in yoke depth. If you know this shallow yoke will not work for you because you are tall or have broad shoulders, you can increase the yoke depth by adding rows worked even between the decrease rounds in the Yoke Decreases section.

back

With longer cir needle, CO 101 (111, 121, 131, 141, 151) sts. Do not join.

NEXT ROW (WS) [P1tbl, k4] 1 (0, 1, 2, 3, 4) time(s), place marker (pm), work set-up row of Body chart (page 124) over center 91 (111, 111, 111, 111, 111) sts as indicated for your size, pm, [k4, p1tbl] 1 (0, 1, 2, 3, 4) time(s).
NEXT ROW (RS) [K1tbl, p4] 1 (0, 1, 2, 3, 4) time(s), slip marker (sl m), work Row 1 of Body chart to m, sl m, [p4, k1tbl] 1 (0, 1, 2, 3, 4) time(s).

Working 5 (0, 5, 10, 15, 20) sts outside markers at each side as for the last 2 rows, work Rows 2–12 once, then rep Rows 1–12 once more—25 chart rows total. Cont in patt until Row 118 of chart has been completed—131 rows total; piece measures about 17½" (44.5 cm) from CO for all sizes. Cut yarn, place first and last 5 (10, 10, 10, 10, 10) sts of row on separate holders, then place rem 91 (91, 101, 111, 121, 131) sts on a third holder.

front

Work as for back—5 (10, 10, 10, 10, 10) sts on holder at each side; 91 (91, 101, 111, 121, 131) center sts on third holder; piece measures about 17½" (44.5 cm) from CO.

sleeves

With longer cir needle, CO 51 (51, 51, 61, 61, 61) sts. Do not join. Beg and ending as indicated for your size, work set-up row of Sleeve chart (page 127) once, then rep Rows 1–12 two times—25 chart rows total. Work Rows 25–36 once—37 chart rows total; piece measures 5" (12.5 cm) from CO.

Shape Sleeve

NOTES *While working the foll shaping, after Row 96 of chart has been completed rep Rows 73–96 of chart thereafter. To avoid having any partial motifs at the top of the sleeve, do not start any new 3-st motifs (the ones that begin with [p1, yo, p1] in same st) in the last 2" (5 cm) of the sleeve; work the st that would have been inc'd to 3 sts as k1tbl on RS and p1tbl on WS instead.*

Inc 1 st each end of needle on next RS row, then every 8th row 7 (0, 0, 0, 0, 0) times, then every 6th row 4 (11, 7, 9, 5, 0) times, then every 4th row 0 (4, 11, 7, 14, 23) times, working new sts into chart patt—75 (83, 89, 95, 101, 109) sts. Work even in patt until piece measures 18 (18, 18½, 18½, 19, 19)" (45.5 [45.5, 47, 47, 48.5, 48.5] cm) from CO or desired length to underarm, ending with a WS row. Break yarn, place first and last 5 (10, 10, 10, 10, 10) sts of row on separate holders, then place rem 65 (63, 69, 75, 81, 89) sts on a third holder. Work second sleeve the same as the first, but do not break yarn.

yoke

JOINING RND With longer cir needle and RS facing, using yarn attached to second sleeve and working sts as they appear (k1tbl the k1tbl's, and purl the purls), *work 65 (63, 69, 75, 81, 89) left sleeve sts, pm; work 91 (91, 101, 111, 121, 131) front sts, pm; rep from * for right sleeve and back—312 (308, 340, 372, 404, 440) sts.

Join for working in rnds; rnd beg start of left sleeve sts.

Raglan Decreases

DOUBLE DEC RND *Ssk, work in patt to 2 sts before next m, k2tog, slip m (sl m); rep from * 3 more times—8 sts dec'd; 2 sts each from each sleeve, back, and front.
SINGLE DEC RND *Ssk, work in patt to 2 sts before next m, k2tog, sl m, knit to next m, sl m; rep from * to end of rnd—4 sts dec'd; 2 sts from each sleeve; no change to back and front.

Rep these 2 rnds 4 (2, 2, 3, 4, 5) more times, then rep only the single dec rnd 3 (3, 1, 1, 1, 2) time(s)—240 (260, 300, 320, 340, 360) sts rem; 39 (45, 55, 57, 59, 61) sts each sleeve; 81 (85, 95, 103, 111, 119) sts each for back and front; yoke measures 1¾ (1¼, 1, 1¼, 1½, 2)" (4.5 [3.2, 2.5, 3.2, 3.8, 5] cm). Sts at each end of sleeves are p4 (p2, p2, p3, p4, k1tbl); sts at each end of front and back are k1tbl (p2, p2, p1, k1tbl, p4); rib patt is continuous around the yoke.

Yoke Short-rows

Working sts as they appear, work short-rows (see Glossary) to raise the back neck as foll:

SHORT-ROW 1 (RS) Work to last 6 sts of left sleeve (6 sts before m where left sleeve meets front), wrap next st, turn.

SHORT-ROW 2 (WS) Work across left sleeve and back, then to last 6 sts of right sleeve (6 sts before m where right sleeve meets front), wrap next st, turn.

SHORT-ROWS 3–6 Work to 5 sts before previously wrapped st, wrap next st, turn—3 wrapped sts at each side.

SHORT-ROW 7 (RS) Work to beg-of-rnd m at start of left sleeve sts.

NEXT RND Work 1 rnd even on all sts, working wraps tog with wrapped sts as you come to them and removing all m except for beg-of-rnd m—yoke measures 2¾ (2¼, 2, 2¼, 2½, 3)" (7 [5.5, 5, 5.5, 6.5, 7.5] cm) at center back; no change to length at center front.

Yoke Decreases

Reposition beg-of-rnd m to be in the center of a p4 column if necessary for your size as foll: Remove m, p2 (p0, p0, p1, p2, [k1tbl, p2]), replace m.

DEC RND 1 P1, *sl 2, k1, p2sso, p3, k1tbl, p3; rep from * to last 9 sts, sl 2, k1, p2sso, p3, k1tbl, p2—192 (208, 240, 256, 272, 288) sts rem; each p4 column has been dec'd to p3.

Work sts as they appear for 8 (10, 12, 14, 12, 12) rnds.

DEC RND 2 P1, *k1tbl, p2, sl 2, k1, p2sso, p2; rep from * last 7 sts, k1tbl, p2, sl 2, k1, p2sso, p1—144 (156, 180, 192, 204,

BODY ROWS 67 to 118

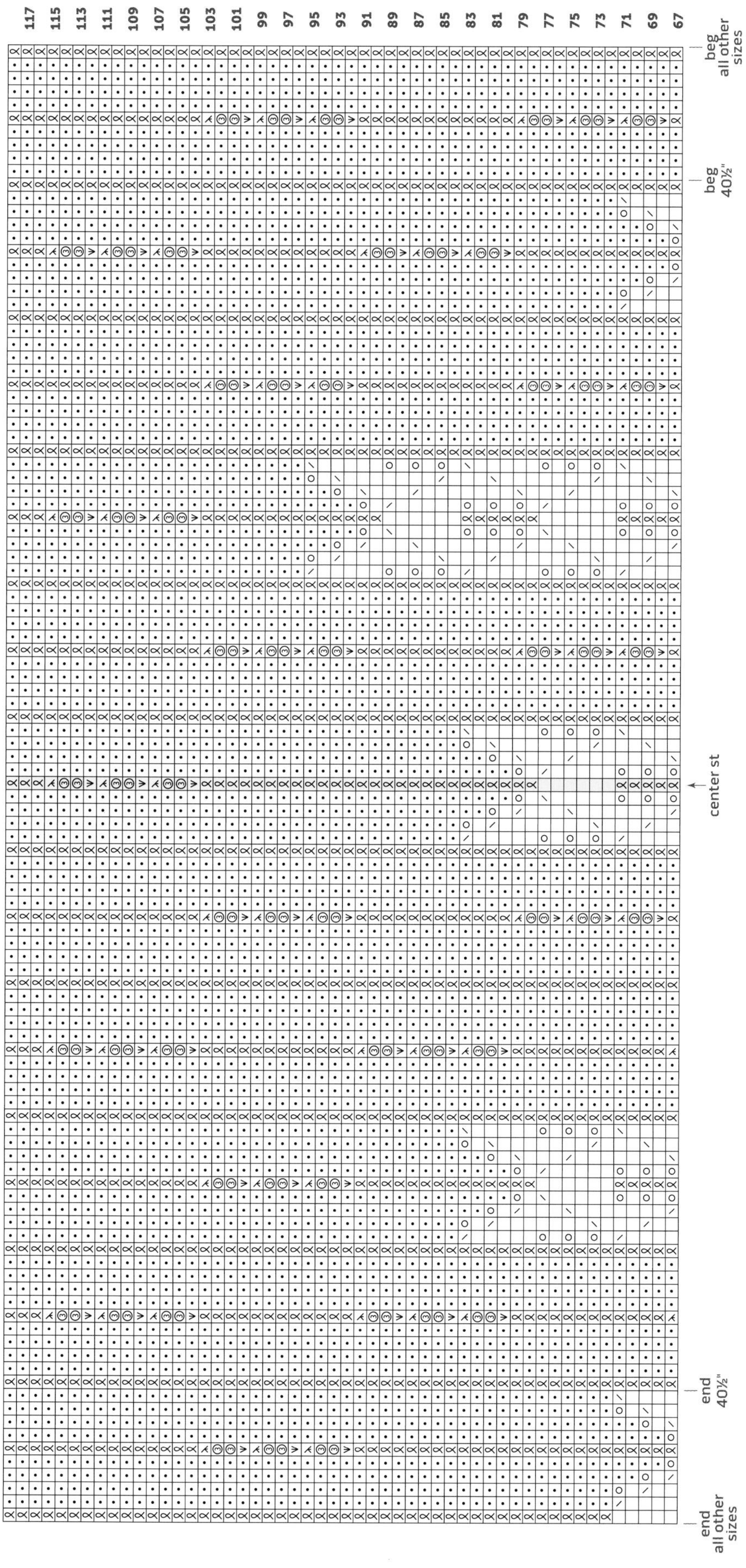
117
115
113
111
109
107
105
103
101
99
97
95
93
91
89
87
85
83
81
79
77
75
73
71
69
67
beg all other sizes
beg 40½"
center st
end 40½"
end all other sizes

☐	knit on RS; purl on WS
•	purl on RS; knit on WS
ℓ	k1tbl on RS; p1tbl on WS
○	yo
/	k2tog
\	ssk (see Glossary)
⋏	sl 1, k2tog, psso
∧	sl 2, k1, p2sso
∨	work [p1, yo, p1] all in same st
③	k3 on RS; p3 on WS

216) sts rem; each p3 column has been dec'd to p2.

Work 6 (8, 10, 12, 10, 10) rnds even. For the foll dec rnds, change to shorter cir needle when there are too few sts to fit comfortably on longer needle.

DEC RND 3 *K2tog, p2, k1tbl, p1; rep from * to last 6 sts, [k2tog tbl, p1] 2 times—119 (129, 149, 159, 169, 179) sts rem.

Work 6 (8, 10, 10, 10, 10) rnds even.

DEC RND 4 *K1tbl, p1, k2tog, p1; rep from * to last 4 sts, [k1tbl, p1] 2 times—96 (104, 120, 128, 136, 144) sts rem.

SIZES 40½ (44½, 48½, 52½)" ONLY
Work 6 rnds even—yoke measures 6¾ (7, 7½, 8¼)" (17 [18, 19, 21] cm). BO all sts.

SIZES (56½, 60½)" ONLY
Work 4 rnds even.

DEC RND 5 *K1tbl, p3tog, [k1tbl, p1] (15, 7) times; rep from *—128 sts rem for both sizes.

Work 6 rnds even—yoke measures (8¾, 9¼)" ([22, 23.5] cm). BO all sts.

finishing

With yarn threaded on a tapestry needle, sew sleeve and side seams. Use the Kitchener st (see Glossary) to graft underarm sts. Weave in loose ends. Block lightly.

passyunk pullover

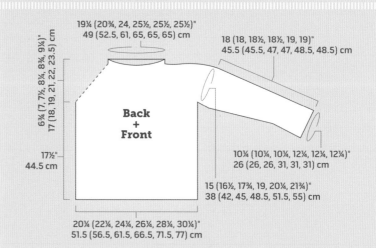

19¼ (20¾, 24, 25½, 25½, 25½)"
49 (52.5, 61, 65, 65, 65) cm

18 (18, 18½, 18½, 19, 19)"
45.5 (45.5, 47, 47, 48.5, 48.5) cm

6¾ (7, 7½, 8¼, 8¾, 9¼)"
17 (18, 19, 21, 22, 23.5) cm

Back + Front

17½"
44.5 cm

10¼ (10¼, 10¼, 12¼, 12¼, 12¼)"
26 (26, 26, 31, 31, 31) cm

15 (16½, 17¾, 19, 20¼, 21¾)"
38 (42, 45, 48.5, 51.5, 55) cm

20¼ (22¼, 24¼, 26¼, 28¼, 30¼)"
51.5 (56.5, 61.5, 66.5, 71.5, 77) cm

knit on RS; purl on WS

purl on RS; knit on WS

k1tbl on RS; p1tbl on WS

yo

k2tog

ssk (see Glossary)

sl 1, k2tog, psso

sl 2, k1, p2sso

work [p1, yo, p1] all in same st

k3 on RS; p3 on WS

SLEEVE

95
93
91
89
87
85 — rep to end
83
81
79
77
75
73
71
69
67
65
63
61
59
57
55
53
51
49
47
45
43
41
39
37
35
33
31
29
27
25
11
9
7 — work 2 times
5
3
1

set-up

beg
52½", 56½",
60½"

beg
40½", 44½",
48½"

center st

end
40½", 44½",
48½"

end
52½", 56½",
60½"

barton cardigan

DESIGNED BY **MARLAINA BIRD**

This intricately patterned cardigan features bottom-up seamless yoke construction, cropped sleeves, and a high closure that allows for movement (and some size variation) at the hips and belly. This sweater is worked in the round with a steek for the front opening so that the knit side is always facing you as you work. In-pattern gussets are used to shape the A-line lower body; the yoke shaping maintains the long vertical lines of the cable pattern. At the back, soft gathers let the fabric fall away from the yoke in a graceful line.

FINISHED SIZE
About 35¾ (38½, 41¼, 46¾, 49½, 52¼, 55)"
(91 [98, 105, 118.5, 125.5, 132.5, 139.5] cm) bust circumference, with fronts meeting in center. Sweater shown measures 49½" (125.5 cm).

YARN
DK weight (#3 Light).

Shown here: Bijou Basin Ranch Bijou Spun Bijou Bliss (50% yak, 50% cormo wool; 150 yd [137 m]/2 oz): natural brown, 10 (12, 12, 13, 15, 15, 16) hanks.

NEEDLES
Size U.S. 3 (3.25 mm): 16", 24", 32", and 47" (40 [60, 80, and 120] cm) circular (cir) and set of 5 double-pointed (dpn).

Adjust needle size if necessary to obtain the correct gauge.

NOTIONS
Cable needle (cn); markers (m); stitch holders; tapestry needle; sewing machine or sharp-point sewing needle with matching sewing thread for securing steek; three 2¼" (5.5 cm) pewter clasps.

GAUGE
32 stitches and 38 rounds = 4" (10 cm) in 22-st cable and lace pattern from Rnds 1–12 of Bust chart, worked in rounds.

notes

+ The lower body and sleeves are worked separately in the round to the underarms, then joined for working the yoke in the round to the neck edge. The steeked center front opening is secured and cut during finishing.

+ The steek stitches are folded to the wrong side to form facings on each side of the front opening. The steek stitches do not count toward the finished measurements and are not shown on the schematic.

+ When increasing for the sleeve, if there are not enough stitches to work each yarnover with its companion decrease, work the stitches in stockinette instead. If there are not enough stitches to work a complete 6-stitch cable, substitute one of the smaller cables to fit the number of stitches available.

+ Review the schematic before knitting; pay special attention to yoke depth and upper sleeve circumferences for your chosen size.

+ If you need a deeper yoke, you can work Yoke chart Rounds 8–19 one additional time (at the beginning of the yoke) to add 1¼" (3.2 cm) in depth.

+ If you want to alter the sleeve circumference, you'll need to add or remove stitches in increments of 22 (the chart repeat), which equals about 3" (7.5) in width. The stitch count before the sleeve increase rounds are multiples of 22 stitches, then 22 stitches are added with the increase rounds, ending again with a multiple of 22 stitches for all sizes. In order to work the yoke in pattern, the ending sleeve stitch count (after 21 stitches are put on hold for underarm) needs to be a multiple of 22 stitches + 1. The amount of stitches remaining after the yoke shaping will change for your size if you change the stitch count. You will need to determine how this will affect the neck circumference and if you need to customize the yoke shaping.

body

With 32" (80 cm) cir needle, use the cable method (see Glossary) to CO 281 (299, 317, 353, 371, 389, 407) sts. Place marker (pm) and join for working in rnds, being careful not to twist sts. Establish steek sts and patt from Rnd 1 of Ribbing chart (see pages 135 to 138 for charts) as indicated for lower body as foll: K5 (steek sts; knit every rnd), pm, work 5 sts before pattern rep box once, work 18-st patt 14 (15, 16, 18, 19, 20, 21) times, work 14 sts after patt rep box once, pm, k5 (steek sts; knit every rnd). Rnd begs at center front in the middle of steek sts. Cont in patt until Rnds 1–4 have been worked a total of 6 times—24 rnds completed. Work Rnds 5 and 6 once, inc as shown in Rnd 6—26 rnds completed; 341 (363, 385, 429, 451, 473, 495) sts; piece measures 2½" (6.5 cm) from CO.

Hip-to-Waist Shaping

Work for your size as foll.

SIZES 35¾ (38½, 46¾, 49½, 55)" ONLY

Establish patts from Rnd 1 of charts as foll: K5; for Right Front chart, work 7 sts before patt rep box once, work 22-st patt 3 (3, 4, 4, 5) times, work 2 sts after patt rep box once; pm, work 27 sts of Gusset A chart, pm; for Back chart work 2 sts before patt rep box once, work 22-st patt 5 (6, 7, 8, 8) times, work 15 sts after patt rep box once; pm, work 27 sts of Gusset A chart, pm; for Left Front chart, work 2 sts before patt rep box once, work 22-st patt 3 (3, 4, 4, 5) times, work 7 sts after patt rep box once; k5.

Cont in chart patts until Rnd 72 of Gusset A chart is complete, ending with Rnd 12 of back and front charts—297 (319, 385, 407, 451) sts rem; 5 steek sts each end of rnd; 75 (75, 97, 97, 119) sts each front; 127 (149, 171, 193, 193) back sts; 5 sts each gusset section; piece measures about 10" (25.5 cm) from CO.

SIZES 41¼ (52¼)" ONLY

Establish patts from Rnd 1 of charts as foll: K5; for Right Front chart work 7 sts before patt rep box once, work 22-st patt 3 (4) times, work 9 sts after patt rep box once; pm, work 35 sts of Gusset B chart, pm; for Back chart work 9 sts before patt rep box once, work 22-st patt 5 (7) times, work 22 sts after patt rep box once; pm, work 35 sts of Gusset B chart, pm; for Left Front chart, work 9 sts before patt rep box once, work 22-st patt 3 (4) times, work 7 sts after patt rep box once; k5.

Cont in chart patts until Rnd 72 of Gusset B chart is complete, ending with Rnd 12 of back and front charts—341 (429) sts rem; 5 steek sts each end of rnd; 82 (104) sts each front; 141 (185) back sts; 13 sts each gusset section; piece measures about 10" (25.5 cm) from CO.

Waist to Underarms

NEXT RND K5, work Rnd 1 of Bust and Sleeves chart as indicated across center 287 (309, 331, 375, 397, 419, 441) sts, leaving m on each side of gusset sections in place, k5.

Work even in patt until 112 (118, 118, 124, 124, 124, 130) chart rnds have been completed above the ribbing, ending with Rnd 4 (10, 10, 4, 4, 4, 10) of Bust and Sleeves chart—piece measures about 14¼ (15, 15, 15½, 15½, 15½, 16¼)" (36 [38, 38, 39.5, 39.5, 39.5, 41.5] cm) from CO.

Divide for Front and Back

NEXT RND (Rnd 5 [11, 11, 5, 5, 5, 11] of chart) Work in patt to 9 (9, 5, 9, 9, 5, 9) sts after first gusset section, place 23 sts just worked on holder for right armhole (center gusset st is in center of held sts; sts on holder beg and end with p1), work in patt to 9 (9, 5, 9, 9, 5, 9) sts after second gusset section, place 23 sts just worked on holder for left armhole (sts on this holder are arranged same as first holder), work in patt to end—5 steek sts each end of rnd; 66 (66, 77, 88, 88, 99, 110) sts each front; 109 (131, 131, 153, 175, 175, 175) back sts.

For sizes 35¾", 38½", 46¾", 49½", and 55", which used 27-st Gusset A chart for waist shaping, there are 6 cable sts next to the armhole gaps for the back and both fronts. For sizes 41¼" and 52¼", which used 35-st Gusset B chart for waist shaping, there are 2 lace sts next to the armhole gaps for the back and both fronts. Do not break yarn. Leave body sts on needle and set aside.

sleeves

With dpn or shortest cir needle, use the cable method to CO 72

(90, 90, 90, 108, 108, 108) sts. Pm and join for working in rnds, being careful not to twist sts. Establish patt from Rnd 1 of Ribbing chart as indicated for your size as foll: Work 4 (4, 13, 4, 4, 13, 4) sts before patt rep box once, work 18-st patt 3 (4, 4, 4, 5, 5, 5) times, work 14 (14, 5, 14, 14, 5, 14) sts after patt rep box once.

Cont in patt until Rnds 1–4 have been worked a total of 6 times—24 rnds completed. Work Rnds 5 and 6 once, inc as shown in Rnd 6—26 rnds completed; 88 (110, 110, 110, 132, 132, 132) sts; piece measures 2½" (6.5 cm) from CO.

Establish patt from Rnd 1 of Bust and Sleeves chart as indicated for your size as foll: Work 6 (6, 17, 6, 6, 17, 6) sts before pattern rep box once, work 22-st patt 3 (4, 4, 4, 5, 5, 5) times, work 16 (16, 5, 16, 16, 5, 16) sts after patt rep box once.

Work 14 more rnds even in patt, ending with Rnd 3 of chart.

NEXT RND Work in patt to last st, pm, M1P (see Glossary), p1, M1P—2 sts inc'd; 3 sts between m at end of rnd.

Working 3 sts between m at end of rnd as p3, work 5 rnds even in patt.

INC RND Work in patt to m, sl m, M1P, work in patt to end, M1P—2 sts inc'd between m at end of rnd.

NOTE *For the foll incs, keep the center st of the marked section as p1 and work*

barton cardigan

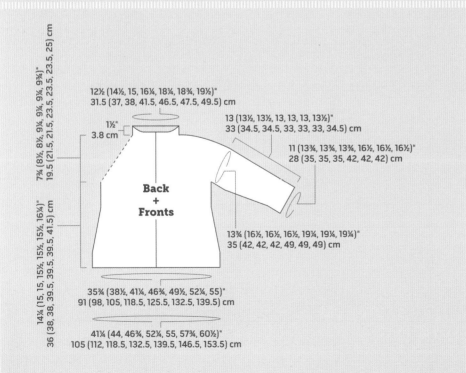

7¾ (8½, 8½, 9¼, 9¼, 9¼, 9¾)"
19.5 (21.5, 21.5, 23.5, 23.5, 23.5, 25) cm

12½ (14½, 15, 16¼, 18¼, 18¾, 19½)"
31.5 (37, 38, 41.5, 46.5, 47.5, 49.5) cm

1½"
3.8 cm

13 (13½, 13½, 13, 13, 13, 13½)"
33 (34.5, 34.5, 33, 33, 33, 34.5) cm

11 (13¾, 13¾, 13¾, 16½, 16½, 16½)"
28 (35, 35, 35, 42, 42, 42) cm

Back + Fronts

14¼ (15, 15, 15½, 15½, 15½, 16¼)"
36 (38, 38, 39.5, 39.5, 39.5, 41.5) cm

13¾ (16½, 16½, 16½, 19¼, 19¼, 19¼)"
35 (42, 42, 42, 49, 49, 49) cm

35¾ (38½, 41¼, 46¾, 49½, 52¼, 55)"
91 (98, 105, 118.5, 125.5, 132.5, 139.5) cm

41¼ (44, 46¾, 52¼, 55, 57¾, 60½)"
105 (112, 118.5, 132.5, 139.5, 146.5, 153.5) cm

new sts into patt (see Notes) on each side of center p1 st.

[Work 5 rnds even, then rep inc rnd] 9 times, changing to next-longest cir needle if necessary—110 (132, 132, 132, 154, 154, 154) sts total; 23 sts between m at end of rnd; piece measures about 10½" (26.5 cm) from CO. Leaving m in place, work even in patt until 100 (106, 106, 100, 100, 100, 106) chart rnds have been completed above the ribbing, ending with Rnd 4 (10, 10, 4, 4, 4, 10) of chart to end with same rnd as lower body before the dividing rnd—piece measures about 13 (13½, 13½, 13, 13, 13, 13½)" (33 [34.5, 34.5, 33, 33, 33, 34.5] cm) from CO.

NEXT RND (Rnd 5 [11, 11, 5, 5, 5, 11] of chart) Work in patt to last 23 sts, remove m, p1, work center 21 sts of marked section and place sts just worked on holder for underarm, p1, remove end-of-rnd m, transfer p1 on right needle after held sts to left needle, break yarn—89 (111, 111, 111, 133, 133, 133) sleeve sts rem.

Sleeve sts for all sizes have p1 next to underarm gap. Sizes 35¾", 38½", 46¾", 49½", and 55" have 6 cable sts next to the p1 at each side. Sizes 41¼" and 52¼" have 2 lace sts next to the p1 at each side. Place sts on spare cir needle and set aside. Make a second sleeve the same as the first.

yoke

Place all sts on longest cir needle with RS facing in this order: 5

steek sts, 66 (66 (77, 88, 88, 99, 110) right front sts, 89 (111, 111, 111, 133, 133, 133) right sleeve sts, 109 (131, 131, 153, 175, 175, 175) back sts, 89 (111, 111, 111, 133, 133, 133) left sleeve sts, 66 (66 (77, 88, 88, 99, 110) left front sts, 5 steek sts—429 (495, 517, 561, 627, 649, 671) sts total.

SIZES 35¾ (46¾, 49½, 52¼)" ONLY
JOINING RND K5, work Rnd 7 of Yoke chart over center 419 (551, 617, 639) sts, k5.

SIZES 38½ (41¼, 55)" ONLY
JOINING RND K5, work Rnd 1 of Yoke chart over center 485 (507, 661) sts, k5.

Cont steek sts as established, work Rnds 2–7 of chart.

□	knit
·	purl
○	yo
╱	k2tog
╲	ssk (see Glossary)
⟍	p2tog
⟍	ssp (see Glossary)
⟋	k3tog
⟍	sssk (see Glossary)
▨	no stitch
□	pattern repeat
⤵	k1f&b (see Glossary)

sl 1 st onto cn and hold in back, k1, k1 from cn

sl 1 st onto cn and hold in front, k1, k1 from cn

sl 2 sts onto cn and hold in back, k1, k2 from cn

sl 1 st onto cn and hold in front, k2, k1 from cn

sl 2 sts onto cn and hold in back, k2, k2 from cn

sl 2 sts onto cn and hold in front, k2, k2 from cn

sl 2 sts onto cn and hold in back, k3, k2 from cn

sl 3 sts onto cn and hold in front, k2, k3 from cn

sl 3 sts onto cn and hold in back, k3, k3 from cn

sl 3 sts onto cn and hold in front, k3, k3 from cn

sl 2 sts onto cn and hold in front or back alternately, k2, k2 from cn (see directions)

sl 3 sts onto cn and hold in front or back alternately, k3, k3 from cn (see directions)

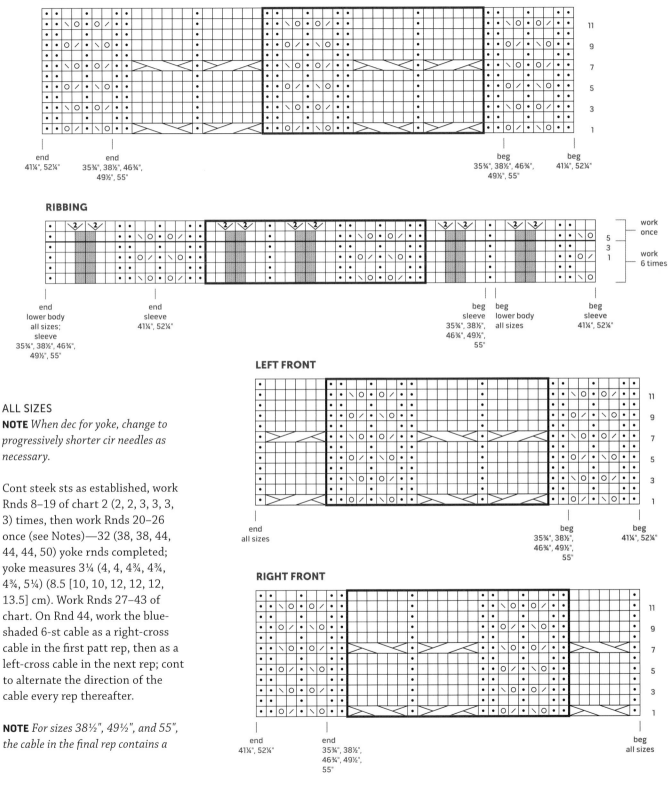

BACK

end
41¼", 52¼"

end
35¾", 38½", 46¾",
49½", 55"

beg
35¾", 38½", 46¾",
49½", 55"

beg
41¼", 52¼"

RIBBING

work
once

work
6 times

end
lower body
all sizes;
sleeve
35¾", 38½", 46¾",
49½", 55"

end
sleeve
41¼", 52¼"

beg
sleeve
35¾", 38½",
46¾", 49½",
55"

beg
lower body
all sizes

beg
sleeve
41¼", 52¼"

ALL SIZES

NOTE *When dec for yoke, change to progressively shorter cir needles as necessary.*

Cont steek sts as established, work Rnds 8–19 of chart 2 (2, 2, 3, 3, 3, 3) times, then work Rnds 20–26 once (see Notes)—32 (38, 38, 44, 44, 44, 50) yoke rnds completed; yoke measures 3¼ (4, 4, 4¾, 4¾, 4¾, 5¼) (8.5 [10, 10, 12, 12, 12, 13.5] cm). Work Rnds 27–43 of chart. On Rnd 44, work the blue-shaded 6-st cable as a right-cross cable in the first patt rep, then as a left-cross cable in the next rep; cont to alternate the direction of the cable every rep thereafter.

NOTE *For sizes 38½", 49½", and 55", the cable in the final rep contains a*

LEFT FRONT

end
all sizes

beg
35¾", 38½",
46¾", 49½",
55"

beg
41¼", 52¼"

RIGHT FRONT

end
41¼", 52¼"

end
35¾", 38½",
46¾", 49½",
55"

beg
all sizes

GUSSET A

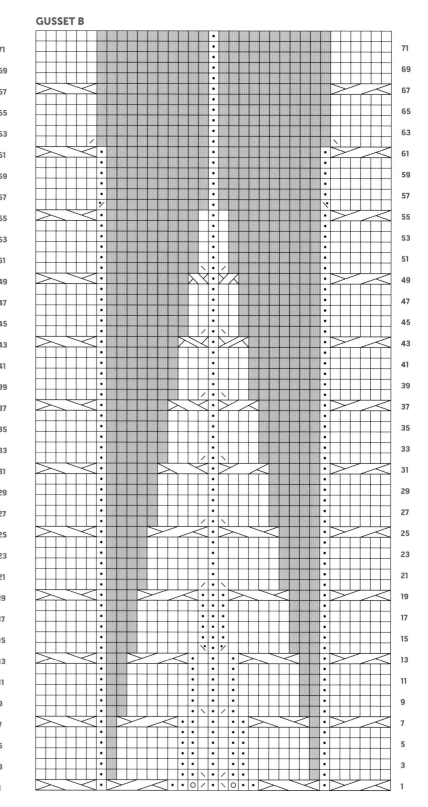

GUSSET B

BUST AND SLEEVES

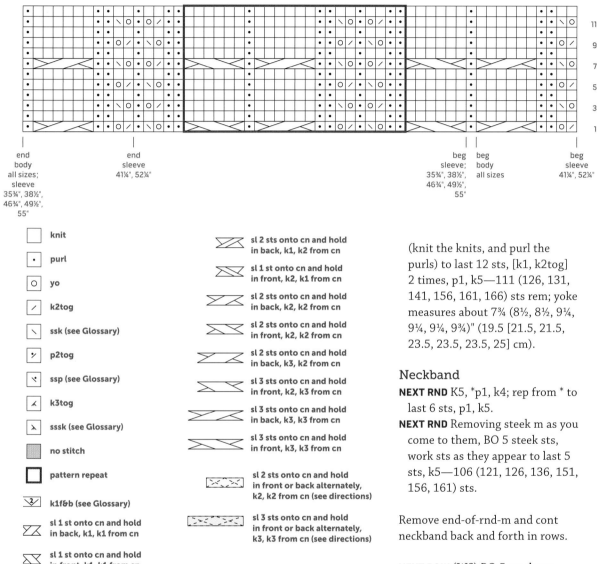

end
body
all sizes;
sleeve
35¾, 38½,
46¾, 49½,
55"

end
sleeve
41¼, 52¼"

beg
sleeve;
35¾, 38½,
46¾, 49½,
55"

beg
body
all sizes

beg
sleeve
41¼, 52¼"

☐	knit
•	purl
○	yo
╱	k2tog
╲	ssk (see Glossary)
╱•	p2tog
╲•	ssp (see Glossary)
╱	k3tog
╲	sssk (see Glossary)
▨	no stitch
☐	pattern repeat
▽	k1f&b (see Glossary)
⧄	sl 1 st onto cn and hold in back, k1, k1 from cn
⧅	sl 1 st onto cn and hold in front, k1, k1 from cn

⧄	sl 2 sts onto cn and hold in back, k1, k2 from cn
⧅	sl 1 st onto cn and hold in front, k2, k1 from cn
⧄	sl 2 sts onto cn and hold in back, k2, k2 from cn
⧅	sl 2 sts onto cn and hold in front, k2, k2 from cn
⧄	sl 2 sts onto cn and hold in back, k3, k2 from cn
⧅	sl 3 sts onto cn and hold in front, k2, k3 from cn
⧄	sl 3 sts onto cn and hold in back, k3, k3 from cn
⧅	sl 3 sts onto cn and hold in front, k3, k3 from cn
⧈	sl 2 sts onto cn and hold in front or back alternately, k2, k2 from cn (see directions)
⧈	sl 3 sts onto cn and hold in front or back alternately, k3, k3 from cn (see directions)

right-cross cable, which is followed by the right-cross cable for the left front edge at end of patt; for all other sizes, the cables alternate right- and left-cross all the way around.

Cont in patt until Rnd 61 has been completed, crossing each blue-shaded cable in Rnds 50 and 56 in the same direction as the cable below it from Rnd 44. Work Rnds 62–68 of chart, crossing each gold-shaded 4-st cable in the same direction as the 6-cables below it—115 (130, 135, 145, 160, 165, 170) sts rem.

NEXT RND K5, p1, [k1, k2tog] 2 times, work sts as they appear (knit the knits, and purl the purls) to last 12 sts, [k1, k2tog] 2 times, p1, k5—111 (126, 131, 141, 156, 161, 166) sts rem; yoke measures about 7¾ (8½, 8½, 9¼, 9¼, 9¼, 9¾)" (19.5 [21.5, 21.5, 23.5, 23.5, 23.5, 25] cm).

Neckband

NEXT RND K5, *p1, k4; rep from * to last 6 sts, p1, k5.

NEXT RND Removing steek m as you come to them, BO 5 steek sts, work sts as they appear to last 5 sts, k5—106 (121, 126, 136, 151, 156, 161) sts.

Remove end-of-rnd-m and cont neckband back and forth in rows.

NEXT ROW (WS) BO 5 steek sts, work in established rib to end—101 (116, 121, 131, 146, 151, 156) sts rem.

Work short-rows (see Glossary) to raise back neck as foll:

SHORT-ROWS 1 (RS) AND 2 (WS)
Work in established rib to last 16 (17, 18, 19, 21, 23, 26) sts, wrap next st, turn.

YOKE

*68
67
65
63
*62
61
59
57
*56
55
53
51
*50
49
47
45
*44
43
41
39
37
35
33
31
29
27
25
23
21
19
17
15
13
11
9
7 ← beg
35¾", 46¾",
49", 52¼"
5
3
1 ← beg
38", 41¼",
55"

*See instructions.

SHORT-ROWS 3–8 Work in patt to 4 sts before previously wrapped st, wrap next st, turn—4 wrapped sts at each side.

SHORT-ROWS 9 AND 10 Work in patt to end, working wraps tog with wrapped sts as you come to them.

BO all sts in patt—neckband measures 1½" (3.8 cm) high at center back neck and ½" (1.3 cm) at front edges.

BO all sts in patt.

finishing
Sew and Cut Steeks

Identify the 2 sts in the center of the 10-st steek. With sewing machine or by hand, sew a line of small straight stitches on each side of these center 2 sts. Sew 2 more lines of straight stitches, each 1 steek st farther out from center than the first 2 stitching lines. Carefully cut open the steek between the 2 center sts. Fold each steek to the WS along the 1-st purl column between the steek and front edge cable to form a facing. With yarn threaded on a tapestry needle, use a whipstitch (see Glossary) to sew facings invisibly to WS of front.

With yarn threaded on a tapestry needle, use the Kitchener St (see Glossary) to graft 23 held body sts and 21 held sleeve sts tog at each underarm, matching purl sts at center of each group, and grafting 2-for-1 to ease in extra body sts. Weave in loose ends. Block to measurements.

Sew clasps to fronts; for the garment shown the clasps are placed 1½", 3½", and 5½" (3.2, 9, and 14 cm) below the first neckband rnd.

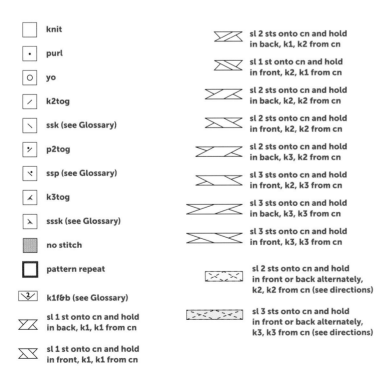

□	knit
•	purl
○	yo
╱	k2tog
╲	ssk (see Glossary)
⟍	p2tog
⟍	ssp (see Glossary)
⟋	k3tog
⟋	sssk (see Glossary)
▨	no stitch
□	pattern repeat
⊻	k1f&b (see Glossary)

sl 1 st onto cn and hold in back, k1, k1 from cn

sl 1 st onto cn and hold in front, k1, k1 from cn

sl 2 sts onto cn and hold in back, k1, k2 from cn

sl 1 st onto cn and hold in front, k2, k1 from cn

sl 2 sts onto cn and hold in back, k2, k2 from cn

sl 2 sts onto cn and hold in front, k2, k2 from cn

sl 2 sts onto cn and hold in back, k3, k2 from cn

sl 3 sts onto cn and hold in front, k2, k3 from cn

sl 3 sts onto cn and hold in back, k3, k3 from cn

sl 3 sts onto cn and hold in front, k3, k3 from cn

sl 2 sts onto cn and hold in front or back alternately, k2, k2 from cn (see directions)

sl 3 sts onto cn and hold in front or back alternately, k3, k3 from cn (see directions)

the dolman
sweater

In a dolman sweater, the sleeve is worked as a seamless extension of the body. The term is used to cover a diverse group of construction styles that can differ drastically from one another. The only common element is that the sleeve is always worked as a continuation of the body.

Dolman sweaters can be used to great effect for plus-size women because the construction creates a roomy fit in the upper body. If this volume is combined with drape-rich fibers, flowing and elegant silhouettes result that cover contours beautifully.

who should wear the dolman style?

Just like a drop-shoulder sweater, anyone can wear a dolman. It typically has a loose fit with a sophisticated style that is attractive on women of all ages. Dolmans have a dramatic goddess aesthetic that is commonly used in commercial plus-size clothing. However, the more fitted dolmans or styles with cropped body lengths may not be as universally wearable—know what shapes look good on you before you begin knitting. And choose yarns carefully—all the dolmans in this book are made with fibers that drape.

All that being said, just because a sweater falls into the broad category of dolman construction, it does not have to have a drapy, robe-like look. A heavily cabled wool sweater with dolman sleeves can be quite attractive. But for plus-size women, especially those on the larger end of the spectrum, the flowy dolman offers a truly wearable silhouette with many possible variations.

dolman construction

Dolmans can be worked side to side, such as the Delsea Pullover on page 146, or they can be worked from the bottom up. In either case, the sleeves are worked as extensions at each edge of the body to create a "T" shape. In general, dolmans are recognizable for their winged kimono-type sleeves and T shape. But the one truism about dolmans is this—there is no standard! Consider the many varieties shown on the following pages.

Because there is a seamless join between the body and sleeve, there isn't an opportunity to tweak the fit between the two. The top of the sleeve circumference is exactly the same as the armhole circumference, which means the depth of the armhole represents half the sleeve circumference at the upper arm, and vice versa. If you have large upper arms, you need a deep armhole in a dolman and therefore a deep yoke. If you have thin upper arms but a large bust, or if you are very tall, your need for a deep armhole will force the sleeve to be relatively wide—something you may not want. Most designers use the dolman style for its tendency to create oversized silhouettes—it's a deliberate aesthetic, so there's no need to worry about these picky fit issues.

notable effects
of seamless yoke construction

+ There is less definition and structure in the upper body of a dolman compared to sweaters that have seams or seamlines.

+ The armhole circumference is the same as the sleeve circumference.

+ The armhole depth is half of the sleeve circumference.

+ There is no underarm span.

+ In more fitted styles, the lack of an underarm span can lead to bunching at the armpit.

+ There is no defined cross-back or shoulder width; you can estimate it by subtracting the sleeve length from the body width.

+ Because there is no armhole shaping to narrow the cross-back, the body will overhang the shoulder similar to a drop-shoulder; the larger the sweater size, the wider the overhang.

+ In dolmans knitted from side to side, the knitting drapes differently (or doesn't drape at all) than in those knitted from bottom up.

+ In bottom-up dolmans, the sleeve stitches run counter to the traditional cuff-up orientation, which will affect stitch patterns, edging treatments, and other design elements.

+ If you select a size that fits your widest part (bust, belly, hip?), the rest of the sweater might end up too oversized.

For a simple bottom-up T-shape dolman, one long cast-on at each side accounts for all the sleeve stitches. In this style, the sleeve does not taper from upper arm to wrist.

For a side-to-side pullover, cast on stitches for the right cuff, work up the right sleeve, across the body, down the left sleeve, and bind off at the left cuff. The right sleeve can be shaped with increases; the left sleeve can be shaped with decreases.

Another fun option is to knit the sweater in a single piece by casting on at the back hem, working bottom-up with sleeve extensions at the sides, split for the neck, then work the front down to the hem. Seam the sides and sleeves, and it's done.

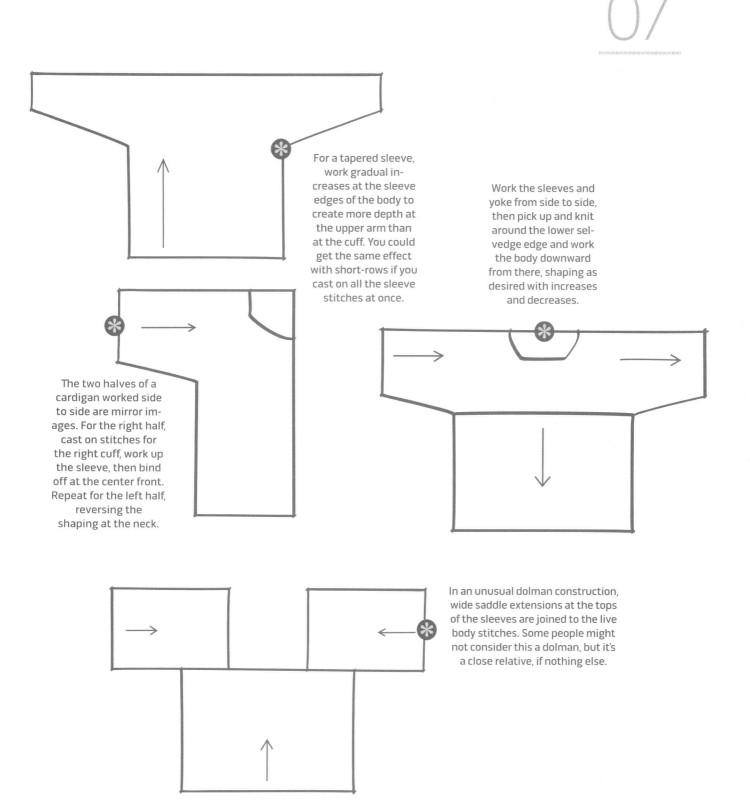

For a tapered sleeve, work gradual increases at the sleeve edges of the body to create more depth at the upper arm than at the cuff. You could get the same effect with short-rows if you cast on all the sleeve stitches at once.

Work the sleeves and yoke from side to side, then pick up and knit around the lower selvedge edge and work the body downward from there, shaping as desired with increases and decreases.

The two halves of a cardigan worked side to side are mirror images. For the right half, cast on stitches for the right cuff, work up the sleeve, then bind off at the center front. Repeat for the left half, reversing the shaping at the neck.

In an unusual dolman construction, wide saddle extensions at the tops of the sleeves are joined to the live body stitches. Some people might not consider this a dolman, but it's a close relative, if nothing else.

SEAGIRT PULLOVER [page 152]

The Sleeve

There is hardly a standard rule for dolman sleeve length. But you can think of the boxy cross-back and capless sleeve similar to that of a drop-shoulder. For a full-length dolman sleeve, aim for a total sleeve length of about 20" to 21" (51 to 53.5 cm).

The sleeves shown on pages 142 and 143 form a clean T-shaped extension of the body, created by casting on a lot of stitches at the beginning of a right-side row, then again at the beginning of the following wrong-side row. There will be some issues with a sleeve that is "shaped" into existence so dramatically. First, the cuff will be as wide as the upper arm. In addition, the 90-degree angle created at the intersection of the sleeve and body will not be maintained when the sweater is worn (unless you hold your arms out from your body in a T shape). Because there is no underarm span (which would notch out the horizontal space for the armhole), there will be some bunching in your armpit as the flat planes of front and back, including the sleeve, are forced around your three-dimensional body.

In a more gradually shaped dolman, the sleeve shaping begins well below the armpit, which creates a kind of webbed arm/body fabric that resembles a wing. The wing will bunch in a different way when your arms are down, but that bunching will occur in the excess fabric of the wing, rather than in your armpit. Drapey fibers and stitch patterns will alleviate the discomfort of all these effects, as will including positive ease to the body.

Side-to-Side Construction

Dolman shaping is particularly suited to side-to-side constructions. The edges of the body (the side seams) will consist of cast-on or bind-off stitches. If you want to avoid sewing seams, work provisional cast-ons that can be joined by grafting or a three-needle bind-off.

The three dolman patterns in this book are all pullovers, but dolman cardigans are also lovely. The Delsea Pullover from page 146 is worked in two mirror-image pieces, each knitted from cuff to midline of the body. The Seagirt and Missimer Pullovers (page 152 and 158, respectively) are both bottom-up T shapes, but each design uses different sleeve shaping: the Seagirt has shorter sleeves that are longer at the shoulder line than under the arm, and the Missimer features one drastic cast-on for each sleeve, with no sleeve taper.

If you do sew the side seams, use a horizontal mattress stitch (see Glossary), matching stitch for stitch along the seam.

Row gauge is important in side-to-side knits—it affects the width of the pieces, not the length as in top-down or bottom-up constructions. And width is of utmost concern for plus-size knitters. Stitch gauge is also very important—it affects the length of the pieces, and once you cast on, there's no adjusting for length. The stitch count along the cast-on edge determines the length from the get-go. So be sure to take accurate gauge measurements before you cast on.

In side-to-side knits, the sleeves can be worked in the round between the cuff and the body (the body can't be worked in the round because the hem and neck need to be open). The steps for shaping side-to-side sweaters are different than for shaping top-down or buttom-up sweaters. A dropped front neck is shaped with the addition and subtraction of rows instead of stitches. Technically, this is done by subtracting stitches at the neck end of rows to create the neck shape. Customizing body shaping is trickier to configure when the body is worked from side to side. To get a wider hip circumference, you'll need to work short-rows, working more rows at the hem edge than the shoulder edge. To make an hourglass shape, you'll need to work short-rows over the bust and hem so that fewer rows are worked over the yoke and waist. Configure this shaping by combining your row gauge and needed measurements and then consider the transition between the narrow and wide areas.

For a side-to-side dolman, you'll need to finish the selvedge edges (hem and neck) in some way. If you're working in stockinette stitch, pick up and knit a ribbed band along the bottom selvedge for a vertically oriented edging. Or, work a knitted-in band by working ribbing, garter stitch, or another non-curling stitch at the hem edge of rows.

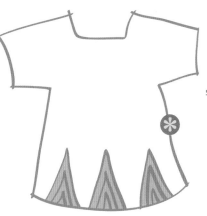

To achieve hourglass shaping in a side-to-side dolman, work short-row insertions at the bust and hips (hem).

To achieve hip shaping in a side-to-side dolman, work short-row wedges at the hem edge.

delsea pullover

DESIGNED BY **LISA SHROYER**

Worked from side to side in two pieces, this pullover lets a luxurious mohair/silk blend drape and cling. Each body half is worked from cuff to center body, then joined with a three-needle bind-off. Wide sleeves, a gently dropped front neck, and seeded rib edges frame large expanses of stockinette. The boxy silhouette is meant to be worn with a good amount of positive ease—err on the side of too-big when choosing a size. This pullover offers just one variant of the dolman-construction style. The standard dolman wing-shape sleeves in this version will help you evaluate how this construction type works for you (and see how fun it is to knit).

FINISHED SIZE
About 44 (48, 52, 56, 60, 64)" (112 [122, 132, 142, 152.5, 162.5] cm) bust circumference (to be worn with positive ease). Sweater shown measures 48" (122 cm).

YARN
Worsted weight (#4 Medium).

Shown here: Stacy Charles Collezione Tivoli (52% silk, 48% mohair; 108 yd [99 m]/50 g): #02 taupe, 10 (11, 12, 13, 13, 14) balls.

NEEDLES
Size U.S. 7 (4.5 mm): 16" and 32" (40 and 80 cm) or longer circular (cir), plus spare long cir needle for three-needle bind-off.

Adjust needle size if necessary to obtain the correct gauge.

NOTIONS
Waste yarn for stitch holders; markers (m); tapestry needle.

GAUGE
17 stitches and 22 rows or rnds = 4" (10 cm) in stockinette stitch.

notes

+ This sweater is worked in two halves, each beginning with the sleeve worked in the round to the start of the body. Then stitches are cast on at each end of the sleeve stitches for the lower body, which is worked back and forth in rows to the center of the body. The live stitches of each half are joined with a three-needle bind-off at center front and back.

+ Because the garment is worked in two pieces, the schematic reflects the measurements of just one finished half. The hip circumference will be the same as the listed finished bust measurement—to determine that from the schematic, multiply the hem width by four (times two to get the total front width, then times two again to get the full body circumference). The back neck width shown represents one-half of the total back neck; multiply this by two to calculate the total width for your size.

+ To determine the upper sleeve circumference, multiply the armhole depth by two.

+ Adjust the body circumference by working more or less length between the side seam provisional cast-ons and the center of the body. Take care to make the same adjustment on both halves. Every half an inch added or removed on each piece will increase or decrease the finished body circumference by about 2" (5 cm). For example, to make a 46" (117 cm) finished bust, follow the directions for size 44" (112 cm) and work 11½" (29 cm) between the sides and center body instead of 11" (28 cm) to add 2" (5 cm) to the finished size.

+ Because the body is worked from side to side, customized body shaping becomes tricky. To get a wider hip circum-ference, you would need to work short-rows at each end of the body sections to create more rows at the hem edge than at the shoulder line. For an hourglass waist, you would need to work short-rows over the bust and hem edge, without adding any extra rows at the waist and shoulder line.

+ If you need greater width at the hip but don't want to work short-rows, shorten the overall body length so that the hem doesn't fall to the widest point of your hips. Reduce the number of stitches in the provisional cast-on at each side of the body, making the same adjustment on both halves. Every 4 stitches removed at each side will shorten the body by about 1" (2.5 cm).

+ The sleeves are the same length for all sizes. As the body sections become wider, the cuff-to-cuff "wingspan" auto-matically becomes longer without the need to increase the sleeve length. Depending on your body proportions, the sleeves may reach farther down your arms than they do on the arms of the model in the photograph. For a quick check on how the sleeves will fit you, add up the sleeve length, shoulder width, and half-neck measure-ments marked on the schematic for your size. Have a friend hold a fabric tape measure from the center of your back neck, over one shoulder, and down your arm, ending when she reaches the sum you just calculated. That is about where the cuff edge will hit your arm. If you want to tweak this point, you can shorten or lengthen the sleeves, recalculating the sleeve shaping to work within that length.

+ The lower edging is not shown on the schematic. It will add about ½" (1.3 cm) to the body length after finishing.

right half
Sleeve
With shorter cir needle, CO 66 (70, 74, 78, 82, 86) sts. Place marker (pm) and join for working in rnds, being careful not to twist sts.

RND 1 Knit.
RND 2 *K1, p1; rep from *.

Rep these 2 rnds 7 more times, then rep Rnd 1 once more—17 rnds total; piece measures about 2¼" (5.5 cm) from CO.

EYELET RND *K2, yo; rep from *—99 (105, 111, 117, 123, 129) sts.

Work 6 rnds even in St st (knit every rnd).

INC RND K1, M1 (see Glossary), knit to last st, M1, k1—2 sts inc'd.

Work 3 rnds even in St st. Rep the last 4 rnds 5 more times, then work the inc rnd once more—113 (119, 125, 131, 137, 143) sts. Work 5 rnds even—piece measures 9" (23 cm) from CO.

body
With waste yarn, longer cir needle, and new strand of working yarn, use the invisible-provisional method (see Glossary) to CO 50 (50, 50, 46, 44, 40) sts. With same working yarn, k113 (119, 125, 131, 137, 143) sleeve sts, join waste yarn at end of sleeve sts, and use the provisional method to CO 50 (50, 50, 46, 44, 40) more sts—213 (219, 225, 223, 225, 223) sts total.

NOTE *The provisional CO sts at beg of RS rows are the front; the new sts at end of RS rows are the back.*

Working back and forth in rows, work all sts in St st (knit RS rows; purl WS rows) until piece measures 4½ (4½, 5, 5½, 6½, 7)" (11.5 [11.5, 12.5, 14, 16.5, 18] cm) from provisional CO, ending with a WS row.

FRONT

K106 (109, 112, 111, 112, 111) for front, place 107 (110, 113, 112, 113, 112) back sts on waste yarn holder. Working on 106 (109, 112, 111, 112, 111) front sts only, purl 1 WS row.

NECK DEC ROW (RS) Knit to last 4 sts, k2tog, k2—1 st dec'd at neck edge. Cont in St st, rep the neck dec row on the next 8 RS rows—97 (100, 103, 102, 103, 102) sts rem. Work even in St st until front measures 11 (12, 13, 14, 15, 16)" (28 [30.5, 33, 35.5, 38, 40.5] cm) from provisional CO, ending with a WS row. Place sts on waste yarn holder.

BACK

Return 107 (110, 113, 112, 113, 112) held back sts to longer cir needle and rejoin yarn with RS facing. Work even in St st until back measures 11 (12, 13, 14, 15, 16)" (28 [30.5, 33, 35.5, 38, 40.5] cm) from provisional CO, ending with a WS row. Place sts on waste yarn holder.

left half

Sleeve and Body

Work as for right half until piece measures 4½ (4½, 5, 5½, 6½, 7)" (11.5 [11.5, 12.5, 14, 16.5, 18] cm) from provisional CO, ending with a WS row—213 (219, 225, 223, 225, 223) sts.

NOTE *The provisional CO sts at beg of RS rows are the back; the new sts at end of RS rows are the front.*

FRONT

K107 (110, 113, 112, 113, 112), then place sts just worked on holder for back; join new yarn and knit across 106 (109, 112, 111, 112, 111) sts of front. Working 106 (109, 112, 111, 112, 111) front sts only, purl 1 WS row.

NECK DEC ROW (RS) K2, ssk (see Glossary), knit to end—1 st dec'd for neck.

Cont in St st, rep the neck dec row on the next 8 RS rows—97 (100, 103, 102, 103, 102) sts rem. Work even in St st until piece measures 11 (12, 13, 14, 15, 16)" (28 [30.5, 33, 35.5, 38, 40.5] cm) from provisional CO, ending with a WS row. Place sts on waste yarn holder.

BACK

Return 107 (110, 113, 112, 113, 112) held back sts onto longer cir needle and rejoin yarn with WS facing. Work even in St st until back measures 11 (12, 13, 14,

delsea pullover

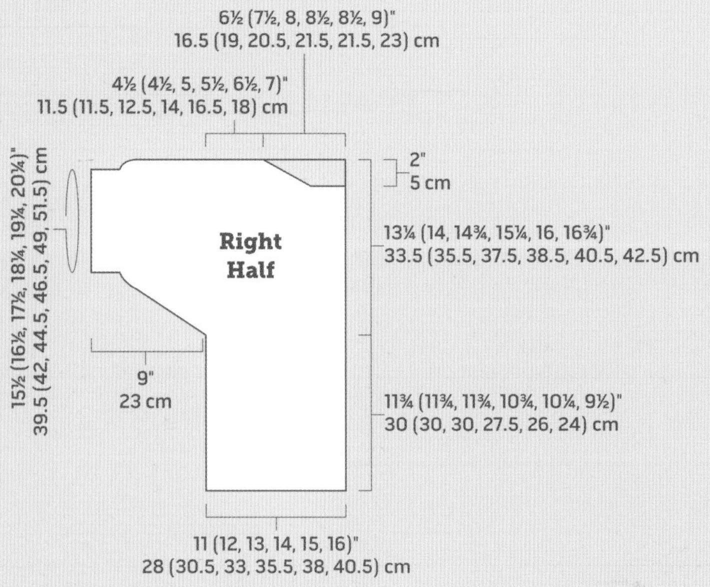
6½ (7½, 8, 8½, 8½, 9)"
16.5 (19, 20.5, 21.5, 21.5, 23) cm
4½ (4½, 5, 5½, 6½, 7)"
11.5 (11.5, 12.5, 14, 16.5, 18) cm
2"
5 cm
15½ (16½, 17½, 18¼, 19¼, 20¼)"
39.5 (42, 44.5, 46.5, 49, 51.5) cm
Right
Half
13¼ (14, 14¾, 15¼, 16, 16¾)"
33.5 (35.5, 37.5, 38.5, 40.5, 42.5) cm
9"
23 cm
11¾ (11¾, 11¾, 10¾, 10¼, 9½)"
30 (30, 30, 27.5, 26, 24) cm
11 (12, 13, 14, 15, 16)"
28 (30.5, 33, 35.5, 38, 40.5) cm

15, 16)" (28 [30.5, 33, 35.5, 38, 40.5] cm) from provisional CO, ending with a WS row. Leave sts on needle.

finishing

Place held back sts of right half on spare long cir needle. Hold pieces tog with RS touching and WS facing out, then use the three-needle method (see Glossary) to BO the right and left halves of the back tog. Place held sts of right and left fronts on two cir needles and hold pieces with RS tog, then use the three-needle method to BO the right and left halves of the front tog. Remove the waste yarn from the provisional CO at left front and carefully place the live sts on a cir needle. Place live sts from left back provisional CO on a second cir needle. With RS held tog, use the three-needle method to BO the sts tog for left side seam. Rep for right side seam.

Lower Edging

With longer cir needle, RS facing, and beg at one side seam, pick up and knit 180 (198, 214, 230, 246, 264) sts evenly spaced around lower body opening (about 3 sts for every 4 rows). Pm and join for working in rnds.

RND 1 *K1, p1; rep from *.
RND 2 Knit.

Rep these 2 rnds once more, then purl 4 rnds. BO all sts pwise—lower edging measures about ½" (1.3 cm) from pick-up rnd with BO edge rolled.

Neckband

With shorter cir needle, RS facing, and beg at center back seam, *pick up and knit 27 (31, 33, 35, 35, 37) sts to shoulder (about 3 sts for every 4 rows), pm, 1 st at side of neck, pm, 54 (62, 66, 70, 70, 74) sts across front neck, pm, 1 st at side of neck, pm, and 27 (31, 33, 35, 35, 37) sts to center back seam—110 (126, 134, 142, 142, 150) sts total. Pm and join for working in rnds.

NOTE *Although the front neck edge is longer than the back neck edge because of shaping, the same number of sts are picked up across both to draw in the neck edge and provide structure.*

RND 1 *K1, p1; rep from *.
RND 2 *Knit to 2 sts before marked st at side of neck, ssk, slip marker (sl m) k1, sl m, k2tog; rep from * once more, knit to end—4 sts dec'd.

Rep Rnds 1 and 2 once, then rep Rnd 1 once more. BO as foll: [K2tog] 2 times, BO 1 st, *k2tog (2 sts on right needle), BO 1 st; rep from * around until 1 st rem on right needle, fasten off last st.

Weave in loose ends, using yarn tails to close any holes at ends of three-needle bind-off seams. Lay sweater flat, spray liberally with water, and allow to air-dry. Turn sweater over and repeat on the other side, if needed.

seagirt pullover

DESIGNED BY **LOU SCHIELA**

A pretty twist-stitch pattern along the back and at the front neck of Lou Schiela's dolman tee provides simultaneous decoration and shaping. Decreases are incorporated into the pattern to produce an A-line shape that flatters full figures. The back and front are worked upward from the lower edges; stitches for the sleeves are cast-on at each side. The sleeves are gradually increased as the body is worked to the shoulder line, then the pieces are grafted together at the shoulders. This style works well for most plus-size women and offers an especially strong option for women in the largest sizes. Bamboo yarn keeps the fabric light and breathable.

FINISHED SIZE
About 37 (41, 45, 49, 53, 57, 61)" (94 [104, 114.5, 124.5, 134.5, 145, 155] cm) bust/chest circumference.

Sweater shown measures 45" (114.5 cm).

YARN
Sportweight (#2 Fine).

Shown here: SWTC Bamboo (100% bamboo; 250 yd [229 m]/100 g): #138 purplexed, 5 (5, 5, 6, 6, 7, 7) balls.

NEEDLES
Size U.S. 5 (3.75 mm): 24" (60 cm) circular.

Adjust needle size if necessary to obtain the correct gauge.

NOTIONS
Markers (m); waste yarn for stitch holders; row counter (optional); tapestry needle.

GAUGE
28 stitches and 34 rows = 4" (10 cm) in stockinette stitch.

stitch guide + notes

RIGHT TWIST (RT)
Insert right needle into second st on left needle as if to knit, yo and draw loop through without removing st from left needle, then insert right needle into first stitch on left needle as if to knit, yo and draw loop through, slip both stitches off left needle.

TWIST AND RIB
(multiple of 5 sts + 4)

ROW 1 (RS) *P1, RT, p1, k1; rep from * to last 4 sts, p1, RT, p1.

ROW 2 (WS) *K1, p2, k1, p1; rep from * to last 4 sts, k1, p2, k1.

Repeat Rows 1 and 2 for pattern.

+ A row counter is strongly recommended for keeping track of when to incorporate new stitches into the twist rib pattern.

+ During front neck shaping, if there are not enough stitches to work a complete two-stitch right twist, work the remaining stitch in stockinette.

+ The sleeves have the same circumference at cuff edge and upper arm. To determine this measurement, take the armhole depth for your size from the schematic and multiply this number by two—that is the sleeve circumference. If you find you need a larger sleeve, you will have to cast on for the sleeve extensions lower on the body than called for in the pattern. This will simultaneously create a deeper armhole and larger sleeve circumference.

+ The A-line shaping is achieved with decreases worked into the twist and rib pattern on both back and front. To eliminate the A-line shape, work the decreases in pattern as is, but work compensating increases at the side edges to keep the stitch count constant. If you do this, the stitch counts in the upper body will all change and you may want to cast on fewer stitches for the sleeves.

back

CO 140 (154, 168, 182, 196, 210, 224) sts. Do not join. Knit 11 rows, beg and ending with a WS row—piece measures about 1" (2.5 cm). Change to St st (knit RS rows; purl WS rows) and work even until piece measures 10 (10, 10½, 10½, 10, 10, 10)" (25.5 [25.5, 26.5, 26.5, 25.5, 25.5, 25.5] cm) from CO, ending with a RS row.

SET-UP ROW (WS) P68 (75, 82, 89, 96, 103, 110), [p2tog] 2 times, purl to end—138 (152, 166, 180, 194, 208, 222) sts rem.

ROW 1 (RS) K67 (74, 81, 88, 95, 102, 109), place marker (pm), p1, RT (see Stitch Guide), p1, pm, knit to end.

ROW 2 Purl to m, slip marker (sl m), k1, p2, k1, sl m, purl to end.

ROWS 3–15 Rep Rows 1 and 2 six more times, then work Row 1 once more.

ROW 16 Purl to 7 sts before m, pm, p1, [p2tog] 2 times, p2, remove m, k1, p2, k1, remove m, p2, [p2tog] 2 times, p1, pm, purl to end—134 (148, 162, 176, 190, 204, 218) sts rem; 14 center sts between m.

ROW 17 Knit to m, sl m, work Twist and Rib patt (see Stitch Guide) over center 14 sts, sl m, knit to end.

ROWS 18–35 Cont in patt, working sts on each side of center Twisted Rib sts in St st, ending with a RS row.

ROW 36 Purl to 7 sts before m, pm, p1, [p2tog] 2 times, p2, remove m, work in established patt to next m, remove m, p2, [p2tog] 2 times, p1, pm, purl to end—130 (144, 158, 172, 186, 200, 214)

sts rem; 24 center sts between m.

ROW 37 Knit to m, sl m, work Twist and Rib over marked center sts, sl m, knit to end.

ROWS 38–52 Work even in patt, ending with a RS row—piece measures 16¼ (16¼, 16¾, 16¾, 16¼, 16¼, 16¼)" (41.5 [41.5, 42.5, 42.5, 41.5, 41.5, 41.5] cm) from CO.

Sleeves

ROW 53 Use the cable method (see Glossary) to CO 33 sts at beg of

row, work new sts as p5, k28, then work in patt to end—163 (177, 191, 205, 219, 233, 247) sts.

ROW 54 Use the cable method to CO 33 sts at beg of row, work new sts as k5, p28, work in patt to last 5 sts, k5—196 (210, 224, 238, 252, 266, 280) sts.

ROW 55 P5, work in patt to last 5 sts, p5.

ROW 56 K5, purl to 7 sts before m, pm, p1, [p2tog] 2 times, p2, remove m, work in established

patt to next m, remove m, p2, [p2tog] 2 times, p1, pm, purl to last 5 sts, k5—192 (206, 220, 234, 248, 262, 276) sts rem; 34 center sts between m.

NOTE *Throughout the foll shaping, maintain 5 sts at each end of row in rev St st (purl on RS, knit on WS) for rolled sleeve edgings.*

Sleeve Shaping + Twist Rib Additions

NOTE *The sleeve increases are worked at the same time as new sts cont to be incorporated into the center Twist Rib patt; read all the way through the foll section before proceeding.*

For sleeve shaping, work 0 (2, 4, 6, 10, 10, 30) rows even.

SLEEVE INC ROW (RS): P5, k1, M1 (see Glossary), work in patt to last 6 sts, M1, k1, p5—2 sts inc'd.

Rep the inc row every 4 (6, 6, 8, 12, 12, 32) rows 20 (13, 12, 9, 6, 6, 2) more times, working new sts in St st—42 (28, 26, 20, 14, 14, 6) sts total added to sleeves; 21 (14, 13, 10, 7, 7, 3) sts added at each side.

At the same time for Twist Rib patt, work Rows 76 and 96 the same as Row 56, dec 4 sts in each row and adding 5 more sts to each

side of marked Twist Rib center section—226 (226, 238, 246, 254, 268, 274) sts after all shaping is complete; 54 center sts between m; 86 (86, 92, 96, 100, 107, 110) sts on each side of marked sts. Work even if necessary for your size until piece measures 10 (10, 10, 10, 11, 11, 12)" (25.5 [25.5, 25.5, 25.5, 28, 28, 30.5] cm) from sts CO for sleeves, ending with a WS row. Place sts on waste yarn holder.

front

Work as for back until Row 56 has been completed—192 (206, 220, 234, 248, 262, 276) sts; 34 center

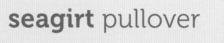

seagirt pullover

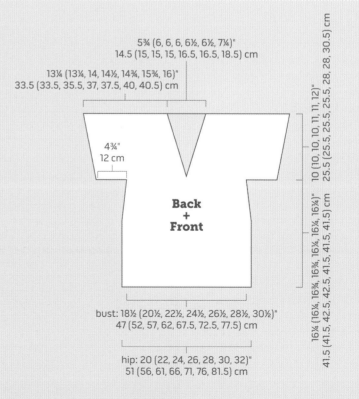

5¾ (6, 6, 6, 6½, 6½, 7¼)"
14.5 (15, 15, 15, 16.5, 16.5, 18.5) cm

13¼ (13¼, 14, 14½, 14¾, 15¾, 16)"
33.5 (33.5, 35.5, 37, 37.5, 40, 40.5) cm

4¾"
12 cm

Back + Front

10 (10, 10, 10, 11, 11, 12)"
25.5 (25.5, 25.5, 25.5, 28, 28, 30.5) cm

16¼ (16¼, 16¾, 16¾, 16¾, 16¼, 16¼)"
41.5 (41.5, 42.5, 42.5, 41.5, 41.5) cm

bust: 18½ (20½, 22½, 24½, 26½, 28½, 30½)"
47 (52, 57, 62, 67.5, 72.5, 77.5) cm

hip: 20 (22, 24, 26, 28, 30, 32)"
51 (56, 61, 66, 71, 76, 81.5) cm

sts between m; piece measures ¼" (6 mm) above sts CO for sleeves.

Neck and Sleeve Shaping + Twist Rib Additions

NEXT ROW (RS) P5, knit to m, sl m, work 14 sts in Twist Rib patt, ssk, k1, join second ball of yarn, k1, k2tog, work 14 sts in Twist Rib patt, sl m, knit to last 5 sts, p5—95 (102, 109, 116, 123, 130, 137) sts at each side; 16 marked sts at each neck edge.

NOTE *Work each side separately while working the sleeve increases and neck decreases and also while incorporating new sts at each side of Twist Rib patts; read all the way through the foll section before proceeding.*

For sleeve shaping, work 1 (1, 3, 5, 9, 9, 29) row(s) even, then inc 1 st at each sleeve edge as for back on the next RS row, then every 4 (6, 6, 8, 12, 12, 32) rows 20 (13, 12, 9, 6, 6, 2) more times, working new sts in St st—21 (14, 13, 10, 7, 7, 3) sleeve sts added at each side.

At the same time for Twist Rib patt work Rows 76 and 96 as foll: (WS) Work in patt to 7 sts before m, pm, p1, [p2tog] 2 times, p2, remove m, work in patt to right neck edge; at left neck edge work in patt to next m, remove m, p2, [p2tog] 2 times, p1, pm, work in patt to end—2 sts dec'd at each side and 5 patt sts added to each side in both rows.

Also at the same time, for neck shaping, dec 1 st at each neck edge every 4 rows 19 (20, 20, 20, 22, 22, 24) times (see Notes)—93 (92, 98, 102,

104, 111, 112) sts rem at each side after all shaping is complete; 7 (6, 6, 6, 4, 4, 2) patt sts at each neck edge.

Work even if necessary for your size until piece measures 10 (10, 10, 10, 11, 11, 12)" (25.5 [25.5, 25.5, 25.5, 28, 28, 30.5] cm) from sts CO for sleeves, ending with a WS row. Place 33 (33, 35, 36, 36, 36, 38) sts closest to each neck edge on waste yarn holder for shoulders, then place rem 60 (59, 63, 66, 68, 75, 74) sts at each side on separate holders for sleeves.

finishing

Block pieces to measurements. With yarn threaded on a tapestry needle, use the Kitchener st (see Glossary) to graft 60 (59, 63, 66, 68, 75, 74) sts at each side of front and back tog for sleeves. To prevent the shoulders from stretching, use the three-needle method (see Glossary) to BO 33 (33, 35, 36, 36, 36, 38) sts tog at each shoulder—40 (42, 42, 42, 46, 46, 50) center back neck sts rem on holder. With yarn threaded on a tapestry needle, sew side and sleeve seams.

Neck Edging

With RS facing and beginning at right shoulder join, pick up and work [k2tog] 20 (21, 21, 21, 23, 23, 25) times across held back neck sts, pick up and knit 40 (45, 45, 45, 47, 49, 49) sts along left neck edge, pm at base of V, pick up and knit 40 (45, 45, 45, 47, 49, 49) sts along right neck edge—100 (111, 111, 111, 117, 121, 123) sts. Do not

join. With WS facing, use the cable method to CO 5 sts at the end of the picked-up sts.

ROW 1 (WS) Sl 1 pwise with yarn in back (wyb), k3, k2tog (last edging tog with 1 st from neck edge), turn work—1 picked-up st joined.

ROW 2 Sl 1 pwise with yarn in front (wyf), p4.

Rep Rows 1 and 2 until 1 st rems before m at center front V.

SHAPE V

Work short-rows without wrapping any sts at the turning points as foll:

SHORT-ROW 1 (WS) Sl 1 pwise wyb, k3, k2tog, remove m, turn work.

SHORT-ROW 2 Sl 1 pwise wyf, p1, turn.

SHORT-ROW 3 Sl 1 pwise wyb, k2tog, turn.

SHORT-ROW 4 Sl 1 pwise wyf, k4.

SHORT-ROW 5 Sl 1 pwise wyb, k1, turn.

SHORT-ROW 6 Sl 1 pwise wyf, p1.

Resume working edging Rows 1 and 2 as before until all picked-up sts have been joined—5 edging sts rem. BO all sts. With yarn threaded on a tapestry needle, sew BO and CO ends of edging tog.

Weave in loose ends.

missimer pullover

DESIGNED BY **KATYA WILSHER**

The butterfly styling of this cropped dolman takes on an elegant dimension when combined with a shimmery linen-blend yarn and a large-scale lace pattern. By working the pattern as an allover tapestry, Katya Wilsher makes a cleaned-lined top that keeps the viewer's eye moving. She chose a simple boat-neck shape so that the pattern could flow uninterrupted from hem to neck with beautiful drape. Waist shaping is a nice option for the curvy woman, but, if you prefer a simple A-line silhouette, omit the waist reshaping and taper the garment gradually from the hip to the bust circumference.

FINISHED SIZE
About 39½ (43, 47, 51½, 55, 59, 63)" (100.5 [109, 119.5, 131, 139.5, 150, 160] cm) bust circumference. Top shown measures 43" (109 cm).

YARN
DK weight (#3 Fine).

Shown here: Louisa Harding Merletto (46% viscose, 34% polyamide, 20% linen; 98 yd [90 m]/50 g): #10 plum, 8 (9, 10, 11, 12, 13, 14) skeins.

NEEDLES
Size U.S. 6 (4 mm): 16" (40 cm) and 24" (60 cm) or longer circular (cir).

Adjust needle size if necessary to obtain the correct gauge.

NOTIONS
Markers (m); tapestry needle.

GAUGE
20 stitches and 31 rows = 4" (10 cm) in Lace pattern from chart; 7 sts of Slip-stitch Rib measure ½" (1.3 cm) wide.

stitch guide + notes

SLIP-STITCH RIB (worked over 7 sts)
ROW 1 (RS) [K1, sl 1 pwise with yarn in front (wyf)] 3 times, k1.
ROW 2 (WS) [Sl 1 pwise wyf, k1] 3 times, sl 1 pwise wyf.
Repeat Rows 1 and 2 for pattern.

+ This design is intended to be worn with positive ease.

+ When establishing the pattern for your size and when working shaping, make sure that each pattern decrease (ssk or k2tog) is accompanied by a corresponding yarnover (yo) increase and that each double decrease (sl 1, k2tog, psso) is accompanied by two yarnover increases. If there are not enough stitches to work the decreases with their companion yarnovers, work the stitches in stockinette instead.

+ In most cases the corresponding yarnovers are situated next to the decreases, but pay close attention on Rows 7, 9, 11, 13, 15, 25, 27, 29, 31, and 33 of the chart, where some yarnover/decrease pairs are separated by 3 stockinette stitches.

+ Because of the dolman construction, the cross-back width (the width of the body minus the sleeve extensions) of each size gets progressively wider, going up to 31" (78.5 cm) for the largest size. This may be a problem if you want to keep the sleeves fairly short—the potential overhang of the body fabric, added to the sleeve length, may cause the cuff edge to fall closer to your wrist. To get a rough idea of where the sleeve cuff will fall, add up the following from the schematic: half the back neck; the shoulder; and the sleeve length. This number is the measurement from the center back neck to the cuff. With a fabric tape measure, measure this length from the center back of your neck, over one shoulder, and down your arm—where it ends is roughly where the sleeve cuff would fall.

+ The sleeves are created by one drastic cast-on at each side of the body. To alter the sleeve length in any way, you need to rework the cast-on number. The sleeve stitches consist of 7 rib stitches (for an edging), then a set number of stitches in the lace pattern. You can work any of the sleeve lengths listed on the schematic—choose a length, then refer to that size's sleeve cast-on and chart starting and ending points.

back

With longer cir needle, CO 105 (113, 123, 135, 143, 153, 163) sts. Purl 1 WS row.

Establish patt from Row 1 of Lace chart (page 164) beg and ending where as indicated for your size as foll (see Notes): (RS) K1 (selvedge st), work 3 (19, 0, 6, 10, 3, 8) sts before patt rep once, work 24-st patt rep 4 (3, 5, 5, 5, 6, 6) times, work 4 (20, 1, 7, 11, 4, 9) sts after patt rep box once, k1 (selvedge st).

Working selvedge sts in St st (knit on RS rows; purl on WS rows), work in patt as established for 5 more rows, beg and ending with a WS row—piece measures about 1" (2.5 cm) from CO.

DEC ROW (RS) K1, ssk, work in patt to last 3 sts, k2tog, k1 (see Notes)—2 sts dec'd.

[Work 5 rows even in patt, then rep the dec row] 5 times—93 (101, 111, 123, 131, 141, 151) sts rem. Work 19 rows even, beg and ending with a WS row—piece measures 7½" (19 cm) from CO.

INC ROW (RS) K1, M1 (see Glossary), work in patt to last st, M1, k1—2 sts inc'd.

[Work 5 rows even in patt, then rep the inc row] 2 times, working new sts into chart patt—99 (107, 117, 129, 137, 147, 157) sts. Cont even in patt until piece measures 11½ (11½, 11½, 11½, 11¼, 10¾, 10¼)" (29 [29, 29, 29, 28.5, 27.5, 26] cm) from CO, ending with a RS row.

NOTE *The largest sizes have shorter lower bodies because they have deeper armholes.*

Shape Sleeves

NEXT ROW (WS) Purl to last st, (pm), p1, use the backward-loop method (see Glossary) to CO 39 (41, 41, 42, 44, 44, 44) sts for right back sleeve—138 (148, 158, 171, 181, 191, 201) sts.

NEXT ROW (RS) Knit across new CO sts to m, sl m, work in established patt to last st, pm, k1, use the backward-loop method to CO 39 (41, 41, 42, 44, 44, 44) sts for left back sleeve—177 (189, 199, 213, 225, 235, 245) sts total; 97 (105, 115, 127, 135, 145, 155) body sts between m; 40 (42, 42, 43, 45, 45, 45) sleeve sts outside m at each side.

NEXT ROW (WS) Sl 1 pwise wyf, purl to last st, sl 1 pwise wyf.

NEXT ROW (RS) Work Row 1 of slip-stitch rib (see Stitch Guide) over 7 sts, pm, beg and ending as indicated for your size (see Notes), work next row of chart patt over all 163 (175, 185, 199, 211, 221, 231) center sts (removing m between sleeve and body sts as you come to them), pm, work Row 1 of slip-stitch rib over last 7 sts.

Working 7 sts at each side in slip-stitch rib, cont in established patt until sleeves measure 8¾ (9, 9¼, 9½, 10, 10¾, 11¼)" (22 [23, 23.5, 24, 25.5, 27.5, 28.5] cm) from sleeve CO, ending with a WS row.

Shape Back Neck + Shoulders

NEXT ROW (RS) Work 68 (72, 76, 83, 88, 92, 97) sts in patt, join a second ball of yarn and BO center 41 (45, 47, 47, 49, 51, 51) sts, work in patt to end—68 (72, 76, 83, 88, 92, 97) sts rem each side.

NOTE *Neck and shoulder shaping are worked at the same time; read the foll section all the way through before proceeding.*

Working each side separately, at each neck edge BO 3 (3, 3, 4, 4, 4, 4) sts once, then BO 2 sts once. *At the same time* at each sleeve edge BO 21 (23, 23, 25, 28, 28, 31) sts once, then BO 21 (22, 24, 26, 27, 29, 30) sts 2 times—no sts rem.

missimer pullover

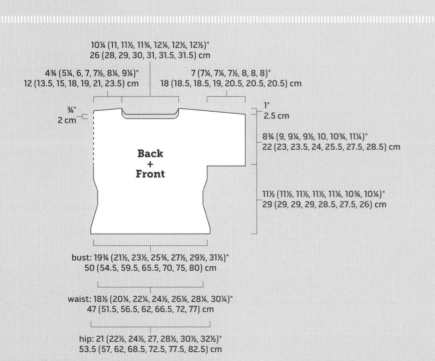

10¼ (11, 11½, 11¾, 12¼, 12½, 12½)"
26 (28, 29, 30, 31, 31.5, 31.5) cm

4¾ (5¼, 6, 7, 7½, 8¼, 9¼)"
12 (13.5, 15, 18, 19, 21, 23.5) cm

7 (7¼, 7¼, 7½, 8, 8, 8)"
18 (18.5, 18.5, 19, 20.5, 20.5, 20.5) cm

¾"
2 cm

1"
2.5 cm

8¾ (9, 9¼, 9½, 10, 10¾, 11¼)"
22 (23, 23.5, 24, 25.5, 27.5, 28.5) cm

Back + Front

11½ (11½, 11½, 11½, 11¼, 10¾, 10¼)"
29 (29, 29, 29, 28.5, 27.5, 26) cm

bust: 19¾ (21½, 23½, 25¾, 27½, 29½, 31½)"
50 (54.5, 59.5, 65.5, 70, 75, 80) cm

waist: 18½ (20¼, 22¼, 24½, 26¼, 28¼, 30¼)"
47 (51.5, 56.5, 62, 66.5, 72, 77) cm

hip: 21 (22½, 24½, 27, 28½, 30½, 32½)"
53.5 (57, 62, 68.5, 72.5, 77.5, 82.5) cm

LACE

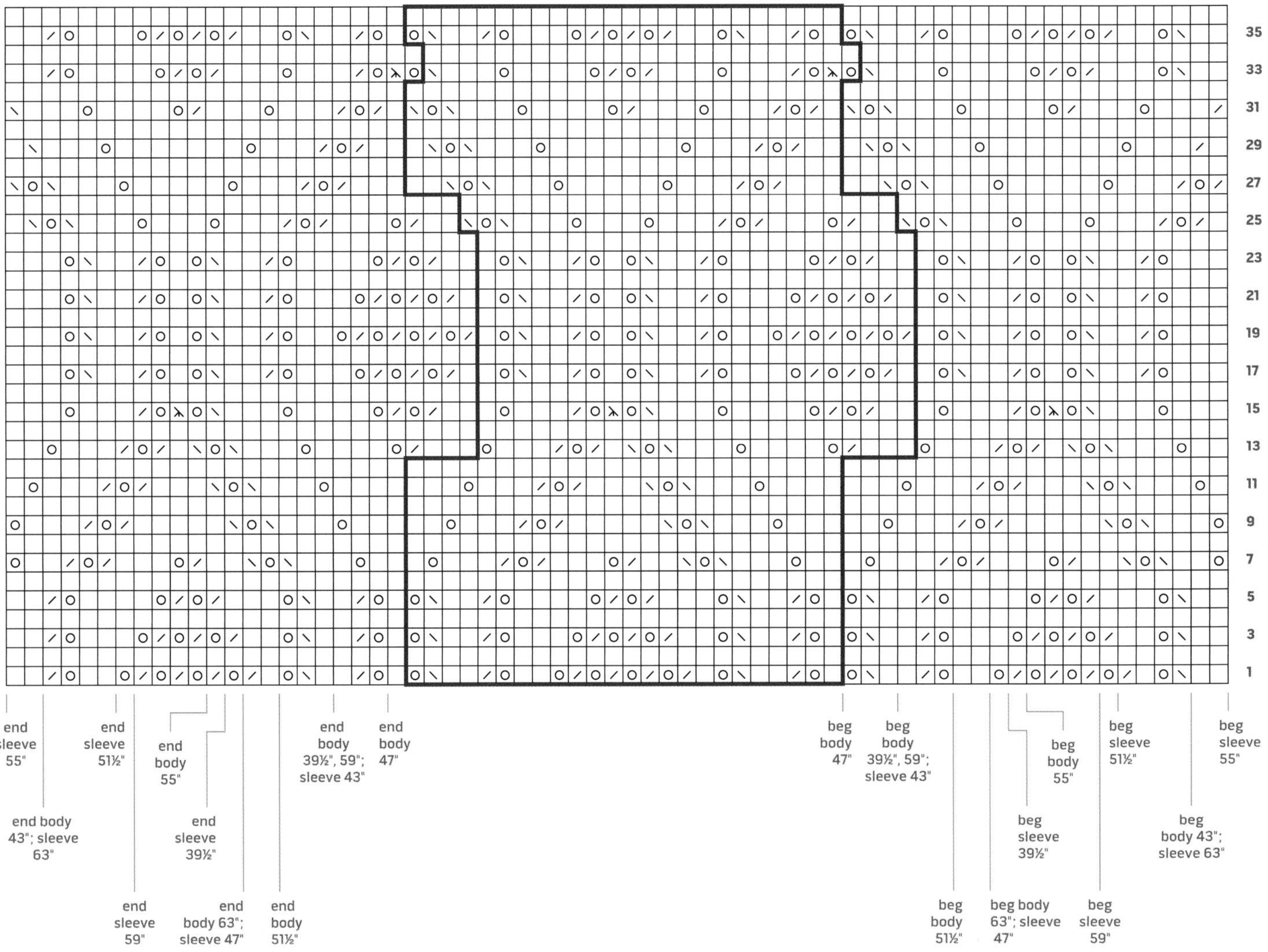
35
33
31
29
27
25
23
21
19
17
15
13
11
9
7
5
3
1
end sleeve 55"
end sleeve 51½"
end body 55"
end body 39½", 59"; sleeve 43"
end body 47"
end body 43"; sleeve 63"
end sleeve 39½"
end sleeve 59"
end body 63"; sleeve 47"
end body 51½"
beg body 47"
beg body 39½", 59"; sleeve 43"
beg body 55"
beg sleeve 51½"
beg sleeve 55"
beg sleeve 39½"
beg body 43"; sleeve 63"
beg body 51½"
beg body 63"; sleeve 47"
beg sleeve 59"

- ☐ **knit on RS; purl on WS**
- ○ **yo**
- ⁄ **k2tog**
- \ **ssk (see Glossary)**
- ⋏ **sl 1, k2tog, psso**
- ▢ **pattern repeat**

front

CO and work as for back until piece measures 8 (8¼, 8½, 8¾, 9¼, 10, 10½)" (20.5 [21, 21.5, 22, 23.5, 25.5, 26.5] cm) from sleeve CO, ending with a WS row—177 (189, 199, 213, 225, 235, 245) sts; 7 sts each side in rib patt; 163 (175, 185, 199, 211, 221, 231) center sts in lace patt.

Shape Front Neck

NEXT ROW (RS) Work 69 (73, 77, 84, 89, 93, 98) sts in patt, join a second ball of yarn and BO center 39 (43, 45, 45, 47, 49, 49) sts, work in patt to end—69 (73, 77, 84, 89, 93, 98) sts rem each side.

Working each side separately, at each neck edge BO 4 (4, 4, 5, 5, 5, 5) sts once, then BO 2 sts once—63 (67, 71, 77, 82, 86, 91) sts rem each side. Cont in established patt until sleeves measure 8¾ (9, 9¼, 9½, 10, 10¾, 11¼)" (22 [23, 23.5, 24, 25.5, 27.5, 28.5] cm) from sleeve CO, ending with a WS row.

Shape Shoulders

Working each side separately, at each sleeve edge BO 21 (23, 23, 25, 28, 28, 31) sts once, then BO 21 (22, 24, 26, 27, 29, 30) sts 2 times—no sts rem.

finishing

Block pieces to measurements. With yarn threaded on a tapestry needle, sew front to back along shoulder line.

Neckband

With shorter cir needle, RS facing, and beg at left shoulder seam pick up and knit 59 (63, 65, 67, 69, 71, 71) sts across front neck edge and 51 (55, 57, 59, 61, 63, 63) sts across back neck edge—110 (118, 122, 126, 130, 134, 134) sts total. Pm and join for working in rnds. Knit 1 rnd. BO all sts.

With yarn threaded on a tapestry needle, sew sleeve and side seams. Weave in loose ends. Block the neck opening. Block the body again, if desired.

abbreviations

beg(s)	begin(s); beginning
BO	bind off
CC	contrasting color
cm	centimeter(s)
cn	cable needle
CO	cast on
cont	continue(s); continuing
dec(s)	decrease(s); decreasing
dpn	double-pointed needles
foll	follow(s); following
g	gram(s)
inc(s)	increase(s); increasing
k	knit
k1f&b	knit into the front and back of same stitch
kwise	knitwise; as if to knit
m	marker(s)
MC	main color
mm	millimeter(s)
M1	make one (increase)
p	purl
p1f&b	purl into front and back of same stitch
patt(s)	pattern(s)
psso	pass slipped stitch over
pwise	purlwise; as if to purl
rem	remain(s); remaining
rep	repeat(s); repeating
rev St st	reverse stockinette stitch
rnd(s)	round(s)
RS	right side
sl	slip
sl st	slip st (slip 1 stitch purlwise unless otherwise indicated)
st(s)	stitch(es)
St st	stockinette stitch
tbl	through back loop
tog	together
WS	wrong side
wyb	with yarn in back
wyf	with yarn in front
yd	yard(s)
yo	yarnover
*****	repeat starting point
******	repeat all instructions between asterisks
( )	alternate measurements and/or instructions
[ ]	work instructions as a group a specified number of times

glossary

bind-offs

Sewn Bind-Off

Cut yarn four times the width or circumference of the knitting to be bound off and thread onto a tapestry needle. Working from right to left, *insert tapestry needle purlwise (from right to left) through the first two stitches **(figure 1)** and pull the yarn through. Bring tapestry needle knitwise (from left to right) through first stitch **(figure 2)**, pull the yarn through, and slip this stitch off the knitting needle. Repeat from * for desired number of stitches.

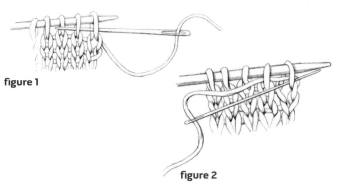

figure 1

figure 2

Three-Needle Bind-Off

Place the stitches to be joined onto two separate needles and hold the needles parallel so that the right sides of knitting face together. Insert a third needle into the first stitch on each of two needles **(figure 1)** and knit them together as one stitch **(figure 2)**, *knit the next stitch on each needle the same way, then use the left needle tip to lift the first stitch over the second and off the needle **(figure 3)**. Repeat from * until no stitches remain on first two needles. Cut yarn and pull tail through last stitch to secure.

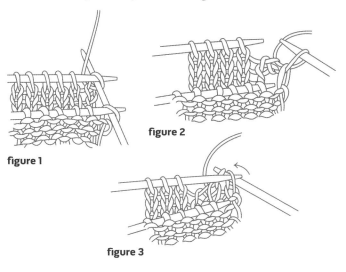

figure 1

figure 2

figure 3

Tubular Bind-Off

Cut the yarn three times the width or circumference of the knitting to be bound off and thread it onto a tapestry needle. Working from right to left, insert the tapestry needle purlwise (from right to left) through the first (knit) stitch **(figure 1)** and pull the yarn through. Then bring the tapestry needle behind the knit stitch (i.e., skip this stitch) and insert it knitwise (from left to right) into the second (purl) stitch **(figure 2)**, then pull the yarn through. *Slip the first knit stitch knitwise off the knitting needle, insert the tapestry needle purlwise into the next knit stitch **(figure 3)** and pull the yarn through. Slip the first stitch purlwise off the knitting needle, then bring the tapestry needle behind the knit stitch (i.e., skip this stitch), and insert it knitwise into the next purl stitch **(figure 4)**, and pull the yarn through. Repeat from * until one stitch remains on the knitting needle, insert the tapestry needle purlwise through the last stitch and pull tight to secure.

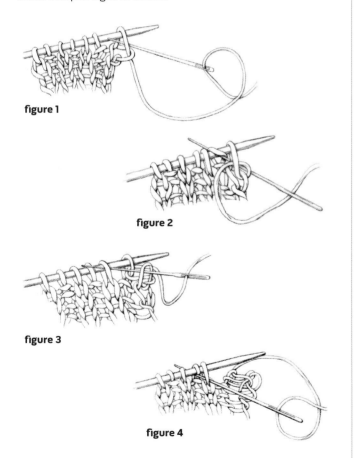

figure 1

figure 2

figure 3

figure 4

buttonholes
Three-Stitch One-Row Buttonhole

Bring the yarn to the front of the work, slip the next stitch purlwise, then return the yarn to the back. *Slip the next stitch, pass the second stitch over the slipped stitch **(figure 1)** and drop it off the needle. Repeat from * two more times. Slip the last stitch on the right needle to the left needle and turn the work around. Bring the working yarn to the back, [insert the right needle between the first and second stitches on the left needle **(figure 2)**, draw up a loop and place it on the left needle] four times. Turn the work around. With the yarn in back, slip the first stitch and pass the extra cast-on stitch over it **(figure 3)** and off the needle to complete the buttonhole.

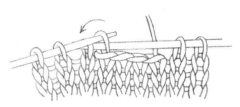

figure 1

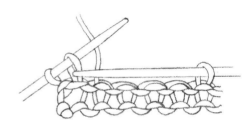

figure 2

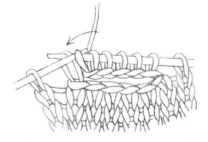

figure 3

glossary

cast-ons

Backward-Loop Cast-On
*Loop working yarn and place it on needle backward so that it doesn't unwind. Repeat from *.

Cable Cast-On
If there are no stitches on the needles, make a slipknot of working yarn and place it on the needle, then use the knitted method to cast-on one more stitch—two stitches on needle. Hold needle with working yarn in your left hand. *Insert right needle *between* the first two stitches on left needle **(figure 1)**, wrap yarn around needle as if to knit, draw yarn through **(figure 2)**, and place new loop on left needle **(figure 3)** to form a new stitch. Repeat from * for the desired number of stitches, always working between the last two stitches on the left needle.

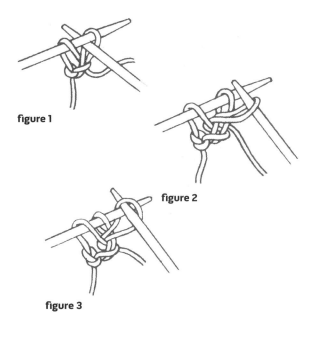

figure 1

figure 2

figure 3

Invisible Provisional Cast-On
Make a loose slipknot of working yarn and place it on the right needle. Hold a length of contrasting waste yarn next to the slipknot and around your left thumb; hold working yarn over your left index finger. *Bring the right needle forward, then under waste yarn, over working yarn, grab a loop of working yarn and bring it forward under working yarn **(figure 1)**, then bring needle back behind the working yarn and grab a second loop **(figure 2)**. Repeat from * for the desired number of stitches. When you're ready to work in the opposite direction, place the exposed loops on a knitting needle as you pull out the waste yarn.

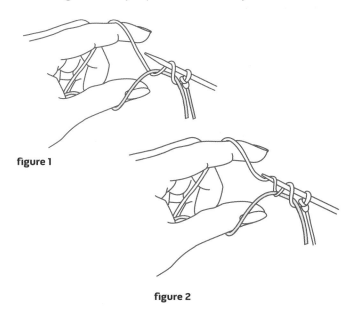

figure 1

figure 2

Knitted Cast-On
Make a slipknot and place it on the left needle if there are no stitches already there. *Use the right needle to knit the first stitch (or slipknot) on left needle **(figure 1)** and place new loop onto left needle to form a new stitch **(figure 2)**. Repeat from * for the desired number of stitches, always working into the last stitch made.

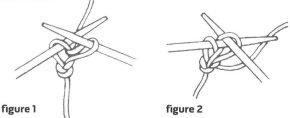

figure 1

figure 2

Long-Tail Cast-On

Leaving a long tail (about ½" [1.3 cm] for each stitch to be cast on), make a slipknot and place on right needle. Place thumb and index finger of your left hand between the yarn ends so that working yarn is around your index finger and tail end is around your thumb and secure the yarn ends with your other fingers. Hold your palm upward, making a V of yarn **(figure 1)**. *Bring needle up through loop on thumb **(figure 2)**, catch first strand around index finger, and go back down through loop on thumb **(figure 3)**. Drop loop off thumb and, placing thumb back in V configuration, tighten resulting stitch on needle **(figure 4)**. Repeat from * for the desired number of stitches.

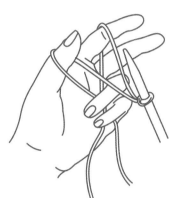

figure 1

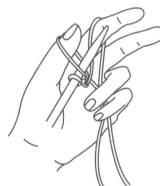

figure 2

figure 3

figure 4

decreases

Slip, Slip, Knit (ssk)

Slip two stitches individually knitwise **(figure 1)**, insert left needle tip into the front of these two slipped stitches, and use the right needle to knit them together through their back loops **(figure 2)**.

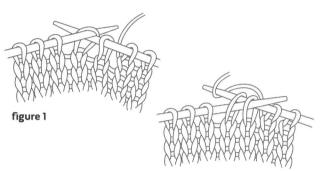

figure 1

figure 2

Slip, Slip, Slip, Knit (sssk)

Work as for ssk but slip three stitches individually knitwise, insert left needle tip into the front of the three slipped stitches, and use the right needle to knit them together through their back loops.

Slip, Slip, Purl (ssp)

Holding yarn in front, slip two stitches individually knitwise **(figure 1)**, then slip these two stitches back onto left needle (they will be twisted on the needle) and purl them together through their back loops **(figure 2)**.

figure 1

figure 2

glossary

grafting
Kitchener Stitch

Arrange stitches on two needles so that there is the same number of stitches on each needle. Hold the needles parallel to each other with wrong sides of the knitting together. Allowing about ½" (1.3 cm) per stitch to be grafted, thread matching yarn on a tapestry needle. Work from right to left as follows:

Step 1. Bring tapestry needle through the first stitch on the front needle as if to purl and leave the stitch on the needle **(figure 1)**.

Step 2. Bring tapestry needle through the first stitch on the back needle as if to knit and leave that stitch on the needle **(figure 2)**.

Step 3. Bring tapestry needle through the first front stitch as if to knit and slip this stitch off the needle, then bring tapestry needle through the next front stitch as if to purl and leave this stitch on the needle **(figure 3)**.

Step 4. Bring tapestry needle through the first back stitch as if to purl and slip this stitch off the needle, then bring tapestry needle through the next back stitch as if to knit and leave this stitch on the needle **(figure 4)**.

Repeat Steps 3 and 4 until one stitch remains on each needle, adjusting the tension to match the rest of the knitting as you go. To finish, bring tapestry needle through the front stitch as if to knit and slip this stitch off the needle, then bring tapestry needle through the back stitch as if to purl and slip this stitch off the needle.

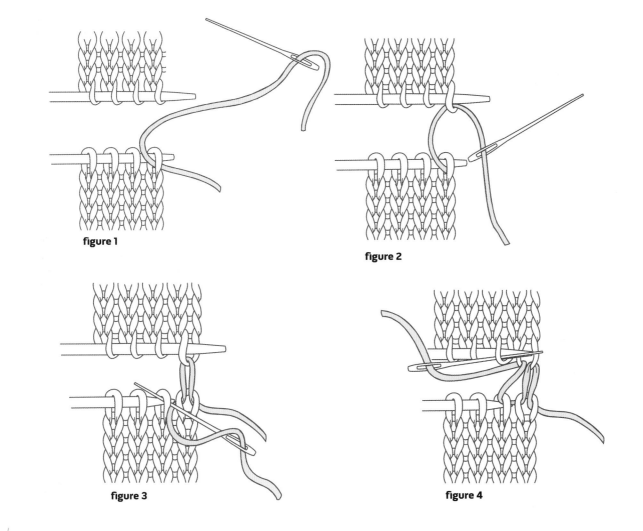

figure 1

figure 2

figure 3

figure 4

increases

Bar Increase (k1f&b)

Knit into a stitch but leave it on the left needle **(figure 1)**, then knit through the back loop of the same stitch **(figure 2)** and slip the original stitch off the needle **(figure 3)**.

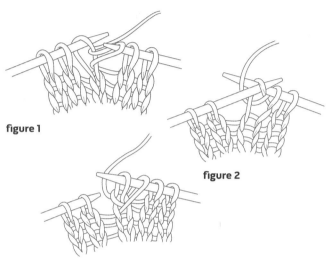

figure 1

figure 2

figure 3

Raised Make One

NOTE *Use the left slant if no direction of slant is specified.*

LEFT SLANT (M1L)

With left needle tip, lift the strand between the last knitted stitch and the first stitch on the left needle from front to back **(figure 1)**, then knit the lifted loop through the back **(figure 2)**.

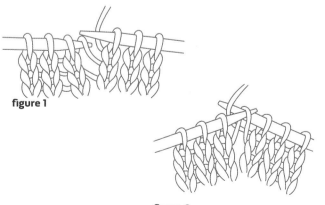

figure 1

figure 2

RIGHT SLANT (M1R)

With left needle tip, lift the strand between the needles from back to front **(figure 1)**, then knit the lifted loop through the front **(figure 2)**.

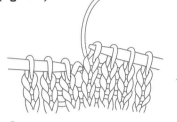
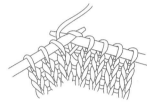

figure 1

figure 2

PURLWISE (M1P)

With left needle tip, lift the strand between the needles from front to back **(figure 1)**, then purl the lifted loop through the back **(figure 2)**.

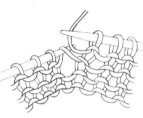
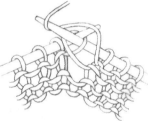

figure 1

figure 2

pick up + purl

With wrong side of work facing and working from right to left, *insert needle tip under selvedge stitch from the far side to the near side **(figure 1)**, wrap yarn around needle, and pull a loop through **(figure 2)**. Repeat from * for desired number of stitches.

figure 1

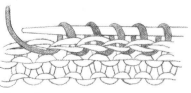

figure 2

glossary

seams

Horizontal-to-Horizontal Seam

With the bound-off edges opposite each other, right sides of the knitting facing you, and working into the stitches just below the bound-off edges, bring threaded tapestry needle out at the center of the first stitch (i.e., go under half of the first stitch) on one side of the seam, then bring needle in and out under the first whole stitch on the other side **(figure 1)**. *Bring needle into the center of the same stitch it came out of before, then out in the center of the adjacent stitch **(figure 2)**. Bring needle in and out under the next whole stitch on the other side **(figure 3)**. Repeat from *, ending with a half-stitch on the first side.

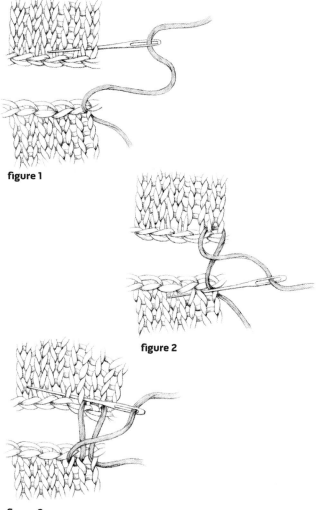

figure 1

figure 2

figure 3

Mattress Stitch

Place the pieces to be seamed on a table, right sides facing up. Begin at the lower edge and work upward as follows for your stitch pattern:

STOCKINETTE STITCH WITH 1-STITCH SEAM ALLOWANCE
Insert threaded needle under one bar between the two edge stitches on one piece, then under the corresponding bar plus the bar above it on the other piece **(figure 1)**. *Pick up the next two bars on the first piece **(figure 2)**, then the next two bars on the other **(figure 3)**. Repeat from *, ending by picking up the last bar or pair of bars on the first piece.

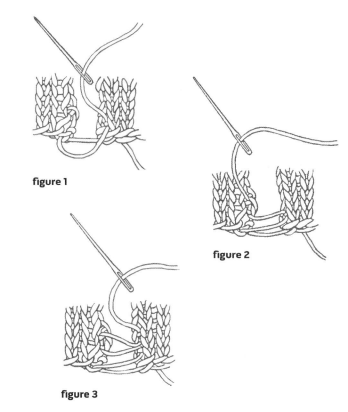

figure 1

figure 2

figure 3

STOCKINETTE STITCH WITH ½-STITCH SEAM ALLOWANCE
To reduce bulk in the mattress-stitch seam, work as for the 1-stitch seam allowance but pick up the bars in the center of the edge stitches instead of between the last two stitches.

Whipstitch

Hold pieces to be sewn together so that the edges to be seamed are even with each other. With yarn threaded on a tapestry needle, *insert needle through both layers from back to front, then bring needle to back. Repeat from *, keeping even tension on the seaming yarn.

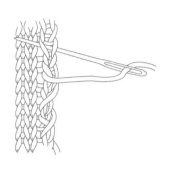

short-rows

Short-Rows Knit Side

Work to turning point, slip next stitch purlwise **(figure 1)**, bring the yarn to the front, then slip the same stitch back to the left needle **(figure 2)**, turn the work around and bring the yarn in position for the next stitch—one stitch has been wrapped and the yarn is correctly positioned to work the next stitch. When you come to a wrapped stitch on a subsequent row, hide the wrap by working it together with the wrapped stitch as follows: Insert right needle tip under the wrap (from the front if wrapped stitch is a knit stitch; from the back if wrapped stitch is a purl stitch **(figure 3)**, then into the stitch on the needle, and work the stitch and its wrap together as a single stitch.

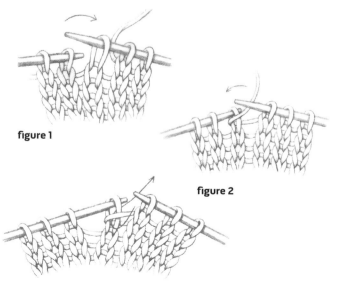

figure 1

figure 2

figure 3

Short-Rows Purl Side

Work to the turning point, slip the next stitch purlwise to the right needle, bring the yarn to the back of the work **(figure 1)**, return the slipped stitch to the left needle, bring the yarn to the front between the needles **(figure 2)**, and turn the work so that the knit side is facing—one stitch has been wrapped and the yarn is correctly positioned to knit the next stitch. To hide the wrap on a subsequent purl row, work to the wrapped stitch, use the tip of the right needle to pick up the wrap from the back, place it on the left needle **(figure 3)**, then purl it together with the wrapped stitch.

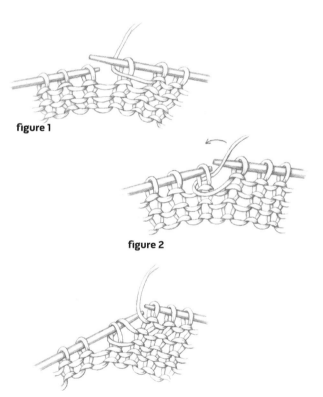

figure 1

figure 2

figure 3

sources

Bijou Basin Ranch
PO Box 154
Elbert, CO 80106
bijoubasinranch.com

Blue Sky Alpacas
PO Box 88
Cedar, MN 55011
blueskyalpacas.com

Brown Sheep Company
100662 County Rd. 16
Mitchell, NE 69357
brownsheep.com

Cascade Yarns
PO Box 58168
1224 Andover Park E.
Tukwila, WA 98188
cascadeyarns.com

Classic Elite Yarns
122 Western Ave.
Lowell, MA 01851
classiceliteyarns.com

Diamond Yarn
9697 Boul. St. Laurent
Ste. 101
Montreal, QC
Canada H3L 2N1
and
155 Martin Ross Ave., Unit 3
Toronto, ON
Canada M3J 2L9
diamondyarn.com

**Knitting Fever Inc.
/Louisa Harding**
PO Box 336
315 Bayview Ave.
Amityville, NY 11701
knittingfever.com

Louet North America
3425 Hands Rd.
Prescott, ON
Canada K0E 1T0
louet.com

Manos del Uruguay
Distributed in the U.S. by:
Fairmont Fibers
PO Box 2082
Philadelphia, PA 19103
fairmontfibers.com

**Southwest Trading
Company**
918 S. Park Ln., Ste. 102
Tempe, AZ 85281
soysilk.com

Tahki/Stacy Charles Inc.
70–30 80th St., Bldg 36
Ridgewood, NY 11385
tahkistacycharles.com
in Canada: Diamond Yarn

**Westminster Fibers/
Rowan**
165 Ledge St.
Nashua, NH 03060
westminsterfibers.com
in Canada: Diamond Yarn

index

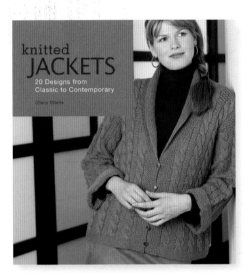
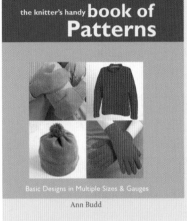

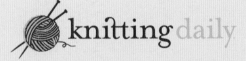